Risk Management in Law Firms:
Mitigate Risk and Enhance Firm Success

EDITED BY KATERINA MENHENNET

Commissioning editor
Katerina Menhennet

Managing director
Sian O'Neill

Risk Management in Law Firms: Mitigate Risk and Enhance Firm Success
is published by

Globe Law and Business Ltd
3 Mylor Close
Horsell
Woking
Surrey GU21 4DD
United Kingdom
Tel: +44 20 3745 4770
www.globelawandbusiness.com

Risk Management in Law Firms: Mitigate Risk and Enhance Firm Success

ISBN 9781787429161
EPUB ISBN 9781787429178
Adobe PDF ISBN 9781787429185

Contents

Executive summary

Effective risk management in law firms has never been more important. Lawyers must contend with the long-standing risks associated with the practice of law, such as anti-money laundering and issues of client confidentiality, as well as new risk areas such as data protection and cyber-security, and increased regulatory burdens. Poor handling of these risks can lead to reputational damage, diminished client relationships, and even regulatory action, and so it is critical for law firms to remain vigilant and put in place robust risk management policies, processes, and systems. *Risk Management in Law Firms: Mitigate Risk and Enhance Firm Success* brings together lawyers, consultants, and other risk and compliance professionals to provide expert and practical guidance on essential risk management topics, and aims to help law firm leaders and all lawyers understand and prepare for the risks they face – as well as effectively handle them when issues do inevitably arise. As observed by many of the authors, effective risk management is not only important for ensuring compliance, but can also positively impact client relationships, recruitment and retention of talent, the firm's reputation, and its continued success and growth.

Our opening chapter considers risk management in the context of the new, hybrid working model, which, while accelerated by the pandemic, seems to be here to stay. William Glynn, legal director, and Niya Phiri, partner at Clyde & Co LLP, set out some of the key considerations law firm risk managers should bear in mind as firms transition to new working arrangements, some of which may require a renewed approach to current risk issues, and others which may demand entirely new practices. The authors cover people risks, including issues relating to health and well-being; operational risks and challenges of "working from anywhere"; data and IT risks, particularly in relation to security and reliability; and legal and regulatory risks, which require an embedding of the right culture. A firm's ability to manage effectively a hybrid working environment is not only important for ensuring compliance, but also for recruitment and retention as talent increasingly expect flexible working opportunities.

In recent years, resilience, corporate social responsibility, and protecting the environment have increasingly been at the forefront of many minds and businesses, and lawyers and law firms are no exception. Chapter two by Alexia Howard, senior associate, and Simon Konsta, partner at Clyde & Co LLP, examines the climate change and ESG risks law firms need to be alive to both in respect of their daily operations and their advice to clients. These include reputational risks, as both clients and legal talent expect robust ESG initiatives from firms; transition and transactional risks – as well as opportunities – as due diligence and commercial awareness become even more crucial; and corporate disclosure and liability risks, with coverage of the Task Force on Climate-related Financial Disclosures and the latest disclosure regulations, including those relating to law firms. The authors also look at the issue of greenwashing and how lawyers can advise their clients to prevent claims, and the importance of diversity and inclusion in the legal profession. They conclude with key pieces of advice for how lawyers can effectively advise their clients in the ESG-focused future, and ensure the resilience of their own firms.

Law firms manage huge volumes of data, and so compliance with data protection laws is a significant regulatory risk that must be managed. Chapter three, written by Nigel Miller, founding partner at Fox Williams LLP, sets out a high-level summary of applicable data protection laws, with a focus on areas that have specific application to law firms. He subsequently provides some best practice points for risk management. The chapter covers the key data protection principles, lawful grounds for data processing and extra considerations for certain categories of data, accountability, data processors, and individual rights of data subjects. The question of what happens when there is a breach is also addressed, as well as restrictions on international data transfers and email marketing, websites, and cookies. Good data protection practices are essential for law firms, not just for compliance and risk management, but also to maintain positive professional relationships, including with clients, by demonstrating firms will secure and respect the personal data entrusted to them.

Another crucial and growing risk area for law firms is cybersecurity, as they are vulnerable to an increasingly sophisticated range of cyberattacks, which could result in catastrophic consequences. Our fourth chapter by Simon Chester, counsel, conflicts and regulatory matters, and Sandy Gill, assistant general counsel at Gowling WLG (Canada) LLP, outlines some of the key cybersecurity risks law firms face and the steps that firms of all sizes can take to protect themselves. They consider the combined pressure from regulators and clients to implement robust cybersecurity measures, and provide guidance on how firms can manage risks specific to how law firms work now, such as in relation to cloud computing and remote working. The authors highlight that human error is a common cause of cyberattacks, and demonstrate how firms can mitigate the human risk, including through comprehensive policies and procedures and training, as well as due diligence for new and departing colleagues. The chapter also covers common security provisions firms can implement, how firms can obtain appropriate cyber insurance, and how to plan for a breach. Finally, the authors provide ten practical steps all firms can take to ensure they are in the best position possible, should an attack occur.

A key risk area firms need to monitor and one that is increasingly in the spotlight is financial crime; firms need to be alert to the issues both in respect of their own obligations and responsibilities and in order to assist their clients. In chapter five, Anousheh Bromfield, senior associate, and Charles Kuhn, partner at Clyde & Co LLP, outline some of the most important factors in criminal finances and investigations, and how firms can prepare for and mitigate these risks. They consider investigations by different regulators and common features such as production orders, dawn raids, and interviews; the impact of legal professional privilege in investigations and where this does (and does not) apply; how to approach appointing and organizing representation; and cross-border issues. The authors also cover specific considerations for certain offences in law firms, particularly in relation to section 330 of the POCA. With increasingly sophisticated measures employed by perpetrators and enhanced action from regulators and authorities, it is more important than ever for firms to implement effective processes and procedures to mitigate risks in this arena.

Our next chapter by Brian Rogers, regulatory director at The Access Group, addresses the ever-present issue of anti-money laundering in law firms, and asks whether enough is being done to protect your firm. The chapter provides insight into the current risks around money laundering; the views and actions being taken by regulators, including the use of thematic reviews and the imposition of sanctions on non-compliant firms; and how firms can practically meet their regulatory obligations, such as through effective AML governance and having thorough risk assessments and clearly documented policies, controls, and procedures in place. The pressure on firms to ensure they reduce the risk of involvement in money laundering activity is not going to alleviate, and so it is vital firms ensure they are meeting their compliance obligations to avoid regulatory action and reputational damage.

Firms and their principals in England and Wales cannot continue practicing without qualifying insurance to cover civil liability claims arising from the work conducted, and so chapter seven by Rebecca Atkinson, director of risk and compliance at Howard Kennedy, goes through some of the key considerations for firms. She analyses how much cover firms should buy and provides top tips for professional indemnity insurance renewal, including how to present your firm well in order to attract the best premium price. Rebecca also advises on the importance of a good and transparent relationship between law firms and their insurers during the renewal process and when notifying possible claims. Additionally, key points that could cause big issues for firms are discussed, including the danger of rectifying your own mistakes in relation to potential own interest conflicts, possible professional indemnity exclusions for sanctioned entities and certain types of work, cybercrime insurance, and limiting liability clauses.

While professional indemnity insurance provides a safety net for partners most of the time, it is not possible to insure against everything that may go wrong in professional life, and it is therefore important to be aware of the gaps in that safety net. In our next chapter, Frank Maher, partner at Legal Risk LLP, identifies the risks that partners may assume are protected while they are practicing and after retirement. He focuses on defensive practice; how to be aware of the exclusions in cover which crop up and how those risks can be managed, including by the two key mechanisms, incorporation and limiting liability contractually. Frank concludes by outlining some of the most important insurance options available to firms.

In England and Wales, solicitors and firms must be authorized by and follow the rules and regulations of the Solicitors Regulation Authority (SRA). In chapter nine, Rebecca Atkinson, director of risk and compliance at Howard Kennedy, takes us through the key regulatory framework, beginning with clarification on when a business needs SRA authorization, and how firms can obtain and retain this through the annual reauthorization process. Rebecca then turns to the SRA Standards and Regulations and outlines some of the most important sets of rules contained within these, including the Principles, Codes of Conduct, and Accounts Rules. The SRA's approach to enforcing these regulations is also considered, such as through its enforcement strategy and the reporting requirements when there is or may be a breach, primarily the responsibility of the compulsorily appointed COLP and COFA. The centrality of ethics to the solicitor profession is acknowledged and guidance provided on how to navigate ethical conundrums lawyers may face. The chapter concludes with an explanation of the SRA warning notices and guidance, materials that can be invaluable in ensuring full understanding of and compliance with these crucial rules and regulations.

Chapter ten by Peter Noyce, head of legal sector at Menzies LLP, looks at how firms can mitigate risk through effective management of the client journey and having appropriate financial disciplines and controls in place. Going through the whole client experience from the take on process, throughout the transaction, to completion of the matter, Peter demonstrates how risk can be taken out at each stage. The focus then switches to financial disciplines and both lock-up and non-lock-up matters are considered in their capacity to reduce overall risk in the business, including cash flow management, salary to fees ratio, succession, and staff engagement. Peter argues that having these controls in place provides the foundation for success in risk mitigation, and should be continually measured by satisfied clients, educated staff, a culture of openness and respect, and a growth in profits, which will ultimately result in the increased value of the practice.

The last decade has seen a significant shift in the power dynamic of attorney–client relationships, and, as a consequence, clients now exert tighter control over outside counsel engagements through the increased use of outside counsel guidelines (OCGs). These govern all elements of an attorney–client relationship, and our next chapter by Noah Fiedler, shareholder and co-leader of the Attorney Risk Management Practice Group at Barron & Newburger, P.C., takes a deep dive into the most common and troubling guidelines for lawyers, namely far-reaching indemnity provisions and changes to the definitions of conflicts of interest. He also provides practical strategies on how to manage OCG risk, such as identification and common review of all OCGs, and negotiations with clients. Noah concludes with the warning that OCGs are here to stay, and so firms need to exercise appropriate care and preparation in order to avoid liability and promote strong, healthy client relationships.

Retaining a focus on client-related risks, in chapter 12, Tracey Calvert, founder and director of Oakalls Consultancy Limited, discusses the reason why conflict and confidentiality management is an essential risk management topic, requiring a robust approach. She begins by outlining what is meant by the terms "conflicts of interest", "confidentiality", and "disclosure", and the outcomes the SRA expects those it regulates to achieve. She then turns her attention to how these risks can be managed, and provides objectives and practical tips firms can use to ensure compliance, as well as potential obstacles to this that firms should be aware of. Finally, she suggests some key compliance solutions for firms and takes a look at the bigger picture to demonstrate that, once again, as well as regulatory concerns, breaches of these duties can result in reputational loss, damaged client relationships, and professional indemnity implications, making understanding and complying with these duties of paramount importance.

Unfortunately, it is impossible to keep every client happy all of the time, and some will have complaints. This issue is addressed in chapter 13 by Rebecca Atkinson, director of risk and compliance at Howard Kennedy. Rebecca first discusses the SRA requirements regarding complaints, and proceeds to provide comprehensive guidance on how to handle complaints effectively. This includes explaining what the complaints handling process should be and who should undertake complaint handling in the firm, considering what a complaint can be about, and practical tips. Complaints made by non-clients are also considered, as well as how to handle online reviews – good or bad. Finally, Rebecca outlines the key features of the Legal Ombudsman and concludes with further guidance from key bodies for the handling of complaints.

Just as important as keeping clients happy is ensuring staff satisfaction within firms. How teams are supervised can have a significant impact on employees and so our next chapter by Jamie Butler, executive coach and facilitator and founder of Jamie Butler Coaching Limited, provides guidance on how effective supervision can be achieved in remote and hybrid teams. He considers the risks, challenges, and opportunities of remote supervision, and the core skills and characteristics of a good remote supervisor. He also demonstrates how to set "ground rules" to establish responsibility and build trust, communicate for effectiveness and productivity, and maximize engagement, inclusion, and wellbeing in remote teams. The chapter also covers the specific opportunities and challenges in relation to hybrid working and the changing face of leadership and management to a more distributed and collaborative model, including the increased use and importance of coaching skills.

Lateral hiring presents a myriad of challenges for law firms, but with careful thought, consideration, and preparation, it is perfectly possible to run a recruitment process without overstepping the mark. Chapter 15 by Ruth Bonino, professional support lawyer, and Chris Holme, partner at Clyde & Co LLP, considers how firms can navigate lateral hiring recruitment to seek to make sure the "right person" has been hired, whilst being aware of (and avoiding) the risks of ethical, legal, and regulatory breaches (particularly in terms of confidential client information). The authors outline the basic legal, ethical, and regulatory obligations of partners, including general ethical and confidentiality duties imposed on them by the SRA, as well as how the various stakeholders in the lateral hiring process should take these legal and regulatory duties into account. They also provide guidance on how law firms can mitigate risks in the due diligence process, what to look out for in pre-employment vetting, how to avoid breaching confidentiality obligations in conflict checks, and integration issues. The chapter concludes with some key rules of the road for a successful lateral hiring process.

Chapter 16 by Jessica Clay, partner, Iain Miller, partner, and Lucinda Soon, professional support lawyer at Kingsley Napley, examines the role culture has to play in risk management. The authors observe how recent SRA activity has put ethical culture under the spotlight, culminating in the latest proposed changes to the SRA Codes of Conduct to address issues relating to wellbeing and unfair treatment at work. These changes will strengthen the SRA's ability to regulate and enforce against poor ethical culture in regulated law firms, but throw up several challenges which the authors analyze, including how to assess unfair treatment, how the new rules will overlap with the remit of the Employment Tribunal, the difficulties in challenging behavior that does not meet the standard, and the prevailing issue of the SRA's reach into attorneys' private lives. The proposed changes are likely to be enforced, and this chapter concludes with tips on how firms can prepare for and adhere to the new requirements.

The SRA has embraced principles-based regulation (PBR) for over a decade, where black and white rules are largely replaced by broad principles and outcomes. In our final chapter, Jonathon Bray, director of Jonathon Bray Limited, explores the commercial opportunities for law firms and individual lawyers presented by this more flexible system of regulation. Despite the lack of certainty and arguably greater compliance burden associated with PBR, it frees up law firms to decide how best to achieve the outcomes required, presenting opportunities for innovation and new ways to service clients. Jonathon discusses how the removal of regulatory barriers such as the "separate business rule" has made it easier for lawyers to work in an unregulated and freelance environment, encouraged them to embrace technology, and helped make legal services more accessible to individuals and small businesses. He also outlines some of the potential new business models that would have been unthinkable before the huge shift brought about by the Legal Services Act 2007, allowing lawyers to go into business with "non-lawyers". Slowly but surely, investment and talent are being attracted to legal services; Jonathon argues that what some may dismiss as an erosion of professionalism nonetheless presents an opportunity for law firms to act like businesses and engage in true legal innovation.

About the authors

Rebecca Atkinson is director of risk and compliance at Howard Kennedy. She leads the firm's internal risk and compliance function and sets the related strategy. Rebecca is a skilled risk and compliance professional with over a decade of experience ensuring businesses are compliant. She is the firm's compliance officer for legal practice, money laundering reporting officer, money laundering compliance officer, anti-bribery officer and whistleblowing officer. She additionally holds the position of data protection officer alongside head of technology and security, Jonathan Freedman. Rebecca is a barrister (non-practicing), New York attorney, and solicitor of England and Wales. Rebecca has authored two books (*Assessing and Addressing Risk and Compliance in Your Law Firm* and *Financial Crime: A Compliance Manual*) and regularly produces written content for compliance publications, as well as Practice Notes for Practical Law Company. Rebecca sits on the Board for the Law Society Legal Compliance Bulletin and is a member of the Law Society Regulatory Processes Committee.

Ruth Bonino is a solicitor with more than 25 years' experience in employment law. She writes regular legal articles for external publications and has contributed to legal textbooks for a number of years. She has a Masters degree in employment law. Ruth's role at Clyde & Co involves keeping her colleagues and the firm's clients up to date on employment law developments by writing client alerts, organizing and preparing client training seminars, and managing and delivering the team's internal training. As a fee earner she was a senior associate at an international law firm based in the City of London where she handled a full case load of both contentious and non-contentious employment cases. Ruth is a member of the Employment Lawyers Association and PEN, the network of professional support employment lawyers.

Jonathon Bray is a recognized adviser to law firms on all aspects of risk and regulation. His consultancy is best known for its work in helping SRA-regulated firms navigate the compliance maze in a friendly and commercial way. Jonathon and his team have helped launch over 100 Alternative Business Structures, working with established practices, new entrants to the market, and international firms. COLPs, COFAs, and anti-money laundering officers all benefit from their direct and practical guidance.

Anousheh Bromfield is a senior associate at Clyde & Co LLP. She has specific experience advising FCA regulated companies and international trading companies on compliance with sanctions, money laundering, and bribery and corruption issues and regulatory issues. Her regulatory practice includes conducting and assisting with internal and external (including SFO, FCA, HMRC, and SRA) investigations, drafting disclosures to and liaising with the relevant authorities, drafting compliance policies, and advising on proposed transactions to ensure compliance with the relevant regulatory framework. She also conducts client training programs on compliance issues. In addition to regulatory work, Anousheh has a range of experience acting in all types of dispute resolution, representing clients in domestic and international arbitrations as well as before the English courts.

Following a 21-year career in the legal sector, **Jamie Butler** now works as an executive coach and facilitator, founding Jamie Butler Coaching Limited in March 2020. Drawing on his background as a solicitor, law school lecturer, and learning and development leader, Jamie coaches individuals and groups, predominantly in law firms. He specializes in people skills and team development, particularly helping to navigate the path to partnership and building coaching skills in managers and leaders. He has also supported clients during the COVID-19 pandemic to develop remote management and supervision skills and with conversations around effective hybrid working. Most recently, Jamie was director of learning and development at Cleary Gottlieb Steen & Hamilton LLP. He is an accredited executive coach and member of the Association for Coaching.

Tracey Calvert is a lawyer and a regulatory, compliance, and ethics specialist. She is the founder and director of Oakalls Consultancy Limited and provides regulatory compliance, consultancy, and training services to lawyers and law firms. She is a regular speaker and trainer on these topics and has delivered presentations both within the UK and internationally. She is the co-chair of the International Bar Association's Professional Ethics Committee and is on the editorial board of the Law Society's *Legal*

Compliance Bulletin. Tracey is a contributor to *Cordery on Legal Services* and has written several books on compliance and ethics. Tracey was previously employed by the Law Society and the SRA as a senior ethics adviser and a policy executive. She has also worked both in private practice and in an in-house role.

Simon Chester is counsel for conflicts and regulatory matters in Gowling WLG's Toronto office. With roots in three continents, Simon is a global lawyer and is qualified in both Europe and North America. His legal career includes a decade of public service, 30 years of experience as a risk partner with large business law firms, and teaching at Canada's largest English language law school. Throughout his career, he has been a pioneer in applying advanced technologies to legal practice. Educated at Oxford and Osgoode Hall Law School, where he held a Canadian Rhodes Trust Foundation Scholarship, he is qualified in Ontario (1982) and England and Wales (1988). Simon was the first non-American to chair the American Bar Association's Tech Show. He also chaired the ABA Law Practice Section's editorial advisory board, its education board and its new media and internet board. He served as president of the College of Law Practice Management and as president of the Oxford University Society in Toronto. He has spoken on law, technology, and professional issues to audiences across Canada, the United States, Australia, Mexico, India, Singapore, Scotland, England, France, Belgium, and the Netherlands.

Jessica Clay is a partner at Kingsley Napley with over a decade of experience specializing in legal services regulation. Her work focuses on advising law firms, partnerships, and their members on a wide range of regulatory matters, including compliance with their regulatory and ethical obligations, changes to business structures and authorization processes, and any internal or regulatory investigations. In addition to her core legal services regulation practice, Jessica regularly advises regulators on their regulatory and disciplinary frameworks, regulatory policy reform, and governance issues, and is involved in a number of drafting projects. Jessica is also the deputy editor of the leading textbook on legal services regulation – *Cordery on Legal Services*. Prior to joining Kingsley Napley, Jessica was the principal lawyer in the General Counsel team at the SRA. Jessica was the day-to-day lead for two major projects – the drafting of the SRA Standards and Regulations and the Solicitors Qualifying Examination (SQE). She also advised the Investigations and Supervision team on case direction.

Noah Fiedler helps lawyers and law firms. He counsels clients on best practices to avoid ethical and liability problems and defends clients against claims. Noah has wide-ranging experience defending lawyers in malpractice, fiduciary duty breach, defamation, and misrepresentation claims and in disciplinary proceedings. He regularly counsels and educates lawyers and firms across the country on ethics, liability, and risk management topics. Noah has developed numerous law firm risk management resources, including Barron & Newburger P.C.'s Attorneys Risk Management program. Noah is a member of the Association of Professional Responsibility Lawyers and teaches Professional Responsibility at the University of Wisconsin Law School.

Sandy Gill is assistant general counsel at Gowling WLG in Canada. Sandy's practice is focused on law firm governance, risk management, innovation, and professional responsibility and ethics in the changing legal and social landscape. She is interested in global trends and regulatory developments related to law practice management. Sandy has previously served as in-house counsel to both public and private companies in Canada and a Canadian university. Sandy completed her JD/MA in 2004 at the University of Toronto and previously practiced large firm corporate and commercial law, with a focus on securities and M&A transactions. She is also chair of the Calgary Public Library Board.

William Glynn is a legal director whose dispute resolution practice focuses on regulatory investigations, disciplinary proceedings, and the defense of complex, multi-party, and high-value civil and commercial claims against lawyers and law firms. He has advised on high value claims involving underlying transactions or disputes in the corporate, finance, real estate, tax, and litigation sectors. In addition to advising on the defense of claims, William also has experience of advising lawyers in relation to disciplinary proceedings before both the Solicitors Disciplinary Tribunal and the Bar Standards Board, and also regularly advises law firms on risk management issues. William's professional practice also extends to defending claims against accountants and construction professionals, and he also has wide-ranging experience of general commercial litigation, acting for both claimants and defendants across a variety of sectors.

Chris Holme is a leading lawyer in the field of employment law, supporting employers with the full range of issues that they face. He works predominately in the financial services and professional services sectors, supporting a number of law firms, accountancy firms, banks, and asset managers. Chris has various management roles at Clyde & Co; he is a member of the firm's UK board and leads the employment team's financial services and professional services groups. Chris carries out some of the most complex and reputationally significant work within the employment area. In particular, Chris works with clients on partnership issues and disputes, particularly alleged discrimination issues, confidentiality issues and partner moves, and disputes between partners in the UK and internationally.

Alexia Howard is a senior associate at Clyde & Co LLP. Alexia qualified into the firm's insurance financial and professional disputes team in 2014. Her practice focuses on the defense of lawyers and firms of solicitors in professional negligence and malpractice proceedings. She also advises on regulatory investigations and risk management issues. As part of Clyde & Co's resilience program, Alexia is developing thought leadership on the effects of climate change and ESG issues on legal professionals. She has presented to clients on these issues and collaborated on climate conscious contractual clause precedents in a climate change action hackathon in conjunction with The Chancery Lane Project. Alexia is a representative on the firm's gender equality committee and its employee communication and consultation group, and is active within the firm's network for achieving cultural and ethnic diversity.

Simon Konsta is a partner at Clyde & Co LLP. He is a specialist professional liability practitioner. He served as Clyde & Co's senior partner and chair of its global management board between 2016 and 2019, having previously headed up its global insurance practice. Simon acts on behalf of multiple global professional services firms in respect of their defense, regulatory, and disciplinary needs. He has acted on a number of landmark actions. Simon has amassed extensive experience of complex and multi-jurisdictional professional liability disputes. He also advises upon risk management issues, confronting professional services firms (and their insurers), as well as spearheading some of Clyde & Co's thought leadership campaigns such as on climate change, automation, and the application of technology.

Charles Kuhn is a regulatory and financial crime specialist who has worked for the Financial Conduct Authority (Enforcement and Financial Crime Division). Charles is experienced in defending complex financial markets and white-collar crime cases. Charles acts for institutions and individuals providing regulatory advice on financial markets cases including working for banks in their capacity as arranger/underwriter. His practice covers insider dealing, market abuse, money laundering, bribery and corruption, sanctions, and securities litigation. He is one of Clyde & Co's MLROs.

Frank Maher is a practicing solicitor and partner in Legal Risk LLP, solicitors specializing in professional regulation and professional indemnity. He is also admitted as a solicitor in the Republic of Ireland, and has a diploma in anti-money laundering and a certificate in data protection. He advises leading US, European, and UK 100 law firms, insurers as far afield as the US and Australia, and members of other professions. Frank has over 38 years' experience of defending many of the UK's largest law firm claims for insurers and has even advised on a claim arising from the death penalty. He advises law firms extensively on the insurance aspects of their mergers and acquisitions, coverage disputes with insurers, disciplinary investigations, and a wide variety of regulatory issues such as conflicts of interests, practicing rights, and international law firm structures. His advice is often sought on "bet the firm" issues, including many examples of firms that have been impacted by activities of rogue partners and staff.

Iain Miller is a partner at Kingsley Napley with over 25 years of experience in legal services regulation. His primary area of practice focuses on providing regulatory advice to law firms, general counsel, COLPs, and partners. Iain's experience cuts across regulatory, public law, and investigations, and includes advising legal services regulators other than the SRA on their regulatory schemes, governance issues, and rule drafting as well as advice in relation to judicial reviews, investigations, and disciplinary prosecutions. Iain is general editor of *Cordery on Legal Services* and past chair of the Association of Regulatory and Disciplinary Lawyers. He was a member of the Advisory Board of UCL's Centre for Ethics and Law Review of the Statutory Framework for Legal Services. He is a member of the City of London Law Society's Professional Rules and Regulation Committee, an officer of the International Bar Association's Professional Ethics Committee, and a member of its International Trade in Legal Services Committee. He is also a member of the Consulting Editorial Board of LexisPSL Practice Compliance, and a member of the Editorial Board of the Law Society's *Legal Compliance Bulletin*.

Nigel Miller is a founding partner of London law firm Fox Williams LLP and leads the firm's technology and data protection group. Nigel is a Certified Information Privacy Professional/Europe (CIPP/E) under the International Association of Privacy Professionals (IAPP). He advises professional services firms (including a number of UK and US law firms), financial services firms, and tech companies on data protection, privacy, and cybersecurity matters, including GDPR advice and compliance programs. Nigel is a fellow, and past chairman, of the UK Society for Computers & Law (www.scl.org). He is also a past president of the International Federation of Computer Law Associations (www.ifcla.org). He is a member of the International Association of Privacy Professionals (IAPP) and the US iTechLaw Association and is a regular speaker at tech and tech law conferences. He is featured in *Who's Who Legal: Data 2022*.

Peter Noyce is head of legal sector at Menzies LLP and author of *Brighter Thinking for Law Firms*. Peter advises law firms of all sizes in respect of strategy and profit improvement along with overseeing compliance assignments. This has seen Peter and Menzies' wider team play a key role in recent law firm mergers, including preparing firms in advance of this process. Peter's advice never loses sight of the fact that law firms must look to take as much risk out of their business as possible. Peter believes there are opportunities for law firms to reduce the inherent risk of their client relationships and the transactions upon which they are advising. Good financial disciplines are also never far away from the successful practice, and combining these will lead to a practice that scores well on any risk profile. It is the ability to drill down into the operation of the business that ensures Peter and Menzies are well placed to advise legal firms on all areas of their business.

Niya Phiri is a partner in the malpractice, regulatory, investigations and disciplinary group at Clyde & Co LLP. For over 16 years, Niya has specialized in advising and defending law firms and legal professionals in complex and high value malpractice disputes. She has extensive experience of civil litigation in the High Court and Court of Appeal as well as arbitration, mediation, and ADR. Her practice also covers regulatory, disciplinary, and investigations work in the increasingly regulated world in which law firms and legal professionals operate, including advising on a wide range of regulatory obligations, and risk management issues including self-reporting, anti-money laundering, conflicts, confidentiality, and privilege, and representing clients in formal contact with the Solicitors Regulation Authority and the Solicitors Disciplinary Tribunal. As part of her practice, Niya has been involved in a number of cases that go beyond the usual parameters of legal malpractice into issues of civil fraud and dishonesty in both litigation and regulatory matters.

Brian Rogers worked as a senior management executive, including as a money laundering reporting officer, in various law firms for 20 years, and was the first non-solicitor to be appointed to a Law Society Council, serving as chair of Regulatory Affairs at Manchester Law Society. He created the Riliance online risk and compliance system for law firms, for which he won the British Chambers of Commerce North-West Region Innovation Through Technology Award. He was a shareholder and director in Riliance Software Limited, providing risk and compliance software solutions, online training, and consultancy services to law firms and other regulated businesses. Brian joined The Access Group in 2019 when it acquired his company as an initial step in creating a new legal division, and as regulatory director is a regulation and compliance subject matter expert. He regularly presents regulation and compliance webinars, speaks at legal sector conferences, contributes articles to various legal publications, and is a prolific LinkedIn blogger on regulation and compliance matters.

Lucinda Soon is a professional support lawyer in the regulatory team at Kingsley Napley. She has over a decade of experience working in professional ethics and legal services regulation, including projects relating to policy development, and advising individuals and law firms on authorization matters, changes to business structures, and regulatory compliance. Prior to joining Kingsley Napley, Lucinda worked in the legal and enforcement and General Counsel Directorates at the SRA, as a professional support lawyer and knowledge management business lead, and subsequently as a consultant solicitor. Her work focused on knowledge development and training, advising on the legal services regulatory framework, and drafting policies and guidance on the SRA Standards and Regulations. Lucinda is a trustee for LawCare, the charity that supports mental health and wellbeing in the UK legal community. She is also a member of the British Psychological Society (MBPsS) and is pursuing her PhD in Organizational Psychology, focusing on law firm culture and wellbeing in the legal profession.

Chapter 1:
Managing risks in the hybrid "office"

By William Glynn, legal director, and Niya Phiri, partner, Clyde & Co LLP

Introduction

The COVID-19 pandemic created, at short notice, significant challenges for law firms, and with those challenges came the potential for new risk issues to emerge. One of the fundamental changes was the shift of most law firm staff to home working in March 2020, and thereafter what is likely to be a permanent move to a hybrid working arrangement for the majority of firms. Whilst working from home and hybrid working come with many benefits to both firms and staff, it also has the potential for new or greater risks for firms. This chapter sets out some of the considerations that law firm risk managers should bear in mind as firms transition into new working arrangements.

People risks

Health and wellbeing

Law firms (as employers) have always had to give careful consideration to the health and wellbeing of their staff. Indeed, given the nature of the services provided by law firms, the people are the firm.

However, most law firms continue to charge fees based on hourly rates. Therefore, the firm's financial interests in utilizing the highest number of hours from each fee-earner (and at the lowest cost appropriate to the task) sits in direct conflict with the need of individuals to have sufficient rest and an appropriate work–life balance. Accordingly, wellbeing in the legal sector is a thorny subject, with firms being criticized for on the one hand trumpeting mental health awareness initiatives and on the other having demanding chargeable hours targets and expectations. Whilst the two are not mutually exclusive, they are potentially in conflict.

It is therefore not surprising that, as discussions around mental health have become increasingly normalized, law firms have faced ever closer scrutiny by regulatory bodies such as the SRA,[1] which in turn raises risk issues. The need for careful management of wellbeing was heightened as the impact of the COVID-19 pandemic took effect, particularly because for a number of firms there was increased demand from clients and limited scrutiny of how staff were dealing with pressured workloads outside of the office environment, whereas for others there were significant decreases in work, resulting in concerns regarding job security and personal finances. As noted later in this section, an additional impact of the pandemic and the shift to working remotely was the difficulty of demarking work and home life.

Risks arising from health and wellbeing issues are broadly two-fold:

- Risks of health issues for individuals (which, quite properly, is of paramount importance but is largely beyond the scope of this chapter); and
- Consequential risks for firms.

The risks to individuals working in law firms predominantly relate to mental health issues resulting from:

- A lack of autonomy;
- An inability to raise issues;
- Toxic culture and practices;
- Unmanageable workloads; and
- Insufficient support and supervision.

A recent report by the legal community mental health charity LawCare[2] identified that the risk of burnout increases where two or more of these issues intersect (for example, younger lawyers who face often the highest workloads but the least autonomy). Burnout also had a higher incidence in women, participants who identified as belonging to an ethnic minority, and participants with a disability. In terms of risk from the firm's perspective, staff who are under significant pressure may be more likely to make errors or misjudgments, which could result in claims being made against the firm or regulatory issues arising. Accordingly, managing the risk to individuals is part and parcel of managing the risk to the firm.

Workplace support measures can include:

- Regular catch-ups and appraisals;
- Training of leaders and managers to identify and support issues of wellbeing; and
- Clear signposting of where individuals can obtain information and support.

The first of these is more challenging in a hybrid environment, whereby managers may not regularly see staff face-to-face. Indeed, the key risk of managing a hybrid office is a lack of visibility and therefore awareness of the health and wellbeing of individuals. Absences may be less easily recorded or noted, and without face-to-face and day-to-day interactions, wellbeing and health issues of employees may be more difficult to identify. In addition to training on mental health awareness for managers, it may be that requiring, where appropriate, regular office attendance and face-to-face meetings can assist in limiting these risks and ensure that employees are able to raise health and wellbeing issues openly and swiftly.

Allocations of work, managing over-performance or under-performance

A further result of less direct face-to-face contact is the increasing challenge of ensuring that work is allocated fairly, not only to ensure efficient use of resources, but also to ensure an equality of opportunity.

Connected to this is the broader challenge of managing both over- and under-performance, which again is more difficult without regular visibility. Whilst most law firms have in place systems that record hours worked and tasks undertaken, that is not necessarily a good indicator of over- or under-performance, relying as it does on the timely and accurate use of the time capture systems. Tendencies of individuals to either over- or under-report their capacity and availability is also likely to compound this problem, and without regular in-person contact it may be difficult to recognize these issues. How firms will deal with these challenges will in part reflect the size of the firm or team, and the availability of resources to measure and record work allocation. Potential ways to mitigate such issues include putting in place a formalized approach to in-person appraisals, regular feedback opportunities, a transparent approach to work allocation, and automated collation of capacity and/or recorded hours.

Invasion of professional life within the home environment

A further issue, which is a common complaint relating to increased working from home, is the difficulty of ensuring that there is a clear demarcation between work and home life. When the first pandemic "lockdown" was announced in March 2020, many employees lived in shared environments, such that "home offices" had to be identified. Often these would be bedrooms where lawyers also slept, or kitchens or sitting room where they and their families also lived. In those circumstances there were potential risks of individuals being unable to properly detach from work, with the added stress and potential exhaustion issues which could pose risks to firms and individuals. Again, these are issues that arose during lockdown and are now part of the hybrid working environment. The forced nature of the initial lockdown did not provide adequate time for lawyers to identify or create dedicated working areas. Whilst over time these initial difficulties may have been (partly) remedied, the issue of demarcation of work and home remains challenging to resolve, and would not exist were all work to be undertaken in an office environment.

Whilst the move to flexible working has many benefits, ensuring that clear lines are kept between home and work is important to the health and wellbeing of lawyers and other law firm staff. In terms of practical tips to assist employees working predominantly from home, discouraging meetings or calls from being scheduled outside of the usual working day will help to demark work and home. In addition, if it is noted that employees are regularly sending emails at times of day or night that indicate that insufficient rest or work–life balance is being achieved, then that will be an issue to be raised with the individuals in relation to their work allocation, capacity, and potential over-performance; of course, it could simply be evidence of employees taking advantage of greater flexibility, but that can only be identified using regular one-to-one communications.

New joiners and departing staff

The hybrid working environment presents challenges for both new joiners and also those who are departing a firm.

In terms of new joiners, the traditional "in person" welcome and introductions may no longer occur, or may occur only after a considerable delay. This means that new joiners may not feel that they are part of the team, may not be identified as having availability to assist with tasks, or they may be overlooked in the allocation of work. Firms should also ensure that risk management (including risks in a hybrid working environment) form part of a formal induction process. This should include clear guidance on who to contact regarding any risk concerns, expectations in terms of protecting client data away from the office, and ensuring that risk considerations form part of the employment contract via inclusion in the staff handbook.

In terms of departing staff, a crucial area of risk management is understanding why individuals are leaving, in case there are issues of culture or management that pose a risk to the firm. It may be that a high volume of departures or a rapid turnover of staff is a precursor to an increase in claims. Departures in the hybrid environment are naturally more difficult to manage as, for example, exit interviews may be conducted remotely if at all. Firms should ensure that there is a formalized exit process, with interviews conducted by appropriate staff or even external agencies.

A further issue relating to departing staff is the need for firms to ensure that they have recovered all documents and data from departing staff, including confidential client data. Again, this is more challenging in the hybrid working environment. Staff may have taken hard copy documents to their home offices, or may have soft copy documents on USB sticks. It is therefore crucial that, as part of the departure process, assurances are obtained from employees to confirm that they have undertaken appropriate searches of their home offices and have provided to the firm copies of all client-related documents in their possession.

Operational risks

Reviewing risk assessments and risk registers to reflect changes in operating conditions

The nature of hybrid working means that firms' traditional ways of identifying and registering risks may no longer be appropriate. Law firms are required, pursuant to paragraph 2 of the SRA Code of Conduct for Firms, to ensure that they have in place effective governance structures, arrangements, systems, and controls so as to ensure that they comply with their regulatory obligations.[3] In particular, firms must identify, monitor, and manage material risks to the business.[4] Records evidencing compliance need to be maintained.[5]

Given the nature of hybrid working, the need to ensure that firms have taken an appropriate view of risk in relation to employees who are predominantly working from home is crucial. As set out further in the following sections, this can encompass issues such as security and data risk, but may also involve issues such as personal risk and potential breaches of confidentiality resulting from home working environments that are not necessarily private. It is important that firms are alive to these potential risks, and have ways of mitigating and recording them.

Challenges of a mobile workforce/working from anywhere

Managing and monitoring a more mobile and flexible workforce is a key challenge of the hybrid office. Whilst flexibility offers considerable benefits, it is not without risk.

The needs of individuals will differ, with some lawyers wanting to work predominantly from home, whereas others may require the space and facilities of an office environment. Age, experience, confidence, and home-working options may all impact on how and when lawyers want to work. Others may have become used to having a more flexible day, so as to undertake caring responsibilities. For firms who are required to monitor the wellbeing of staff this can present a number of challenges.

As noted, one potential issue is the difficulty of employees working in environments that are not necessarily confidential. This may be a particular issue with junior employees who are (for example) sharing houses with other professionals, some of whom may work for different law firms or indeed even on different sides of the same transaction or case. The potential risk of conflicts of interest or breaches of confidentiality arising are obvious, but may not be easily identified by the firm unless specifically raised by the individual. Improving risk awareness and training is key to mitigating this issue.

A further risk of the "working from anywhere" option is jurisdiction. Whilst a number of people may have travelled abroad during the COVID-19 pandemic in order to work from holiday homes or warmer climates, that in turn came with risks of jurisdictional challenges being raised regarding employment status and taxation. Another issue to have considered in this context is the viewing of remote hearings from outside of the jurisdiction, and whether appropriate permissions were obtained in advance; this is addressed further below.

Managing a hybrid team

Individual responses to the option to work on a hybrid basis will have varied. In some instances there will be a reluctance from employees to be physically back in offices, either from a work–life balance perspective or due to ongoing concerns regarding risks to health posed by travelling on public transport. On the other hand, there may be team members who wish to work only in the office environment to maintain a demarcation between work and home. It is important that managers of hybrid teams recognize both extremes of this position, that there is sufficient support both for those who wish to be in the office full-time and those who wish to be at home full-time, and everything in between. Firms need to be conscious of not inadvertently discriminating against those who may be less physically present in offices, in terms of work allocation, supervision, inclusion, and promotion.

It may be that some tasks must be undertaken only in offices and under a controlled environment. This may include, for example, hard-copy document review or dealing with particularly sensitive information where a greater level of security and oversight may be appropriate.

Data/IT risks

Data and IT in the home/hybrid environment

In light of the move to working from home, and the subsequent shift to hybrid working, it is highly likely that lawyers will now have client documents at home. This represents a considerable risk to firms, because they are obliged pursuant to paragraph 6.3 of the SRA Code of Conduct for Solicitors to maintain client confidentiality.[6]

There are limited options for ensuring the protection of client information in remote offices. Whilst firms can encourage a paper-free approach there will inevitably be some practitioners who prefer to work with hard copy documents. How those documents are protected and ultimately disposed of represents a risk to the firm. Firms should ensure that they have clear document destruction policies and could, for example, offer regular courier collections of client documents for confidential shredding, or provide staff working from home with a paper shredder.

In terms of electronic data, again firms will only have limited options in terms of monitoring the security of home Wi-Fi networks. Accordingly, the routes to accessing client data must be protected by the firm through its own server rather than through individuals' Wi-Fi or other virus protection regimes.

Of course it is not just "working from home" that poses such risks; solicitors and law firm staff are much more likely now to be "working from anywhere", such as public spaces, shared working environments, cafes, and trains. Again, whilst risks arising from such working practices existed pre-COVID, they are likely now to be much more widespread. Undertaking confidential and sensitive work in public areas risks breaches of regulatory obligations to keep client data secure, and also has reputational risks.

Dependence on technology

One of the issues that every practitioner has faced during the pandemic has been difficulties relating to technology, whether that be internet outages, connectivity issues, or difficulties in accessing video conferencing facilities and being seen and/or heard. These issues have the potential to pose risks for law firms. If, for example, a lawyer misses a court hearing as a result of a technical difficulty the firm may face an order for wasted costs, a claim from a client, or disciplinary action. Whilst there may initially have been some leeway for such issues, that period has now passed. In addition, it may be that notes of client meetings will not be accurate if the note taker was unable to see or hear those who are speaking throughout the meeting. This is a risk that simply did not arise in the traditional office environment.

In terms of mitigating the risk, it may be prudent to have at least two lawyers attending each virtual hearing or meeting, so that there is some level of back-up. Undertaking technical checks in advance of a hearing (with colleagues or the judge's clerk) may also provide opportunities to iron out technical issues before they cause any significant problems.

Unauthorized video, audio, or photo recordings

One novel difficulty that represents a further risk to law firms is the prospect of individuals viewing court hearings remotely, which in turn provides opportunities for illicit recordings to be made that would have been far more difficult in a traditional court setting. Whilst that would be an obvious contempt of court, and subject the individual to sanction, such behavior could also represent a risk to law firms in relation to regulatory and reputational risk. Again, in the pre-COVID environment, such events would be incredibly rare because of the oversight of the physical courtroom by the court clerk, the judge, and the attendees at the hearing.

A similar risk arises in relation to covert recordings of meetings held remotely, including without prejudice meetings, by those who may then wish to make inappropriate or impermissible use of such content. Again, this is a risk that arises far more prominently in relation to remote meetings as opposed to in-person meetings.

A further issue in this context is the prospect of remote hearings being accessed and viewed from outside the jurisdiction without the appropriate consent from the court first being obtained. Whilst this may be a result of a misunderstanding or error (such as a link to a hearing being forwarded to another employee in another office) it nonetheless risks a contempt of court. Whereas in open court it would be obvious if, for example, someone was attempting to record the proceedings, that is far less easy to control in relation to remote hearings. Whilst it should be expected that solicitors will understand that remote hearings should be treated in precisely the same way as in-person hearings, firms may nonetheless consider issuing guidance to fee-earners to ensure that there are no inadvertent breaches of rules that risk contempt proceedings, which could occur in relation to recording a hearing or sending a remote hearing link to a third party (or to someone outside of the jurisdiction) without the requisite permission having first been obtained.

Use of social media platforms

Social media did not arise from the COVID-19 pandemic and the shift to the hybrid working environment. However, it is another example where the usual checks and balances that a firm may have can perhaps be more easily overcome as a result of more limited oversight.

Whilst many firms take advantage of social media networks for promotional purposes, there is a real risk of adverse publicity, particularly if an error or mistake reaches the mainstream media. In addition, the ability of third parties to comment on social media posts poses a risk of inadvertent breaches of regulatory obligations, for example, client confidentiality. Accordingly, a clear and coherent policy relating to social media is a crucial factor for risk management for law firms. Firms' social media accounts should be tightly controlled with appropriate two-factor approvals required. There should also be in place appropriate automated notifications to bring comments to the immediate attention of firms so that any issues can be remedied as soon as possible.

A further risk to consider is the rapid rise of the legal "influencer". Whilst having employees with large social media platforms can provide significant opportunities, it can also result in unforeseen conflicts of interest arising (for example, the individual being asked to undertake promotions unrelated to the firm). In addition, the reach of some influencers can have an unintended consequence if an error or issue arises, because of the size of the possible audience.

Legal/regulatory risks

Supervision

Pursuant to paragraph 4.4 of the SRA Code of Conduct for Firms and paragraph 3.5 of the SRA Code of Conduct for Solicitors, there is an obligation to ensure that there is adequate supervision of those providing legal services.[7] Providing adequate supervision is perhaps the greatest challenge of remote or hybrid working simply because more people are working alone and, ergo, unsupervised.

The risk of unsupervised solicitors undertaking work for which they are not adequately qualified, or advising clients in an unsupervised way, is considerably higher when those solicitors are less able to discuss issues with colleagues. In order to comply with their regulatory obligations, and to limit exposure to risk of claims, firms should have in place rigorous procedures to record and monitor how junior fee earners are being supervised and by whom. There needs to be the remote equivalent of an "open door" policy such that queries can be raised and addressed. Ensuring that more senior solicitors are copied to client and inter-partes correspondence (and that they have manageable workloads such that they can properly engage with each matter) will reduce the scope of errors arising or going unnoticed.

Training and professional development

Whilst the need to record a fixed number of professional development hours is no longer a requirement of qualified solicitors, firms and solicitors are nonetheless still required to ensure that they are professionally competent and undertake suitable professional development training to maintain that level of competence.[8] Most firms will have in place ways of recording professional development activities, and offer a range of seminars and presentations that can be either undertaken in person, live, or through watching a recording. Again, whilst this flexibility is welcome, it can lead to a risk that busy solicitors do not in fact dedicate sufficient time to professional development. Firms should ensure that as part of regular interaction with staff the issue of professional development is explored, and if gaps are identified then they need to be addressed.

Importance of embedding a risk averse, ethically focused, and regulatory compliant culture

Law firm culture ultimately derives from how more junior staff see their leaders behaving. A culture of risk taking and unethical behavior by partners is likely to foster the same approach throughout the firm.

With appropriate supervision, recording, and monitoring in place, behaviors that do not meet the high standards expected of solicitors should be capable of identification at an early stage before any damage is done. However, there is always a risk of "rogues" in positions of trust, and those who are intending to act in bad faith may be more easily able to do so in a hybrid working environment where there is less oversight. Accordingly, firms must be alive to the risks of hybrid working and should already have, for example, banking policies that require multi-factor authentication and senior approval before transfers are made.

Most important, however, is having a culture of openness where errors can be admitted without risk of blame or sanction. There have been a number of regulatory prosecutions relating to attempts to conceal a relatively minor mistake, including by creating false documents, which have resulted in solicitors being struck-off for dishonesty. Accordingly, the "cover-up" more often than not leads to a greater regulatory penalty than the error itself. Ensuring that employees are adequately supported if errors occur is therefore an important factor in potentially preventing more significant issues in the long run.

Aligned with this, issues of risk and compliance should form part of regular training and professional development updates, either by the firm's in-house counsel teams or by way of briefings from external advisors.

Conclusion

In conclusion, whilst the move to hybrid working was accelerated by the pandemic, it is clearly the model that is here to stay. It requires a renewed approach to some risk issues, and may also result in entirely new issues that firms need to consider. In these circumstances, it is important that firms review and update their risk management structures to reflect this new working model, and future adaptation to it, to ensure that they remain comprehensive and appropriate. Given that it is increasingly clear that staff expect firms to adopt flexible working structures, a firm's ability to manage effectively a hybrid working model will also likely be a key issue when it comes to recruitment and retention.

References

1. See, for example, the Solicitors Regulation Authority, Workplace Culture Thematic Review, issued in February 2022, www.sra.org.uk/sra/research-publications/workplace-culture-thematic-review/.
2. Life in the Law 2020/21, www.lawcare.org.uk/media/14vhquzz/lawcare-lifeinthelaw-v6-final.pdf.
3. Solicitors Regulation Authority, Code of Conduct for Firms, 25 November 2019, www.sra.org.uk/solicitors/standards-regulations/code-conduct-firms/, paragraph 2.1.
4. *Ibid*, paragraph 2.5.
5. *Ibid*, paragraph 2.2.
6. Solicitors Regulation Authority, Code of Conduct for Solicitors, RELs and RFLs, 25 November 2019, www.sra.org.uk/solicitors/standards-regulations/code-conduct-solicitors/.
7. *Ibid* 3 and 6.
8. *Ibid* 3, paragraph 4.3, and 6, paragraph 3.3.

Chapter 2: Climate change and ESG risks for lawyers

By Alexia Howard, senior associate, and Simon Konsta, partner, Clyde & Co LLP

Introduction

In recent years, the world has faced many challenges. Resilience, corporate social responsibility, and protecting the environment have increasingly been at the forefront of many minds and businesses. The 17th edition of the World Economic Forum's Global Risks Report referred to "climate action failure" as being one of the most severe risks anticipated for the coming decade.[1] Key messages that came out of the 2021 United Nations Climate Change Conference (COP26) in Glasgow appear to be that the climate crisis is urgent, and that each and every one of us must play our part now to ensure the safety and prosperity of our planet.[2]

Lawyers and law firms are no exception to the need for all businesses to adapt, to improve corporate social responsibility as much as their carbon footprint. The remit is wide ranging – care and attention towards these issues might be taken in respect of firms' daily operations, and lawyers' advice to their clients. Horizon-scanning for the developing risks will be important to protect our businesses in this changing environment.

What is ESG?

In April 2006, the United Nations Principles for Responsible Investment were launched.[3] These comprise principles on Environmental, Social, and Governance issues, which are now used by many businesses to evaluate their corporate consciousness and commitment to climate and social responsibility. Prospective clients, new investors, and socially conscious job applicants will be increasingly alive to these credentials.

Environmental

The environmental aspect focuses on the contribution an entity makes to the planet and change in climate through, for example, its fossil fuel emissions, waste disposal, and energy practices. This aligns with commitments nations and companies are making to reach net zero emissions. Section

1 of the Climate Change Act 2008 provides that: *"It is the duty of the Secretary of State to ensure that the net UK carbon account for the year 2050 is at least 80 percent lower than the 1990 baseline."*[4] Section 32 established the Committee on Climate Change, which advises the Secretary of State on the 2050 target and carbon budgets. The 9 December 2020 carbon budget set an ambitious target of 78 percent reduction in greenhouse gas emissions by 2035.[5]

Social

The social pillar of the ESG acronym seeks to highlight the importance of diversity and inclusion within firms and across sectors. Its relevance is wide-ranging, including issues of human rights, community engagement, and working conditions. One key focus is supply chains – companies are becoming increasingly alive to the possibility of being embarrassed by those who supply them, and perhaps even any companies that they themselves supply if it transpires that a connected entity is a big carbon emitter or associated with slave labor.

Governance

The final element concerns corporate governance, and the implementation of good environmental and social practices within a firm. This would require the embedding of guidance and principles that explain the employees' rights and responsibilities. Implementation turns on appropriate risk management, strategy, communication, and interaction from board level through to business services.

Reputational risks

We have all seen the myriad headlines in recent years that focused increasingly on sustainability and ESG.[6] In light of the concerns raised, clients will be emboldened to do more homework on their advisers and expect them to reflect their own values and stance on those areas. That also applies for law students and prospective job applicants, who are increasingly focused on sustainability.

Activism and student movement

In February 2020, Harvard and Yale Law School students staged protests at events hosted by Paul, Weiss, Rifkind, Wharton & Garrison LLC, on account of the firm's representation of Exxon Mobil Corporation.[7] That spring, Yale Law School students established an organization named *"Law Students for Climate Accountability"*, which published *"The 2020 Law*

Firm Climate Change Scorecard" in October 2020. The scorecard assigned climate scores (A to F) to each Vault 100 ranked firm,[8] according to their respective alleged roles in the climate change crisis, further to an analysis of those firms' litigation, transactional, and lobbying work between 2015 and 2019.

The UK has seen similar scenes. In February 2020, magic circle firm Slaughter and May was targeted by Lawyers for Extinction Rebellion (LER), on account of the firm's retainer by Premier Oil plc in relation to its North Sea expansion.[9] In September 2020, LER protested outside the Law Society, the Solicitors Regulation Authority, and the Bar Council to demand that further attention be paid to climate change.[10] In August 2021, it was reported that LER also planned to target City law firms that allegedly contributed to the climate crisis.[11]

These developments highlight a growing trend amongst activists and prospective and junior lawyers of questioning the green credentials of firms' client bases and practices. Firms should be alive to this and seek to retain top talent and clients, such as by considering if new instructions present potential climate change risks (as Clifford Chance has resolved to do).[12]

Climate change resolution

On 31 October 2021, the Law Society published its climate change resolution (the "Resolution"). This echoed the American Bar Association climate change policy and resolution adopted in August 2019,[13] the Climate Crisis Statement published by the International Bar Association in May 2020,[14] and the sentiments of the United States Special Presidential Envoy for Climate, John Kerry, in his 5 August 2021 address to the ABA in which he said: *"In short, you are all climate lawyers now, whether you want to be or not… there's a place for lawyers to help hold back the tide and create new pathways."*[15]

The Resolution encourages the legal profession to reclaim that sense of having a crucial part to play in the world's trajectory. Through it, the Law Society resolves to develop plans, targets, and action consistent with restricting global warming to 1.5°C; guide the profession on how to adopt the above into their business; *"engage in climate conscious legal practice"*;[16] and encourage lawyers *"to take a holistic and proactive approach to mitigating the climate crisis and promoting climate change adaptation"*.[17]

The Resolution is easily accessible on the Law Society's website and was well publicized. It will not go unnoticed by clients and competitors. A failure to implement it could expose lawyers to potential criticism and reputational weakness.

Transition and transactional risks

Environmental due diligence in corporate transactions, reports on title in real estate transactions, and advice around capital raising activities such as IPOs require lawyers to be alert to developing environmental risks. Banking lawyers may also see greater responsibilities arising in finance transactions around climate and socially-conscious investments.

General Electric

General Electric's acquisition of Alstom is an example of how an entity and transaction may suffer from the changing environment. At the relevant time, the gas turbine market had collapsed as wind and other renewable resources became affordable. Within two years of the acquisition completing, the relevant GE division headed into a steep downturn. GE's 2014 annual report had noted that: *"Excess capacity in developed markets and macroeconomic and geopolitical environments result in uncertainty for the industry and business."*[18] Despite this ominous footnote, the transaction completed in 2015 for approximately US$10.6 billion.[19] A report by the Institute for Energy Economics and Financial Analysis confirms that between 2016 and 2018, GE lost US$193bn (74 percent) of its market capitalization, largely due to the collapse of the global thermal power market, and that US$23bn of goodwill was written down in GE's power division in 2018, chiefly due to the Alstom acquisition.[20]

Considering this transaction through the lens of today's heightened focus on renewable energy and transition generally demonstrates how the transition will condition the commercial setting against which commercial lawyers will be advising in the future. With that hindsight, potential areas of exposure for the lawyers advising on this transaction would include the due diligence seemingly missing issues with the underlying cash flow assumptions, but also any commercial advice that failed to warn GE sufficiently of the scale of change in the energy market, in which the transaction ultimately was doomed to fail. Given market changes, lawyers may need to advise on legal issues arising from unextracted fossil fuel resources that appear as assets on companies' ledgers ("stranded assets"). However, the dividing line between legal and commercial industry sector issues can sometimes be blurred, making it harder to know exactly how detailed advice needs to be to protect against any future liability.

Transactional scrutiny

Other aspects of transactional work that may come under scrutiny in today's environment include contractual warranties, indemnities, and property valuations. Mergers and acquisitions involving energy and transport businesses may be the obvious candidates, but any purchase of new property or contracts with new suppliers, for example, may also involve further due diligence. Questions should be asked as to a property's energy sources and efficiency, suppliers' labor standards, and sourcing of materials, and much more.

Financial investments will also need to be undertaken responsibly. In March 2019 the Loan Market Association published the Sustainability Linked Loan Principles, to encourage borrowers to improve ESG performance in exchange for aligned loan terms (such as in relation to margins).[21] As green savings bonds become increasingly popular, lawyers will need to advise financial clients carefully on the risks of continuing to fund oil companies and fossil fuel developments. Increasing advances in technology alongside global warming mean stranded assets may suffer from unexpected or premature devaluation or write-down. Lawyers will need to keep abreast of relevant legal and regulatory developments, particularly if instructed on claims involving investee companies as the UK's 2050 net zero deadline approaches.

Corporate disclosure and liability risks

The Task Force

The Financial Stability Board announced the establishment of the Task Force on Climate-related Financial Disclosures (TCFD) in 2015.[22] The TCFD aims to improve and increase corporate reporting of climate-related financial information to markets and stakeholders, to assist climate change risk management, investment, and underwriting decisions. The TCFD takes the form of 11 recommended disclosures under four pillars (governance, strategy, risk management, and metrics and targets) as published in 2017.[23]

Disclosure consultation

In December 2020, the Financial Conduct Authority (FCA) introduced a new Listing Rule for commercial companies with a UK premium listing to make disclosures, on a comply or explain basis, consistent with the recommendations of the TCFD (see FCA Policy Statement 20/17).[24] That came into effect for accounting periods beginning on or after 1 January 2021. In December 2021, the Listing Rule was extended to issuers of standard listed shares and standard listed global depository receipts representing equity shares for accounting periods commencing on or after 1 January 2022 (see FCA Policy Statement 21/23).[25]

In parallel, from 24 March 2021 to 5 May 2021, the Department for Business, Energy and Industrial Strategy (BEIS) ran a consultation seeking views on proposals to require a broader spectrum of entities, namely LLPs, publicly quoted and large private companies to make mandatory climate-related financial disclosures aligned with the four pillars of the TCFD.[26] Further to that consultation, a draft statutory instrument was laid before the House of Commons on 28 October 2021.[27] The Companies (Strategic Report) (Climate-related Financial Disclosure) Regulations 2022 SI 2022/31, which came into force on 6 April 2022 and apply for accounting periods commencing on or after that date,[28] require climate-related financial disclosures to be made in strategic company reports, which broadly align with the four overarching pillars of TCFD.

The FCA has also introduced mandatory TCFD-aligned disclosure requirements on certain asset managers, life insurers, and FCA-regulated pension providers with a phased introduction from 1 January 2022 (see FCA Policy Statement 21/24[29] and ESG sourcebook within the FCA Handbook[30]). Further, the FCA launched a consultation, in November 2021, in relation to the new sustainability disclosure requirements and labelling system for sustainable investment products.[31] The Law Society has responded, emphasizing the need for the disclosure requirements to have a clear link to the underlying legal position.[32]

Finally, in the occupation pensions space, the Occupational Pension Schemes (Climate Change Governance and Reporting) Regulations 2021 came into force on 1 October 2021, which introduced new TCFD-aligned climate risk governance and reporting obligations on trustees of large occupational pension schemes.[33]

Lawyers advising corporate clients would do well to keep abreast of commentary and developments, to ensure their advice is current and sufficiently comprehensive. In addition, some law firms will be caught by The Limited Liability Partnerships (Climate-related Financial Disclosures) Regulations 2022,[34] which also came into force on 6 April 2022, and thus will need to consider these reporting requirements for their own account as well.

Compliance

In order to comply with increased disclosure obligations, businesses will need to embed a climate conscious culture. BEIS's consultation paper suggested this would be essential to ensure that the issue of climate change is considered at each and every level of the business.[35] That might be achieved through increased collaboration between employers and employees, and a review of the employment relationship to maximize sustainability.

Compliance will be crucial in order to avoid regulatory scrutiny. Environmental law charity ClientEarth has already reported non-compliance complaints to UK financial regulators requiring companies, including Just Eat, to disclose any "material risks" that may influence their investors' decisions.[36]

Climate litigation

The importance of focusing on good corporate governance is also clear to see when we consider the steep rise in climate litigation. Remedies are being sought worldwide under tort, human rights, corporate, constitutional, and other areas of the law, on the grounds of alleged negligence, nuisance, or product liability.

May 2021 saw a convergence of landmark climate litigation findings, activist and inter-governmental organization publications. The International Energy Agency released a report, *"Net Zero by 2050: A Roadmap for the Global Energy Sector"*,[37] which called for an end to new oil and gas projects and coal mines. On 26 May 2021 the District Court of The Hague handed down its judgment in the case of *Milieudefensie et al. v. Royal Dutch Shell PLC*, which ordered Shell to reduce its global group carbon emission figures *"by at least net 45 percent at end 2030, relative to 2019 levels"*.[38] This was the first instance of a court ordering a private corporation to reduce emissions in line with the Paris Agreement. The same day, activist hedge fund Engine No. 1 unseated two Exxon Mobil Corporation board members, in an attempt to make the corporation's business strategy more climate-conscious.[39] All this suggests that investors, consumers, governments, and judicial systems are moving towards the enforcement of more positive action amongst corporations.

Lawyers advising clients on managing liability risks should also be aware of the range of legal grounds and systems under which a claim might be brought. As climate is a global issue, it is open to claimants to forum shop. Further, climate disputes typically involve individuals or groups seeking to hold governments or corporations to account; and the latter will have far greater lifespans and resources than the former. Business principles and human rights frameworks already place a duty on corporations to remedy any negative consequences of their actions on the enjoyment of human rights.[40] Lawyers may be expected to anticipate and understand these issues, and to seek to mitigate asymmetries between parties to ensure proper and fair functioning of the Law and avoid coming under criticism.

Greenwashing

What is greenwashing?

In line with international commitments to achieving net-zero, public and private entities are increasingly publishing climate statements, advertising clean energy investments, and pledging emission reduction targets. One of the biggest trends in climate-related litigation in recent years is allegations against companies for greenwashing – making unsupported, misleading statements or disclosures in relation to environmental performance or targets, for commercial gain. Further to COP26 scrutiny of the content of climate and ESG-related statements and pledges will increase. That focus, alongside mounting stakeholder pressure, means that "climate-washing" litigation is likely to increase exponentially.

Dieselgate and other examples

There are already several renowned examples of where corporations have been held to account for misleading climate-related advertising. The "Dieselgate" scandal, which concerned tampering with emissions tests of cars sold by the Volkswagen Group over a period of nearly ten years, to achieve results within acceptable emissions limits, resulted in the United States levying a record $4.3bn in criminal and civil penalties on the manufacturer.[41] In 2019, ClientEarth filed a complaint against British Petroleum in relation to its misleading "Keep Advancing" and "Possibilities Everywhere" campaigns that focused on BP's lower carbon energy products, and did not conform to guidelines for multinational enterprises issued by the Organization for Economic Cooperation and Development.[42] Similarly, the first climate-washing complaint to the Federal Trade Commission was made in 2021, jointly filed by Earthworks, Global Witness, and Greenpeace USA, relating to allegedly misleading advertising placed in the *New York Times* by multinational energy corporation Chevron that stated natural gas usage had resulted in "*unprecedented reductions in US energy-related carbon emissions*".[43] The FTC complaint claimed this had been said despite the fact that the corporation's business relied predominantly on fossil fuels.[44] Whilst the advertisement mentioned carbon emissions, it made no mention of another greenhouse gas, methane. An Earthworks press release concerning the FTC complaint stated that fieldwork conducted by Earthworks showed Chevron was "*regularly polluting methane*",[45] which has over 50 times the warming potential of carbon dioxide within 20 years of its emission.[46]

Airlines have also been criticized for "climate-washing". In 2020, the

Advertising Standards Authority (ASA) determined that Ryanair advertisements claiming that customers would have lower personal carbon dioxide emissions than with other carriers were misleading, unsubstantiated, and breached the UK Code of Non-broadcast Advertising and Direct & Promotional Marketing.[47]

Lessons to be learnt

Companies would be well advised to review any advertisements they wish to put out with their lawyers, alongside those companies' net-zero or other climate pledges, to ensure the publication of accurate information and mitigate the risk of potential greenwashing claims. Lawyers would be well advised to get to grips with their jurisdiction's laws and regulations prohibiting false advertising and consumer protection, in order to advise their clients on those accordingly. Failure to do so could substantially increase the risk of negligence claims against those firms for a lack of appropriate advice in this increasingly litigious climate.

Diversity and inclusion

One consequence of the COVID-19 pandemic has been to accelerate changes across the profession, in the way we work and travel for business. The necessity of remote working also highlighted the importance of connectivity, collegiality, and mentoring. That in turn has led professionals to take stock of their surroundings and consider where there might be room for improvement.

The statistics

On 1 February 2022, the SRA published data on diversity in the profession.[48] On the gender balance, it was found that 52 percent of the profession as a whole, and 61 percent of solicitors, are women, but that women only represent 35 percent of partners. Only five percent of lawyers had declared a disability (even though 14 percent of the wider UK working population had reported a disability). At the largest firms, only eight percent of partners were found to be Black, Asian, or of ethnic origin. Evidently, progress is needed – in many areas, and for myriad reasons.

Obligations to clients and the profession

Firms should be aware of the nine protected characteristics and key forms of discrimination under the Equality Act 2010,[49] and promote equality, diversity, and inclusion in accordance with Principle 6 of the SRA's Standards and Regulations.[50] Since the Equality Act 2010, further developments have included the right of all employees to ask for flexible working,[51] the introduction of shared parental leave,[52] and the legal requirement to accurately report gender pay gap data (if the firm employs 250 or more people).[53] There is an increasing risk of reputational damage – and potential liability – for firms that do not meet these requirements.

The issue is also key, reputationally, to business development, recruitment, and retention. Prospective trainees and pupils will scrutinize all available resources to establish whether future employers have, and are meeting, diversity and inclusion targets. Mere lip service and window dressing will not suffice. Speaking to the House of Commons in March 2014 in relation to judicial appointments, Lord Neuberger highlighted the *"risk that having a high proportion of minority group in junior positions can mislead as to the extent to which there is real inclusiveness throughout an organisation"*.[54] The same is true for many clients, who may increasingly prefer to send their business to firms and lawyers who truly represent them and their values. To that end, insurers now increasingly look to retain legal advisers on their panels who will understand and reflect their ESG standards, including in relation to diversity, given the equivalent industry expectations they face on these issues.[55]

The sense of appropriate representation goes above and beyond the case of an individual client or firm. Lord Neuberger's March 2014 Commons speech highlighted the need to deepen the pool of judicial candidates through greater inclusivity: *"the bigger that pool the higher the quality of judges"*.[56] The Lammy Review, published on 8 September 2017, equally highlighted that a representative judiciary and body of legal professionals is crucial to achieving fair outcomes and greater trust in the legal sector.[57]

The theme for International Women's Day 2022, "Breaking the Bias", calls for the profession to strive to be free of bias, stereotypes, and discrimination. As most biases are held unconsciously, addressing this requires conscious effort and focus through appropriate training. The risks of not doing more to address it include restricted vision and perspectives that may lead us to make assumptions; potential allegations being brought against legal professionals for discrimination; and potential complaints being notified to the SRA.

Conclusion

Lawyers are highly experienced in managing known risks and crafting clauses to record and reflect necessary actions and achieve best outcomes for their clients. The challenges around climate change and ESG are nascent, and intricate. However, if properly addressed, they may also provide opportunities for lawyers to give back to their communities, support their environment, and improve their firms' resilience.

Lawyers would do well to equip themselves with the insight and tools to support clients and their own businesses in the transition to net zero. Whilst it is no mean feat, we need not act alone in this endeavor. The Law Society's climate change resolution[58] and the Legal Sustainability Alliance[59] both seek to promote best practice and guide their members in supporting the profession and clients in the field of climate and sustainability. The Chancery Lane Project has compiled a net zero toolkit that provides precedent climate-conscious contractual clauses, applicable to a wide range of practice areas, for lawyers and firms to incorporate into commercial agreements.[60] These and many other ideas provide a creative mechanism via which lawyers can advise clients sustainably and steer them towards net zero.

There are also steps firms can take on each of the ESG pillars to ensure resilience. Increased recycling, investment in renewable energy, and a wider variety of locally-sourced food options (minimizing carbon footprint) are examples of ways to improve environmental sustainability. Taking on pro bono instructions, volunteering with the local community and mentoring would inspire greater social support and mobility. Linking ESG to appraisal criteria and empowering employees to consider sustainability in their work may be positive steps towards good corporate governance.

References

1. See WEF Global Risks Report 2022, p.7, available at: www3.weforum.org/docs/WEF_The_Global_Risks_Report_2022.pdf.
2. See comments in, for example, the United Nations' online piece, "*COP26: Together for our planet*" available at: www.un.org/en/climatechange/cop26.
3. See United Nations' press release of 27 April 2006 regarding the launch, available at: https://press.un.org/en/2006/sg2111.doc.htm.
4. Climate Change Act 2008, Section 1, "*The target for 2050*", available at: www.legislation.gov.uk/ukpga/2008/27/part/1/crossheading/the-target-for-2050/made.
5. See the Government's press release of 20 April 2021, "*UK enshrines new target in law to slash emissions by 78% by 2035*" at: www.gov.uk/government/news/uk-enshrines-new-target-in-law-to-slash-emissions-by-78-by-2035.
6. A few recent examples include the *Financial Times*' article of 18 July 2022, "*Chief sustainability officers prosper as ESG risks mount*", available at: www.ft.com/content/918fee50-5c3c-46eb-af6b-41f2d4393307; Reuters' 28 July 2022 article, "*Positive ESG performance improves returns globally, research shows*", available at: www.reuters.com/business/sustainable-business/

positive-esg-performance-improves-returns-globally-research-shows-2022-07-28/; and EY's insight of 12 June 2020, "*Why sustainability and ESG are now more important than ever*", available at www.ey.com/en_us/assurance/why-sustainability-and-esg-are-now-more-important-than-ever.

7. See, for example, Yale News, "*YLS students protest firm's Exxon ties*", 9 February 2020 at: https://yaledailynews.com/blog/2020/02/09/yls-students-protest-firms-exxon-ties/.
8. See the Law Firm Climate Change Scorecard (2020), p.1, available at: https://static1.squarespace.com/static/5f53fa556b708446acb4dcb5/t/5f755753f217027860728759/1601525603800/Law+Firm+Climate+Change+Scorecard.pdf.
9. See, for example, The Lawyer, "*Extinction Rebellion targets Slaughter and May to protest BigLaw 'blood money'*", 28 February 2020 at: www.thelawyer.com/extinction-rebellion-protests-slaughters-blood-money/.
10. See, for example, Legal Cheek, "*Extinction Rebellion lawyers perform 'theatrical and arrestable' protest outside Law Society office*", 4 September 2020 at: www.legalcheek.com/2020/09/extinction-rebellion-lawyers-perform-theatrical-and-arrestable-protest-outside-law-society-office/.
11. See, for example, The Law Society Gazette, "*Extinction Rebellion confirms plans to target City law firms*", 24 August 2021 at: www.lawgazette.co.uk/news/extinction-rebellion-confirms-plans-to-target-city-law-firms/5109589.article.
12. See, for example, The Lawyer, "*Clifford Chance to scan new matters for climate change risks*", 20 January 2022 at: www.thelawyer.com/clifford-chance-to-scan-new-matters-for-climate-change-risks/.
13. See the American Bar Association's October 2019 Washington Letter, "*Climate Change Takes Center Stage*", available at: www.americanbar.org/advocacy/governmental_legislative_work/publications/washingtonletter/october_2019_wl/climate_article_oct_wl//, and the American Bar Association's Resolution and Policy Report at: www.americanbar.org/content/dam/aba/directories/policy/annual-2019/111-annual-2019.pdf.
14. See the International Bar Association's Climate Crisis Statement at: tinyurl.com/2ruev22a.
15. See transcription of John Kerry 2021 ABA Hybrid Annual Meeting Keynote Speech, produced by Ava Walrond for the Legal Pathways to Deep Decarbonization Project, p.2, available at: https://lpdd.org/wp-content/uploads/2021/08/John-Kerry-Keynote-Speech-2021-ABA-Hybrid-Annual-Meeting.pdf.
16. See The Law Society of England and Wales climate change resolution, section 3, available at: https://f.datasrvr.com/fr1/121/72710/The_Law_Society__Climate_Change_Resolution.pdf?utm_source=law_society_rel_man&utm_medium=email&utm_campaign=Local+Law+Society+Bulletin_11%2F03%2F2021.

17. *Ibid*, section 5.
18. See General Electric Company's 2014 Annual Report, Form 10-K, page 33, available at: www.ge.com/sites/default/files/GE_AR14.pdf.
19. See GE's 3 November 2015 press release, "*GE Completes Acquisition of Alstom Power and Grid Businesses*", available at: www.ge.com/news/press-releases/ge-completes-acquisition-alstom-power-and-grid-businesses.
20. Institute for Energy Economics and Financial Analysis, "*General Electric Misread the Energy Transition: A Cautionary Tale*", June 2019, at pages 1 and 12, available at: https://ieefa.org/wp-content/uploads/2019/06/General-Electric-Misread-the-Energy-Transition_June-2019.pdf.
21. See the Loan Market Association's 20 March 2019 press release, "*The LMA, APLMA and LSTA publish Sustainability Linked Loan Principles*", available at: www.lma.eu.com/news-publications/press-releases?id=162.
22. See the Financial Stability Board's 4 December 2015 press release, "*FSB to establish Task Force on Climate-related Financial Disclosures*", available at: https://assets.bbhub.io/company/sites/60/2015/12/12-4-2015-Climate-change-task-force-press-release.pdf.
23. See the Final Report, "*Recommendations of the Task Force on Climate-related Financial Disclosures*", June 2017, available at: https://assets.bbhub.io/company/sites/60/2021/10/FINAL-2017-TCFD-Report.pdf.
24. The FCA "*Proposals to enhance climate-related disclosures by listed issuers and clarification of existing disclosure obligations*" Policy Statement PS20/17, December 2020, is available at: www.fca.org.uk/publication/policy/ps20-17.pdf.
25. The FCA "*Enhancing climate-related disclosures by standard listed companies*" Policy Statement PS21/23, December 2021, is available at: www.fca.org.uk/publication/policy/ps21-23.pdf.
26. See the UK government's published consultation outcome, "*Mandatory climate-related financial disclosures by publicly quoted companies, large private companies and LLPs*", available at: www.gov.uk/government/consultations/mandatory-climate-related-financial-disclosures-by-publicly-quoted-companies-large-private-companies-and-llps#full-publication.
27. See the UK Parliament's online record of the Companies (Strategic Report) (Climate-related Financial Disclosure) Regulations 2021 Statutory Instrument being laid before Parliament on 28 October 2021: https://statutoryinstruments.parliament.uk/instrument/1OcNLYNq/.
28. See The Companies (Strategic Report) (Climate-related Financial Disclosure) Regulations 2022 SI 2022/31 at: www.legislation.gov.uk/uksi/2022/31/made. See also The Limited Liability Partnerships (Climate-related Financial Disclosures) Regulations 2022 SI 2022/46, which apply to LLPs and are particularly relevant to large law firms which are caught by its provisions, and will need to report accordingly; available at: www.legislation.gov.uk/uksi/2022/46/contents/made.

29. The FCA "*Enhancing climate-related disclosures by asset managers, life insurers and FCA-regulated pension providers*" Policy Statement PS21/24, December 2021, is available at: www.fca.org.uk/publication/policy/ps21-24.pdf.
30. The FCA "*Environmental, Social and Governance sourcebook*" within the FCA Handbook, March 2022, is available at: www.handbook.fca.org.uk/handbook/ESG.pdf.
31. FCA, Sustainability Disclosure Requirements and investment labels Discussion Paper DP21/4, November 2021, available at: www.fca.org.uk/publication/discussion/dp21-4.pdf.
32. The Law Society, "*Sustainability disclosure requirements and investment labels - Law Society response*", available at: www.lawsociety.org.uk/Campaigns/Consultation-responses/Sustainability-disclosure-requirements-and-investment-labels.
33. The Occupational Pension Schemes (Climate Change Governance and Reporting) Regulations 2021 SI 2021/839 are available at: www.legislation.gov.uk/uksi/2021/839/contents/made.
34. The Limited Liability Partnerships (Climate-related Financial Disclosures) Regulations 2022 SI 2022/46 are available at: www.legislation.gov.uk/uksi/2022/46/contents/made.
35. See the Department for Business, Energy & Industrial Strategy, "*Consultation on requiring mandatory climate-related financial disclosures by publicly quoted companies, large private companies and Limited Liability Partnerships*", p.12, at: https://assets.publishing.service.gov.uk/government/uploads/system/uploads/attachment_data/file/972422/Consultation_on_BEIS_mandatory_climate-related_disclosure_requirements.pdf.
36. See ClientEarth press release, "*ClientEarth files complaints against Just Eat and Carnival over climate failings*", 18 August 2021 at: www.clientearth.org/latest/press-office/press/clientearth-files-complaints-against-just-eat-and-carnival-over-climate-failings/.
37. See report by the International Energy Agency, "*Net Zero by 2050 A Roadmap for the Global Energy Sector*", IEA Publications, May 2021 at: https://iea.blob.core.windows.net/assets/deebef5d-0c34-4539-9d0c-10b13d840027/NetZeroby2050-ARoadmapfortheGlobalEnergySector_CORR.pdf.
38. See *Milieudefensie et al. v. Royal Dutch Shell PLC* C/09/571932 / HA ZA 19-379, paragraph 5.3, available at: https://uitspraken.rechtspraak.nl/inziendocument?id=ECLI:NL:RBDHA:2021:5339.
39. See, for example, Reuters, "*Exxon loses board seats to activist hedge fund in landmark climate vote*", 27 May 2021 at: www.reuters.com/business/sustainable-business/shareholder-activism-reaches-milestone-exxon-board-vote-nears-end-2021-05-26/.
40. See, for example, the United Nations Guiding Principles on Business and Human Rights, 2011 at: www.ohchr.org/sites/default/files/documents/publications/guidingprinciplesbusinesshr_en.pdf.

41. See press release of The United States Department of Justice, "*Volkswagen AG Agrees to Plead Guilty and Pay $4.3 Billion in Criminal and Civil Penalties; Six Volkswagen Executives and Employees are Indicted in Connection with Conspiracy to Cheat U.S. Emissions Tests*", 11 January 2017 at: www.justice.gov/opa/pr/volkswagen-ag-agrees-plead-guilty-and-pay-43-billion-criminal-and-civil-penalties-six.
42. See ClientEarth, "*Complaint against BP in respect of violations of the OECD Guidelines*", December 2019 at: www.clientearth.org/media/4npme1i1/ncp-complaint-clientearth-v-bp-complaint-submission-and-annex-a-ce-en.pdf.
43. See the advertisement in The New York Times, "*How Abundant Energy Is Fueling U.S. Growth*" at: www.nytimes.com/paidpost/chevron/how-abundant-energy-is-fueling-us-growth.html?section=header&subsection=1.
44. See details on the complaint from Greenpeace, USA "*Greenpeace jointly files FTC complaint against Chevron*", 16 March 2021 at: www.greenpeace.org/usa/news/greenpeace-jointly-files-ftc-complaint-against-chevron/.
45. See Earthworks' press release, "*Accountability groups file first of its kind FTC complaint against Chevron for misleading consumers on climate action*" of 16 March 2021, at: https://earthworks.org/releases/accountability-groups-file-first-of-its-kind-ftc-complaint-against-chevron-for-misleading-consumers-on-climate-action/.
46. Based on figures from the 2022 United Nations Framework Convention on Climate Change, Global Warming Potentials (IPCC Second Assessment Report) at: https://unfccc.int/process/transparency-and-reporting/greenhouse-gas-data/greenhouse-gas-data-unfccc/global-warming-potentials.
47. See ASA ruling, The Advertising Standards Authority, "*ASA Ruling on Ryanair Ltd t/a Ryanair Ltd*", 5 February 2020 at: www.asa.org.uk/rulings/ryanair-ltd-cas-571089-p1w6b2.html.
48. See the Solicitors Regulation Authority news release, "*Diversity in the profession continues to improve, but more to do*", 1 February 2022 at: www.sra.org.uk/sra/news/press/diversity-data-2021-published/.
49. See the Equality Act 2010, Chapter 1 in relation to protected characteristics (at: www.legislation.gov.uk/ukpga/2010/15/part/2/chapter/1) and Chapter 2 in relation to prohibited conduct (at: www.legislation.gov.uk/ukpga/2010/15/part/2/chapter/2).
50. See the Solicitors Regulation Authority's Standards and Regulations, Principle 6, at: www.sra.org.uk/solicitors/standards-regulations/principles/.
51. See the UK government website's flexible working overview confirming all employees' legal right to request flexible working, at: www.gov.uk/flexible-working.
52. See the UK government website's guide for employers on the introduction of shared parental leave, at: www.gov.uk/shared-parental-leave-and-pay-employer-guide/starting-shared-parental-leave.
53. See the UK government website's guidance on pay gap reporting requirements: www.gov.uk/guidance/the-gender-pay-gap-information-employers-must-report.

54. See The Supreme Court, "*Rainbow Lecture 2014 on Diversity*", paragraph 25, by Lord Neuberger on 12 March 2014 at: www.supremecourt.uk/docs/speech-140312.pdf.
55. See, for example, the insight, "*Insurers Take the Lead on ESG/Sustainability Initiatives*" published by JD Supra on 1 October 2021, at: www.jdsupra.com/legalnews/insurers-take-the-lead-on-esg-6954367/ and the Prudential Regulation Authority's proposal in August 2017 that all Solvency II firms should produce a diversity policy – see: www.thepfs.org/media/7768067/cii_policy_briefing_diversity.pdf.
56. *Ibid* 54, paragraph 15.
57. See produced by David Lammy MP, *The Lammy Review*, commissioned by David Cameron and Theresa May at: https://assets.publishing.service.gov.uk/government/uploads/system/uploads/attachment_data/file/643001/lammy-review-final-report.pdf and published on the UK government's website on 8 September 2017, at: www.gov.uk/government/publications/lammy-review-final-report.
58. The Law Society's climate change resolution is available at: www.lawsociety.org.uk/topics/climate-change/creating-a-climate-conscious-approach-to-legal-practice.
59. The Legal Sustainability Alliance: https://legalsustainabilityalliance.com/.
60. The Chancery Lane Project and its net zero toolkit available at: https://chancerylaneproject.org/toolkit/.

Chapter 3:
Data protection

By Nigel Miller, founding partner, Fox Williams LLP

Introduction

Compliance with data protection laws is a key regulatory risk for law firms, just as it is for clients. Law firms manage huge volumes of data relating to their clients, which can be both sensitive and confidential. Law firms are subject to a general duty of confidentiality to keep the affairs of clients confidential unless disclosure is required or permitted by law or the client consents. In addition to this, law firms must comply with data protection laws.

The risk of getting it wrong can be severe. Aside from substantial fines, more damaging can be the adverse publicity, damage to reputation, and loss of goodwill that can flow from a data breach or regulatory action. This chapter sets out a high-level summary of applicable data protection laws, with a focus on areas that have specific application to law firms, and provides some best practice points for risk management.

Overview

Applicable law

The GDPR applies to all UK organizations that handle personal data. Since Brexit, we refer to the EU GDPR[1] and the UK GDPR.[2] In the UK, the Data Protection Act 2018 (DPA) applies alongside UK GDPR. In this chapter we refer generically to the GDPR.

While the GDPR applies only to "personal data", law firms handle considerable volumes of information that may not fall within the definition of personal data (for example, confidential corporate information). Some of the disciplines imposed by the GDPR in respect of personal data (for example, data security) can also be helpful in terms of protection of such other information.

In the UK, the Information Commissioner's Office (ICO) is the national data protection authority.

Awareness

It is important to ensure that the firm's decision-makers and personnel who handle personal data are aware of the extensive obligations imposed by the data protection regime. The firm should adopt a data protection compliance policy to make sure all staff are aware of their obligations. Compliance with data protection laws should be recorded as a risk in the firm's risk register.

Many data breaches arise as a result of human error. Crucially, therefore, all staff should receive training to ensure awareness of data protection laws and cyber risks. This can be done remotely using elearning programs.

Law firms as controller or processor

The GDPR distinguishes between "controllers" and "processors". In any transaction involving personal data, it is essential to identify the roles correctly (e.g. processor, independent controller, or joint controller) as this determines the obligations of each party under data protection laws.

The controller is the party *"which, alone or jointly with others, determines the purposes and means of the processing of personal data"*.[3] The ICO describes this as the party that decides what data to process and why.[4]

A processor is a body *"which processes personal data on behalf of the controller"*.[5] Typically, a processor is a service provider for the controller.

The main obligations under GDPR fall on the controller. However, a processor also has some standalone obligations (such as record keeping and data security).

Some clients assume that their law firm is a processor and request that the firm enters into a data processing agreement as they would with other service providers. Generally, this is not appropriate as it is considered that law firms process personal data on behalf of their clients as independent controller and not as processor. This is because law firms provide independent advice and have their own professional and regulatory responsibilities that can impact on their processing of the data. The Law Society has also cautioned that contractual obligations imposed upon a law firm in a data processor agreement could put the firm in conflict with its professional duties.[6]

Registration

In the UK, controllers need to register with the ICO and pay the data protection fee.[7] You are at risk of receiving a fine and attracting adverse publicity if you fail to register. Registration is a relatively straightforward step. On the other hand, failure to pay the fee is publicly visible – because firms that have registered are on the searchable register on the ICO website – and could also betray a failure to comply with data protection requirements more generally.

There is no need to register if you only carry out "exempt processing"[8] of personal data, such as staff administration, advertising, marketing and PR, and accounts and record keeping. Even if you are exempt from registration, you must still comply with the requirements of data protection law and best practice is to register voluntarily for public transparency and in case any of your processing extends beyond the scope of the limited exemptions (so as to avoid receiving a fine).

It's good practice to have a process in place to pay the data protection fee on an annual basis. This can be done by setting up a direct debit with the ICO so that the registration is auto-renewed.

Data protection principles

There are seven data protection principles that form the core of the GDPR regime.[9] These are:

1. The lawfulness, fairness and transparency principle – see further below, under "Transparency".
2. The purpose limitation principle – data should be collected only "*for specified, explicit and legitimate purposes and not further processed in a manner that is incompatible with those purposes*".
3. The data minimization principle – you should hold only the minimum amount of personal data you need to fulfil your purpose.
4. The accuracy principle – "*personal data must be accurate and, where necessary, kept up to date; every reasonable step must be taken to ensure that personal data that are inaccurate, having regard to the purposes for which they are processed, are erased or rectified without delay*".
5. The storage limitation principle – see further below.
6. The integrity and confidentiality (data security) principle – see further below.
7. The accountability principle – see further below.

Transparency

Providing privacy information is a fundamental requirement of the GDPR. In practice this means providing a privacy notice to anyone whose personal data you collect. Law firms will typically require privacy notices for clients and prospective clients, for partners and other members of staff, for candidates, for marketing contacts such as users of the website or people you meet at networking events, for visitors to the office and for suppliers.

Under the GDPR, a privacy notice also has to be provided to individuals whose personal data you receive from someone else; for example, information you receive from the client. This may include family members, or people on the other side of a transaction or dispute. In this case, however, there are exemptions that are helpful for law firms. Privacy information does not need to be provided where:

- *"[T]he provision of… information proves impossible or would involve a disproportionate effort,… or in so far as… is likely to render impossible or seriously impair the achievement of the objectives of that processing"*;[10] or
- A claim to legal professional privilege or, in Scotland, confidentiality of communications, could be maintained in legal proceedings in respect of the personal data;[11] or
- The personal data is subject to a duty of confidentiality owed by a professional legal adviser to a client of the adviser.[12]

In practice, the professional duty of confidentiality will make the exemption available.

Storage limitation

The "storage limitation" principle means that personal data must be kept "*for no longer than is necessary*" for the purposes for which the personal data are processed.[13]

As such, each firm needs to establish and document its data retention policy. It is for each firm to decide how long personal data should be retained, taking into account legal and tax requirements, data protection laws, liability limitation periods, business needs, and professional obligations.

Once a retention period has expired, the data or record should be reviewed and securely destroyed if it is no longer needed. Keeping data for longer than is necessary, aside from breaching this principle, unnecessarily exposes the firm to continuing risk (e.g. in the event of a data breach) in relation to the data which it is holding.

Data security

The security of the data (both personal data and confidential corporate data) that law firms process will be an ongoing concern for the management of the firm. A breach of data security can lead to substantial reputational damage, as well as potential loss of business, liabilities, costs, and regulatory action.

Under the GDPR, controllers and processors are required to implement *"appropriate technical and organizational measures to ensure a level of security appropriate to the risk".*[14] The GDPR takes a risk-based approach such that there is no "one size fits all" requirement for data security. You can take into account the state of the art, costs of implementation, and the nature of the processing as well as the risk of varying likelihood and severity for the rights and freedoms of the data subjects.

The "state of the art" will be determined by reference to relevant industry standards of good practice including the ISO 27000 series, the National Institutes of Standards and Technology (NIST), the various guidance from the ICO, the National Cyber Security Centre (NCSC), the Solicitors Regulatory Authority (SRA), Lexcel, and "NCSC Cyber Essentials".

Organizational measures will include development and regular review of the firm's IT security policy, including physical and digital access controls, strong password policies, staff training, and a process for regularly testing and evaluating the effectiveness of the measures put in place.

Technical measures can include implementing encryption of personal data when personal data is in transit (including on storage devices and laptops) and multi-factor authentication. In the event of the loss or theft of the device, the risk of the data being compromised is much reduced and as such there may be no need to report the loss or theft to the ICO as a personal data breach (see below). In addition, ensuring systems are kept up to date with virus protection, timely implementation of software security patches, and maintaining robust data back-up processes are essential.

In March 2022, the ICO fined Tuckers Solicitors LLP £98,000 for contravention of the data security principle following a personal data breach that resulted from a ransomware attack involving the encryption by the attacker of 972,191 files, some of which were then released on the dark web. The ICO identified a number of areas where Tuckers had failed to comply with the data security principle, including use of single factor authentication when multi-factor authentication should have been applied, failing to implement a free patch for four months after it was released (thus allowing a software vulnerability to be exploited), and failing to encrypt data stored on the firm's archive server.[15]

Lawful ground for processing

You can only process personal data if you have a lawful ground for doing so under Article 6 of GDPR. The main lawful grounds for processing are:

- Consent;
- Performance of a contract;
- Compliance with a legal obligation; and
- Necessary for the purpose of legitimate interests.

Under the GDPR, consent must be freely given, specific, informed, and unambiguous. Consent also has to be a positive indication of agreement to personal data being processed – it cannot be inferred from silence, pre-ticked boxes, or inactivity. A separate distinct (granular) consent is needed for different purposes and types of processing. Because of the high bar for obtaining a valid consent, and because consent can always be refused or revoked, it is not normally the preferred ground. Furthermore, consent of employees in the HR context is not normally considered to be valid because of the imbalance in the relationship such that employees may not have an effective free choice.

Where you rely on "legitimate interests", you need to document a legitimate interests assessment (LIA). The ICO provides a template to assist with this.[16]

You have to explain your lawful ground for processing in any privacy notice and when you answer a data subject request.

Special category personal data

If you are processing special category personal data, you will need to identify an additional ground under Article 9. Special category data is personal data revealing racial or ethnic origin, political opinions, religious or philosophical beliefs, or trade union membership; genetic or biometric data processed for the purpose of uniquely identifying a natural person; and personal data concerning health, sex life or sexual orientation.

There are a number of potential grounds for processing special category data, including:

- The data subject has given explicit consent to the processing;
- The processing is necessary for the purposes of compliance with the obligations of an employer under employment law;

- The processing is necessary for the establishment, exercise or defense of legal claims; and/or
- The processing is necessary for reasons of substantial public interest (with a basis in law).

In respect of the substantial public interest condition, there are a number of particular circumstances. The following may be particularly relevant:

- Equality of opportunity or treatment;
- Racial and ethnic diversity at senior levels;
- Preventing or detecting unlawful acts;
- Protecting the public;
- Regulatory requirements;
- Preventing fraud; and/or
- Suspicion of terrorist financing or money laundering.[17]

If you rely on one of the substantial public interest conditions, you will also need an "appropriate policy document".[18] This is a document outlining your compliance measures and retention policies for special category and criminal offence data.

It's good practice to review all the data you process (see below, data mapping) and identify your lawful ground for doing so for each category of data, paying particular attention to special category personal data.

Criminal convictions and offences

The GDPR gives extra protection to personal data relating to criminal convictions and offences. This covers a wide range of information about criminal activity, allegations, investigations, and proceedings. You can only process criminal offence data if you meet one of the 28 possible conditions[19] that are available for the processing of criminal offence data similar to those that apply in relation to special category data. As with special category data, you will need an "appropriate policy document".

Accountability

The concept of accountability is central to the GDPR. The controller is responsible for, and must also be able to demonstrate, compliance with the data protection principles.

In practice, this involves implementing policies, keeping good records and documentation, and having appropriate contracts in place with data processors and other parties with whom you share personal data. It also involves the following specific elements.

Data mapping

You must create a record of your personal data processing, including the information set out in Article 30 of the GDPR. In the event of any issue arising, you may need to make this record available to the ICO on request.

As part of this, it's good practice to create a data map. There is no particular form for this but the ICO offers a template.[20]

There is an exemption from the obligation to keep a record of data processing for organizations employing fewer than 250 people. However, the exemption does not apply in wide-ranging circumstances (for example, where the processing is "not occasional" (not just a one-off occurrence or something you do rarely) or includes special categories of data).[21] As such, the exemption is unlikely to apply to most law firms and, in any event, irrespective of the size of the firm, it is good practice to keep a record of data processing.

Data Protection Officer (DPO)

You must appoint a DPO[22] if your core activities consist of:

- Large-scale processing of special categories of data or data relating to criminal convictions and offences; or
- Processing operations that require the regular or systematic monitoring of data subjects on a large scale.

Law firms, therefore, need to make a determination as to whether the firm is required to appoint a statutory DPO. When considering if processing is on "a large scale", regulator guidelines[23] say you should take into consideration the number of data subjects concerned as well as the volume of personal data being processed.

Even if you are not required to appoint a DPO, it's good practice to appoint someone to take responsibility within the firm for data protection matters and so you may choose to appoint one voluntarily. But if you appoint a DPO on a voluntary basis, that individual becomes subject to the same requirements of the GDPR as a compulsorily appointed DPO. Therefore, if you do not need or want to appoint a formal DPO, consider appointing a data privacy manager or similar alternatively titled role.

Data protection impact assessments (DPIA)

You must carry out a DPIA[24] in respect of certain higher risk processing, especially when implementing new technologies.

Generally, a DPIA should be conducted at the start of a project that could have significant data protection or privacy implications, e.g. rolling out a customer relationship management (CRM) or human resources system. The ICO provides a sample DPIA template.[25]

Data protection by design and by default

"Data protection by design" is an approach to ensure privacy and data protection issues are considered at the design phase of any system, service, product, or process and then throughout the lifecycle. "Data protection by default" requires controllers to implement appropriate technical and organizational measures to ensure that, by default, personal data is only processed as necessary to achieve a specific purpose.[26]

Data processors

Law firms may engage with a range of providers to obtain services that may include processing of personal data on their behalf. Such services could include use of software as a service (SaaS), outsourced IT services, payroll, or hosting of data. The GDPR[27] requires that such processing must be governed by a written contract containing certain minimum obligations on the processor (and requiring that the processor flows down such obligations to any sub-processors it may have). It is, therefore, necessary to keep under review the list of processors that the firm engages and ensure that the appropriate compliant contracts are in force.

Individual rights

The individuals (data subjects) whose personal data you process have a range of rights – known as data subject rights. The main data subject rights that will be applicable to law firm data processing are:

- Access (data subject access request (DSAR)) – the right to access and receive a copy of their personal data.[28]
- Rectification – the right to have inaccuracies corrected.[29]
- Erasure – the right to have information erased, also known as the "right to be forgotten".[30]
- Objection to direct marketing – individuals have the absolute right to object to the processing of their personal data for direct marketing purposes.[31]

- Objection based on legitimate interests – an individual can also object to the processing where you rely on "legitimate interests". This is not an absolute right, and you can refuse to comply if you can demonstrate compelling legitimate grounds for the processing, which override the interests, rights, and freedoms of the individual, or if the processing is for the establishment, exercise, or defense of legal claims.[32]
- To prevent automated decision-making and profiling, individuals have the right not to be subject to a decision based solely on automated processing (without human involvement in the decision-making process) which produces legal effects or similarly significantly affects him or her. This could apply, for example, to online recruitment tests that may use defined criteria to filter out certain applications.[33]

In practice, the DSAR is the right most exercised. If a controller receives a DSAR, they must provide the information requested "*without undue delay and in any event within one month of receipt of the request*".[34] Exceptionally, that period may be extended by two further months where necessary, taking into account the complexity and number of the requests.[35]

There are a number of exemptions to the right of access to information. Importantly, one person's right of access has to be balanced against another person's rights to protection of their personal information. Under the DPA, a controller is not obliged to disclose information to the extent that doing so would involve disclosing information relating to another individual who can be identified from the information, unless: "*(a) the other individual has consented to the disclosure of the information to the data subject, or (b) it is reasonable to disclose the information without the consent of the other individual*".[36]

A further exemption that will be helpful to law firms and their clients provides that the right of access does not apply to personal data that consists of: "*(a) information in respect of which a claim to legal professional privilege or, in Scotland, confidentiality of communications, could be maintained in legal proceedings, or (b) information in respect of which a duty of confidentiality is owed by a professional legal adviser to a client of the adviser*".[37]

It is good practice, therefore, to review your internal processes for dealing with DSARs and implement a policy to enable staff to recognize a DSAR and define how you will handle requests within the timescales specified by the GDPR and apply the various exemptions.

Personal data breach

The GDPR imposes a requirement to notify a personal data breach to the ICO.[38] Not all breaches have to be notified – only those where data subjects are likely to suffer some form of damage, e.g. through identity theft or a confidentiality breach.

When notification to the ICO is required, it must be done *"without undue delay and, where feasible, not later than 72 hours after having become aware of it"*.[39] A justification must be provided if this timeframe is not met.

In addition, if the personal data breach is likely to result in a high risk to the rights and freedoms of individuals, the controller must also communicate the personal data breach to the data subject *"without undue delay"*.[40]

Law firms suffering a personal data breach may also need to report the matter to the Solicitors Regulation Authority and, in appropriate cases, to their insurers.

It is essential, therefore, both for compliance and to mitigate liability, to implement and maintain a data breach incident response plan to detect, investigate, and report, and manage the consequences of, a personal data breach.

Whether or not a personal data breach is reportable, it needs to be documented in a personal data breach register, including the facts relating to the breach, its effects, and the remedial action taken.[41]

International data transfers

The EU GDPR restricts[42] transfers of personal data to a separate organization located outside of the European Economic Area,[43] unless the rights of the individuals in respect of their personal data are protected. The UK GDPR similarly restricts transfers outside of the UK. Transfers are permitted where:

- The receiver is located in a third country covered by an "adequacy decision". Currently, following Brexit, the UK is covered by an adequacy decision of the EU, and UK adequacy regulations include the EEA and all countries covered by EU "adequacy decisions";[44]
- Appropriate safeguards are in place – such as the standard contractual clauses for international data transfers as approved by the EU or the UK;[45] or
- A derogation is in place, such as the individual has given explicit consent to the transfer, or (for occasional transfers) the transfer is necessary for the establishment, exercise, or defense of legal claims.[46]

Reliance on standard contract clauses is commonplace in transactions involving data transfers. However, this has become more complex following the case of *Schrems II*.[47] It is now necessary to carry out and document a transfer impact assessment and, if the assessment is that the appropriate safeguard does not provide the required level of protection, you may need to include supplemental measures.

In the context of the data mapping (see above), it is good practice as a first step to map your international data flows and identify any transfers of personal data outside the UK/EEA, the parties involved, and the purposes of the transfers.

Marketing and cookies

Email marketing

In addition to the GDPR, under the ePrivacy Directive/ePrivacy Regulations (PECR),[48] firms must comply with PECR when sending unsolicited texts or emails to generate marketing. What is permitted by PECR depends on whether the direct marketing is aimed at a business or an individual. Generally, it is not permitted to send unsolicited texts or emails to individuals without their specific consent, save in limited situations when marketing similar products or services to existing clients or contacts who have expressed an interest in your products or services, and who have not objected. Marketing emails to corporate email addresses do not require prior consent.

As referred to above (Individual rights), data subjects have the right to object at any time to their personal data being processed for direct marketing purposes. Every marketing email should include an email address or web link where individuals can easily unsubscribe from future emails. Firms need to have a process in place to ensure that opt-outs are respected.

Websites and cookies

PECR also provides that website owners that set cookies or access information on their users' equipment are required to:

- Provide users with clear and comprehensive information about the purposes for which cookies are stored and accessed; and
- Obtain users' consent.[49]

There are limited exemptions for cookies that are "strictly necessary" for the provision of the service requested by the user.[50]

It is good practice to carry out a cookie audit to determine what cookies are used on your website and the purposes of each. Details should then be set out in a Cookie policy published on the website and a mechanism included on the site to ensure that cookies that are not "strictly necessary" are not set unless and until the user has specifically opted-in.

Conclusion

Good data protection practices and policies are essential for compliance and risk management. However, there are many other sound business reasons why they are important, including to maintain the confidence of clients and others with whom you deal that you will secure and respect the sensitive personal data that they entrust to you.

References

1. Regulation (EU) 2016/679 of the European Parliament and of the Council of 27 April 2016 on the protection of natural persons with regard to the processing of personal data and on the free movement of such data (General Data Protection Regulation).
2. The version of the GDPR transposed into UK law pursuant to the European Union (Withdrawal) Act 2018.
3. Article 4(7) GDPR.
4. See www.ico.org.uk/for-organisations/guide-to-data-protection/guide-to-the-general-data-protection-regulation-gdpr/key-definitions/controllers-and-processors/#3.
5. Article 4(8) GDPR.
6. Law Society Guidance for solicitors in law firms (GDPR and the Data Protection Act), September 2019.
7. Under the Data Protection (Charges and Information) Regulations 2018.
8. As defined in the Schedule to The Data Protection (Charges and Information) Regulations 2018.
9. Article 5 GDPR.
10. Article 14(5)(b) GDPR.
11. DPA Schedule 2 Part 4 paragraph 19(a).
12. DPA Schedule 2 Part 4 paragraph 19(b).
13. Article 5(1)(e) GDPR.
14. Article 32 GDPR.
15. www.ico.org.uk/action-weve-taken/enforcement/tuckers-solicitors-llp-mpn/
16. www.ico.org.uk/media/for-organisations/forms/2258435/gdpr-guidance-legitimate-interests-sample-lia-template.docx

17. DPA, Schedule 1, Part 2.
18. Data Protection Act 2018, Schedule 1, Part 2, Paragraph 5.
19. DPA, Schedule 1, Part 1, 2 and 3.
20. www.ico.org.uk/media/for-organisations/documents/2172937/gdpr-documentation-controller-template.xlsx
21. Article 30(5) GDPR.
22. Article 37 GDPR.
23. Guidelines on Data Protection Officers (DPOs) WP 243 rev.01, as last revised and adopted on 5 April 2017.
24. Article 35 GDPR.
25. www.ico.org.uk/media/for-organisations/documents/2553993/dpia-template.docx
26. Recital 78 and Article 25 GDPR.
27. Article 28 GDPR.
28. Article 15 GDPR.
29. Article 16 GDPR.
30. Article 17 GDPR.
31. Article 21(2) GDPR.
32. Article 21(1) GDPR.
33. Article 22 GDPR.
34. Article 12(3) GDPR.
35. Article 12(3).
36. DPA Schedule 2, Part 3, Paragraph 16.
37. DPA Schedule 2, Part 4, Paragraph 19.
38. Article 33 GDPR.
39. *Ibid*.
40. Article 34 GDPR.
41. Article 33(5) GDPR.
42. Article 44 GDPR.
43. EU countries and also Iceland, Liechtenstein, and Norway.
44. Article 45 GDPR.
45. Article 46 GDPR.
46. Article 49 GDPR.
47. Data Protection Commission v. Facebook Ireland and Maximillian Schrems, 16 July 2020, Case C-311/18.
48. The Privacy and Electronic Communications (EC Directive) Regulations 2003 (as amended).
49. *Ibid*, Regulation 6.
50. *Ibid*, Regulation 6(4)(b).

Chapter 4:
Cybersecurity: an existential risk for law firms

By Simon Chester, counsel, conflicts and regulatory matters, and Sandy Gill, assistant general counsel, Gowling WLG (Canada) LLP

Your law firm is vulnerable to an increasingly sophisticated range of cyberattacks. When attackers succeed, you risk myriad losses at a stroke – liability, reputation, financial, and regulatory. One would be catastrophic. Combined, it will end your business. This chapter explores:

- A critical framework for thinking about the growing risk;
- The need for an enterprise risk management approach; and
- Steps law firms of all sizes can take to protect themselves.

The sole constant in this massive topic is uncertainty. Firm leaders must fully appreciate and address cybersecurity as one of the most serious enterprise risks that they will confront. Any prescription written in the summer of 2022 would be obsolete upon publication – and a comprehensive account would be ten times the length of this volume. Cybersecurity threats develop so rapidly that the response must be immediate and similarly dynamic. What matters most is the ongoing stance firm leadership takes to ensure effective action whenever it is needed.

This issue must be dealt with at the highest levels of firm leadership and throughout the entire firm. The temptation to delegate to overworked security and information technology personnel without the involvement of firm leadership is to be resisted at all costs. This is about anticipating and mitigating a constant and severe risk, which, if not caught and addressed, could mean the end of your firm. Firm leaders must invest resources in hardware, software, consulting, and staffing to build a security response team. They, together with leadership, must drive action through these four interrelated risk management themes:

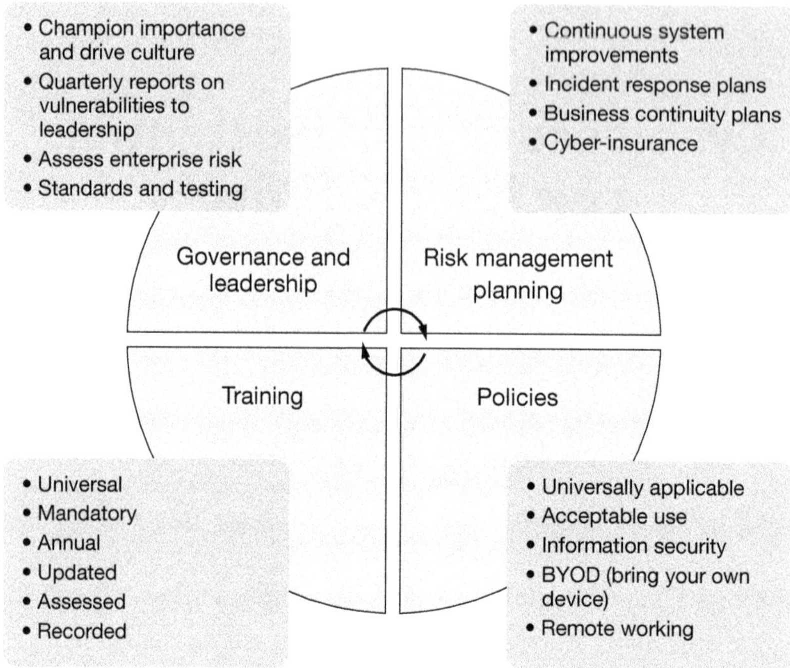

Why is cybersecurity a risk management priority? In a recent Statista report, the most serious future risk (65 percent) faced by all businesses surveyed was cyber-incidents.[1] Recent news reports suggest that law firms, specifically, are highly targeted:

- A global law firm's network was down for ten days after being infected by the NotPetya malware.[2]
- A major Chicago firm announced that it was the victim of a sophisticated and aggressive malware attack that appeared to be ransomware.[3]
- A Latin American law firm experienced the largest data breach ever reported (2.6TB of client information).[4]
- A New York City-based entertainment law firm found that its client files, involving prominent celebrities, were exposed.[5]
- A mid-size English law firm lost £150,000 of billable time due to a single network breach.[6]
- A 2021 American Bar Association survey revealed 29 percent of law firms had experienced virus and/or malware attacks.[7]

- Accounting firm PriceWaterhouseCooper's 2021 Law Firms' Survey revealed that 90 percent of the top 100 UK law firms were extremely concerned about their vulnerability.[8]

These nightmare scenarios are all possible:

- Computers frozen and data inaccessible – firm is incapacitated;
- Funds stolen;
- Personal data compromised;
- Regulatory inquiries from data protection and legal profession regulators;
- Costs for public relations/crisis management and reputational damage; and
- Civil liability to clients.

Regulatory requirements

Far beyond the normal business imperative of keeping secrets, our profession rests on a foundation of protecting client confidentiality. Clients entrust their most sensitive information to us, expecting that we will keep it safe through applicable privilege and rigorous security precautions. In recent years, regulators have been asking whether and how we meet clients' expectations.[9]

Like all businesses, law firms must comply with the General Data Protection Regulation[10] or equivalent local legislation. Law firm breaches exposing personal client information must be promptly reported to the regulators.

Professional conduct rules impose a separate line of responsibilities. In England and Wales, the Solicitors Regulation Authority's Code of Conduct for individuals (Rule 4.2) and the Code of Conduct for firms (Rule 5.2) articulate a duty on the entire profession to "*safeguard money and assets entrusted to you by clients and others*".[11] Among those assets are confidential client information, which is in turn the subject of separate obligations.

The American Bar Association's Model Rules of Professional Conduct, Rule 1.1 (Competence) includes a Comment requiring technological competence,[12] and Rule 1.6 defines the duty of confidentiality:

> *"A lawyer shall not reveal information relating to the representation of a client unless the client gives informed consent, the disclosure is impliedly authorized in order to carry out the representation or the disclosure is permitted by [defined exceptions]."*[13]

In 2012, a new subsection C added: "*a lawyer shall make reasonable efforts to prevent the inadvertent or unauthorized disclosure of, or unauthorized access to, information relating to the representation of a client*".[14]

Helpfully, Comment 18 to Rule 1.6 explains what reasonable efforts entail:

> *"Factors to be considered in determining the reasonableness of the lawyer's efforts include, but are not limited to, the sensitivity of the information, the likelihood of disclosure if additional safeguards are not employed, the cost of employing additional safeguards, the difficulty of implementing the safeguards, and the extent to which the safeguards adversely affect the lawyer's ability to represent clients (e.g. by making a device or important piece of software excessively difficult to use)."*[15]

From this we learn that perfection is neither expected nor realistic. As cyber-threats evolve, firms inevitably scramble to keep pace. The ABA Comment stresses that reasonable precautions will be assessed on a risk management basis. Failure to do anything is an ethical violation that brings serious consequences. As the threat landscape evolves, so does regulatory focus and duties of care for professional negligence.

Client pressures

If internal business concerns were insufficient to drive law firms to confront cybersecurity, clients are increasingly asking whether their data, entrusted to their law firm, is safe. At Gowling WLG in Canada, we centrally monitor client Outside Counsel Guidelines: of our 720 sets of terms, almost a quarter require security assessments, ranging from simple checklists to external audits or complex questionnaires.

Although sound risk management principles suggest treating different enterprises differently, in our experience regulators may require clients in highly regulated sectors to ensure that everyone in their supply chain is meeting the regulator's industry requirements, even if the risks are different. This may lead to extraterritorial compliance requests for law firms outside the US to meet federal laws that simply do not apply or, for example, to be Payment Card Industry compliant, even if they never deal with credit cards. Client confidentiality owed to other clients may limit audits. Your firm may need to prepare clients for enhanced verification or security protocols that may appear unfriendly and explain why they are necessary to protect confidential data and to ensure secure communication.

Some clients deploy extensive questionnaires aimed generically at all service providers without considering the special situation of law firms.

Here a conversation with the client, ideally the in-house legal team, is needed. Providing actual detailed information on deployed security measures could be a road map to any vulnerabilities. Rather, if pressed, firms should show that they have a cybersecurity policy, responsive insurance policies, and certifications from standards organizations (see Planning for breach, below). This documentation is best disclosed through screen sharing, rather than moving files outside the law firm – where the firm can have no confidence in how they might be used. We have also experienced an increase in inconsistent demands – where meeting what Client A wants will mean failing to meet Client B's expectations. A common framework would be welcome and efficient.

The best response may be to show that the firm meets an international standard like ISO 27001 that covers all the client's concerns.[16]

Cloud computing

Cloud computing stores data on remote secure servers, accessible over the internet (hosted on services such as Microsoft Azure or Amazon Web Services). A decade ago, cloud storage might have been seen to present serious risks. It now offers a more secure storage location than servers located on a firm's physical premises. Cloud storage also provides automatic software updates and redundancy that would be cost prohibitive in an on-premise solution. North American legal regulators accept that if appropriate precautions are taken, client data can be safeguarded properly within the cloud.[17] Of course, best-practice configuration recommendations must be adopted. Firms will also want to know where data is stored, whether it will be automatically encrypted, and that safeguards exist in the cloud provider contracts to ensure immediate notification and cooperation if a breach occurs. Check what the cloud provider's policies provide if third parties – especially sovereign governments – seek access to firm and client data. Implement cloud solutions carefully, knowing that according to the latest Hiscox Cyber Readiness Report criminals increasingly aim their attacks onto cloud servers (41 percent most common method of entry).[18]

Before committing to cloud-based services, check:

- Where the data will be stored. Does applicable law or your clients' policy prohibit storage outside the jurisdiction?;
- Whether the cloud provider has a long-standing track record and reputation for reliability;
- Whether the cloud provider is ISO 27001 accredited;

- Do back-up procedures follow industry guidelines such as NIST SP 800-209 – Security Guidelines for Storage Infrastructure?;[19]
- Whether data is encrypted at rest and in transit; and
- Who holds the master decryption key – preferably your firm would hold this key.

Remote working

The move to hybrid working in March 2020, with the global pandemic, is now permanent. Yet recent surveys show that only a small majority of law firms (58 percent) have rethought their policies and procedures in the light of that reality.[20] The rush to remote working meant that cyber-precautions were often an afterthought. According to the EY Global Information Security Survey, 43 percent of IT leaders say they have never been more concerned about their ability to manage cyber risk.[21]

Given the combination of mobile devices and related technologies available on laptops, tablets, and smartphones that we have learned to apply in the hybrid environment, legal professionals now have greater freedom than ever before to work from virtually anywhere, anytime – but it has introduced potential vulnerabilities that require consideration in the firm's cyber security protocols. The physical and technological safeguards within the law firm environment, including monitoring and response, need to be omni-present whenever professionals work remotely.

As far as you can, outlaw the use of devices, networks, apps, or software not approved or provided by your firm. It is essential to proactively identify and invest in the tools your firm's professionals need and provide those tools in a manner that is aligned with the firm's cyber security protection program. These should be updated as necessary, to account for how lawyers work now, and will likely work in the years to come. You do not want to create a gap that a professional may have no choice but to fill with an easily available, but potentially unsafe, workaround.

Together with the now-basic need for law firms to have adequate cyber insurance coverage, firms will also need to review the fine print on insurance policies to ensure that agile remote working is as fully insured as working in the office.

Policies and procedures

All law firms must implement robust, up-to-date, cyber security policies supported by reliable, consistent fraud and breach detection, prevention and response procedures. Although no standard policy that provides impermeable protection in all circumstances exists, established best practices and industry standards do provide an essential baseline for risk mitigation. These are the eight policies that we believe all law firms should have in place, to alert everyone to the firm's obligations and expectations:

1. Acceptable use policy;
2. Information management policy;
3. Information security policy;
4. Remote access policy;
5. Records and data retention;
6. Social media policy;
7. BYOD – personal technology; and
8. Employee privacy.

These policies must apply to every member of the law firm, without exception, and to any third party vendor with access to the firm's systems, including consultants. At least one major cyberattack on a law firm arose through access given to a third party vendor.[22] The policies should cover cryptography, device and network security, acceptable use of technology, password security, training, and enforcement. The policies and procedures need to be updated regularly, and integrated into all aspects of firm operations. Initial training when onboarding, and on an ongoing basis, is critical to ensure the policy is understood and applied. Require attestation to ensure that policies and procedures are read and understood and that there is a compliance commitment.

To illustrate, our firm advises our staff as follows:

- Avoid using removable media (like a flash drive) to transport data. If using removable media is required by a client, ensure the data is encrypted and that the client is warned of the dangers.
- When away from the office, never leave your device out of your sight.
- Ensure that confidential conversations cannot be overheard and turn off devices like Amazon's Alexa and Google's voice assistant.
- Always protect the contents of your computer screen from unauthorized viewing.
- Lock your computer screen whenever you step away and use an automatic screen locking timer when inactive.

- Never use public Wi-Fi or hotspots to conduct client business. Public Wi-Fi is not secure and can be easily hacked. Establish a VPN (Virtual Private Network) for those working remotely.
- Password-protect video conferences and supply passwords to attendees separately.
- Never forward firm related emails and attachments to a personal email account.
- Never store confidential information in public cloud-based services like DropBox or Google Drive.
- Do not print client work at home unless absolutely necessary.

Review your trust accounting procedures to require that funds may never be disbursed electronically without:

- Verification from the financial institution that the funds have actually been collected;
- A telephone call to a number known – independently of the apparent source of instructions – to belong to the recipient confirming the details of the transfer; and
- Review by two experienced senior firm members.

Ontario's legal malpractice insurer, LawPro, observes that attacks tend to coincide with the end of the week or bank holidays, when staff may be distracted or busier than usual.[23]

Finally, even the best data security encryption or server security policy is easily undermined if users are selecting weak passwords. To avoid this, require unique, robust passwords for access to all systems, and update passwords regularly – the latest CIS Password Policy Guide suggests mandatory annual changes.[24] But resist client requirements for more frequent changes. If possible, implement two-factor authentication.

More broadly, firm leadership needs to support efforts to embed cybersecurity policies and procedures into all aspects of the firm, creating a collaborative, proactive, non-punitive culture of cyber risk mitigation and prevention. Blaming and shaming for lapses may lead to covering up future incidents.

Insider risks

The most authoritative surveys of cyberattacks identify human error as a much more likely cause than technological failure. Busy law firm members can make mistakes – indeed, senior partners are just as likely as junior staff when clicking on a seemingly innocuous link and letting malware infect the law firm network.

According to a Verizon Survey, ten times more records were compromised by human error within businesses than external sources.[25] The Solicitors Regulation Authority states that 80 percent of the cybercrime reports it received in 2021 involved email mistakes.[26] Along with simple human error, malicious or discontented individuals may lurk within a firm. So, some clients demand that firm staff be subject to detailed background checks, to the extent legally permitted. Firms are revising their standard contracts of employment to include detailed security and confidentiality clauses as a result.

Everyone in the firm should understand how their actions can cause vulnerabilities and how they can help the firm mitigate risk:

- Worry about human error;
- 76 percent of breaches involve internal mistakes;[27]
- Falling for social engineering scams;
- Clicking recklessly;
- Opening documents without knowing source;
- Trying to sneak past firm precautions;
- Weak passwords;
- Sharing passwords; and
- Resisting multi-factor authentication.

Law firm failures and vulnerabilities result from poor business and cyber practices and how law firm members interact with information systems and client data. Only continuous commitment to cybersecurity training for all personnel – including partners – can reduce this vulnerability. Mandatory cybersecurity training should be at least annual, with periodic questions to avoid people running the training program in the background without paying due attention to its messages. Avoid abstract or overly technical discussions and include real-life stories. Examples of real email frauds are available at LawPro's avoidaclaim.com.

A robust training program covers:

- How the firm is affected by their actions or inactions;

- Spotting common scams and phishing communications;
- Device and password management;
- Avoiding public Wi-Fi;
- Encryption tools; and
- Wire transfer processes and protocols to verify transactions and protect trust funds.

Rigorously train all new firm members on the firm's cybersecurity protocols. Identity and access control is a fundamental aspect of any security program. Adopt "Least Privilege" when granting access to new personnel. This approach provides access to systems and information required to perform in the role or practice area for which the individual is being onboarded. Be just as rigorous when transferring or offboarding personnel. Disable accounts and system access promptly for all departing personnel and adjust access for those transferring to new roles. Automating your access procedures ensures repeatable results. Role-based access and user groups are generally accepted as best practice methods. LawPro has a useful checklist on its PracticePro website.[28]

Consider at least the following due diligence steps for departing firm members:

- Wipe personal data from all firm devices;
- Retrieve firm devices, including security tokens;
- Change all passwords and reset accounts; and
- Forward mail within the firm.

Assessing precautions

Unfortunately, you will find gaps in your armor. The American Bar Association's TechReport 2021, the most comprehensive recent survey, shows how law firms were addressing cyber vulnerabilities.[29] Though it reflects American law firms, presumably firms elsewhere are similar.

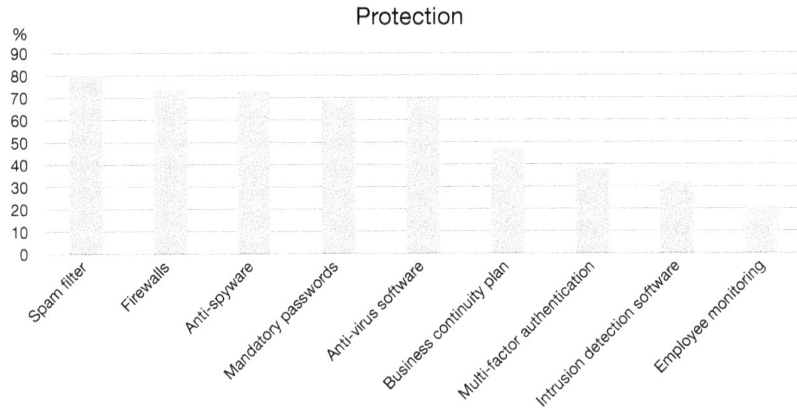

Multi-factor authentication (MFA) is vital, even if annoying. MFA prompts users for a single-use code (a password, token, or biometric control) with every login. If a password is stolen, compromised, or guessed, MFA prevents unauthorized access or breach. According to the Solicitors Regulation Authority in England and Wales, over 60 percent of firms surveyed use MFA.[30] Your firm would be wise to enable MFA everywhere possible.

Recent figures reveal that 80 percent of successful attacks involve ransomware.[31] Ransomware is most commonly delivered by phishing email that contains a link, if clicked, that will download malicious code or it may contain an attachment that will launch the attack if opened. On successfully breaching the network, the attacker will either take control of the network until a substantial ransom is paid or threaten to sell or leak clients' secrets. In the first quarter of 2021, over 3.2 billion records were disclosed.[32] Ransoms constitute 75 percent of cyber insurance claims[33] and the average ransom paid was around $228,000.[34] In the UK, 56 percent of businesses have policies not to pay ransoms,[35] a stance the Law Society of England and Wales recently endorsed in response to a UK National Cyber Security Centre and the Information Commissioner inquiry letter.[36] Because correcting the problems may cost much more than the demanded ransom, one may be tempted to quietly pay up, a stance criticized by the US Treasury Department, the FBI, and police and regulators around the world.[37] The best defense against a ransomware attack is the following:

- Assume vulnerability – adopt Zero Trust;
- Encrypt networks;

- Implement multi-factor authentication;
- Mandate strong passwords and encourage password management software;
- Update and patch software constantly;
- Comprehensive email security;
- Back-up data offsite or to the cloud – follow guidelines for storage infrastructure;
- Mandatory annual cyber risk training for all in the firm; and
- Adopt endpoint detection on all exterior access points.

Insurance

Law firms should carefully investigate available cyber insurance. Extremely scarce a decade ago, cyber-insurance now is an evolving product, with coverage and pricing in flux. Firms should talk to their insurance advisors about appropriate and needed coverage. The two main types of policy are outlined below:

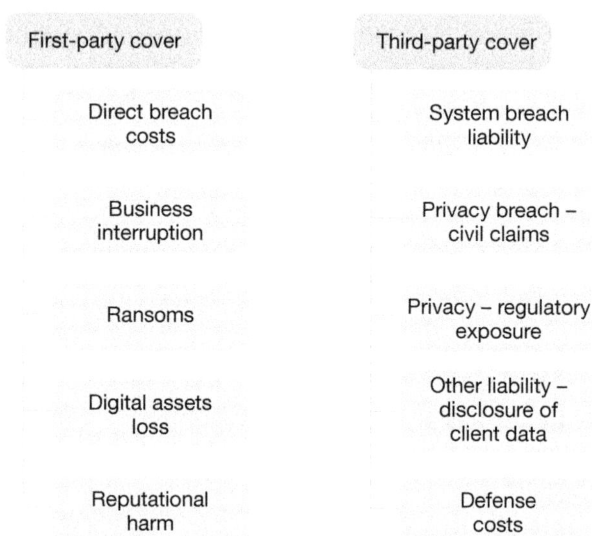

The firm's insurance advisors need to carefully review the firm's circumstances and risk profile to assess the appropriate insurance available to meet those needs. According to the American Bar Association Law Practice

Division's Legal Technology Survey Report 2021 Cybersecurity, only 42 percent of American law firms surveyed had cyber liability coverage.[38] The US Government General Accounting Office reported 47 percent of a major insurer's clients had such coverage, which dropped to 40 percent when only professional service firms were examined.[39]

Reassess the firm's coverage annually, looking closely at any insurance exclusions, limits, sub-limits, and deductibles. You should never rely on other insurance policies for comprehensive cyber insurance coverage. Other policies lack depth and breadth, were not designed for the precise risks you face, and do not have first party costs coverage or offer access to third party cyber security experts if a breach occurs. In July 2019, Lloyds issued a mandate to clarify coverage and reporting issues. Always adhere strictly to insurer requirements for coverage.[40]

Check gaps in coverage carefully. Any gaps may require separate endorsements with additional costs. Consider whether the policy covers:

- Ransomware;
- Business email compromises;
- Social engineering fraud;
- System failure;
- Systemic infrastructure failure;
- Loss of funds; and
- If the firm has offices in multiple territories, also consider whether the coverage territory matches the firm's operations.

Communication with the insurer is a critical component of risk management. The application process alone imposes discipline that can help a firm assess the adequacy of existing security controls. Cyber insurers also offer security consulting services and can help during and after incidents. Equally importantly, cyber insurers can help drive the importance of taking these risks seriously within the firm.

Planning for breach

Given the prevalence of cyberattacks, any risk management strategy must include steps beyond reducing the risk of a breach. No matter how robust the preventive measures, a breach remains possible, perhaps even likely. As part of its preparation, law firm management should insist on having a business-focused crisis management plan. According to American Bar

Association figures, only 36 percent of law firms have a formal incident management plan.[41]

Planning is critical. Successful attacks happen fast. To prevent scrambling, law firms should identify and empower a qualified team with clear responsibilities, capable of acting surely and swiftly. Although every conceivable scenario the firm may face cannot be predicted, simulating crisis response scenarios can identify gaps and bottlenecks and create organizational muscle-memory for the initial steps to take, particularly when information about the extent and impact of the breach may be limited.

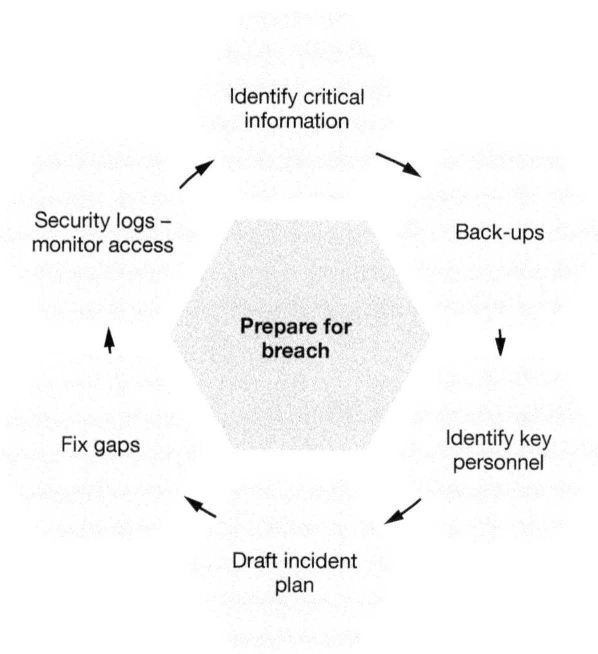

An incident plan should be continually reviewed. All information technology personnel should be knowledgeable and empowered to act. The plan should not only address the technical details, but also sketch out a crisis decision framework and communication strategy. Determine well in advance how to reach personnel, assemble the response team, establish hotlines, and communicate with key clients. The plan should include a list of the following key contacts:

- Insurance provider;
- Legal regulators;

- Government entities, such as data protection and law enforcement authorities;
- Banking contacts;
- Experts on responding to ransom demands;
- Data breach experts or forensic firm;
- Privacy or technology lawyer or expert on legal requirements for breach notification;
- Key service providers, including software vendors and managed security service providers; and
- Public relations or communications professionals.

Identify critical information and ensure that access to sensitive data is strictly limited. Set up a logging system to help identify suspicious activity and create mechanisms for law firm members, clients, and third parties to report suspicious activity. If a firm is compromised, a client may be the first to notice. If a breach occurs, access steps can be retraced to discover how the intrusion occurred.

Keep both a protected digital format and hard copy of the plan in your office and offsite, available externally to all response team members. A plan locked within a compromised system that cannot be accessed is useless.

As with any other substantial business, major law firms are best protected by systems and safeguards assessed according to internationally accepted standards, such as:

- ISO 27001 and the related ISO 27031;[42]
- NIST Cybersecurity Framework;[43]
- Centre for Internet Security Critical Security Controls;[44] and
- Cyber Essentials Plus.[45]

The ISO 27001 review process is an investment worth considering for both assessing and remediating vulnerabilities and satisfying client concerns by meeting an objective, international, rigorous standard.

A periodic readiness assessment of the incident response plan by a qualified third party is recommended and is worthwhile for both assessing and remediating potential gaps and satisfying client concerns.

Next steps

Planning for cybersecurity is a complex process that must be tailored to each firm's environment and requirements. Even so, the following ten practical steps will help all firms increase their confidence that when the inevitable attacks happen, they are in the best position to protect their client's information and the firm's business.

1. Form a team to create a robust breach response plan for the firm, including clearly assigned individual roles and responsibilities with appropriate authority to take swift action and define mechanisms for reliable, confidential communication. The incident response plan should be integrated with the firm's business continuity and crisis communications plan.
2. Review the firm's back-up procedures, which should include three copies of all important data on at least two separate resources offsite. Automated back-ups should be maintained incrementally on a daily basis with full back-ups performed at least weekly. Conduct periodic checks to test integrity and ensure that files can be recovered.
3. Only allow approved and vetted software. Diligently install software and operating systems updates and patches.
4. Store less. Delete more. Implement a firm retention, storage, and deletion policy.
5. Implement multi-factor authentication to reduce risks from the compromise of credentials.
6. Ensure the security and reliability of your key suppliers, especially any with access to your network. Remember that 19 percent of breaches happen because of vulnerabilities elsewhere in the supply chain.[46]
7. Make a robust password manager available to all in the firm and require strong and unique master passwords. Password managers help store and secure online credentials with robust encryption.
8. Consider ISO 27001 certification or engage an independent and credible third party auditor to identify vulnerabilities and mitigation strategies. Conduct regular security risk assessments focused on security precautions, infrastructure, and current controls. Review personnel, processes, and technology to identify vulnerabilities.
9. Enable encryption on all devices, especially media leaving the firm such as USB devices. Turn on tracking for mobile devices so that they can be locked or wiped if lost.
10. Assess whether procedures and policies, which may have been

rushed to enable remote working during the global pandemic, actually meet current security requirements.

All in all, managing cybersecurity risks is a never ending task. Critically reassess the firm's approach often and at least annually to remain responsive to changes in work arrangements, advances in technology, evolving client expectations, and the increasing sophistication of bad actors.

Be patient, persistent, and prepared. Cybersecurity is a work continually in process.

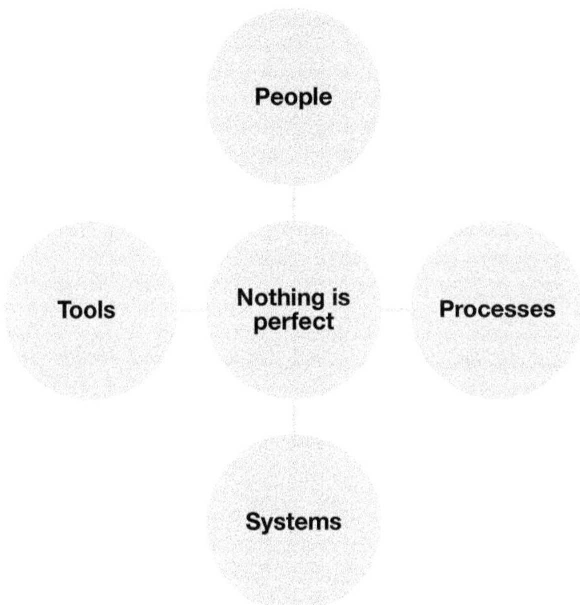

We thank our friends David Bilinsky, Anthony E. Davis, Michael Herman, Nick Jones, Steve Lundy, Ginevra Saylor, and Merrilyn Astin Tarlton who all helped to educate us and provide peer review. This chapter represents our personal opinions, not theirs nor those of our firm.

References

1. www.statista.com/statistics/1293502/most-significant-risks-to-businesses-global/
2. www.dlapiperwin.com/export/sites/win/events/materials/2019/downloads/MelbourneIHCD12March2019-4B_Everything_you_need_to_know_about_cyber-atta....pdf; https://medium.com/resolve-cyber/the-impact-of-cyber-crime-on-the-legal-sector-f8bc8ded1a48.
3. https://web.archive.org/web/20201018102620/https://www.seyfarth.com/malware-attack-information.html

4. www.icij.org/investigations/panama-papers/new-panama-papers-leak-reveals-mossack-fonsecas-chaotic-scramble/
5. https://senseient.com/ride-the-lightning/law-firm-hackers-up-ransom-demand-to-42-million-claim-to-have-dirt-on-trump/
6. www.sra.org.uk/globalassets/documents/sra/research/cyber-security-a-thematic-review.pdf?version=4a48a2, p3.
7. American Bar Association, Law Practice Division, Legal Technology Survey Report 2021 Cybersecurity, www.americanbar.org/groups/law_practice/publications/techreport/2021/cybersecurity/, part 3.
8. PwC Law Firms' Survey 2021, www.pwc.co.uk/industries/law-firms/law-firm-survey-report-2021.pdf, p16 and 30.
9. See e.g. SRA: www.sra.org.uk/sra/research-publications/risk-outlook-2020-21/information-and-cyber-security/; Law Society of British Columbia: www.lawsociety.bc.ca/Website/media/Shared/docs/initiatives/LawFirm/PilotProjectReport-AppA.pdf and www.lawsociety.bc.ca/about-us/news-and-publications/news/2020/notice-to-the-profession-take-action-to-protect-a/; and South Australia: www.lawsocietysa.asn.au/Public/Publications/Resources/CyberSecurity.aspx.
10. https://gdpr-info.eu/
11. Solicitors Regulation Authority, SRA Code of Conduct for Solicitors, RELs and RFLs, 25 November 2019, www.sra.org.uk/solicitors/standards-regulations/code-conduct-solicitors/; SRA Code of Conduct for Firms, www.sra.org.uk/solicitors/standards-regulations/code-conduct-firms/.
12. www.americanbar.org/groups/professional_responsibility/publications/model_rules_of_professional_conduct/rule_1_1_competence/comment_on_rule_1_1/
13. www.americanbar.org/groups/professional_responsibility/publications/model_rules_of_professional_conduct/rule_1_6_confidentiality_of_information/, paragraph (a).
14. Ibid, paragraph (c).
15. www.americanbar.org/groups/professional_responsibility/publications/model_rules_of_professional_conduct/rule_1_6_confidentiality_of_information/comment_on_rule_1_6/
16. www.iso.org/isoiec-27001-information-security.html
17. www.lawsociety.bc.ca/Website/media/Shared/docs/practice/resources/guidelines-cloud.pdf; www.lawsociety.sk.ca/wp-content/uploads/2020/04/lsscloudcomputingchecklist.pdf; and www.clio.com/blog/cloud-computing-lawyers-ethics-opinions/.
18. Hiscox Cyber Readiness Report 2022, www.hiscoxgroup.com/sites/group/files/documents/2022-05/22054%20-%20Hiscox%20Cyber%20Readiness%20Report%202022-EN_0.pdf, p9.

19. https://csrc.nist.gov/publications/detail/sp/800-209/final
20. https://info.menlosecurity.com/rs/281-OWV-899/images/IRN-Menlo-Cybersecurity-Legal-Research%20Report-May-22.pdf, p5.
21. EY Global Information Security Survey, 2021, www.ey.com/en_gl/cybersecurity/cybersecurity-how-do-you-rise-above-the-waves-of-a-perfect-storm.
22. www.dlapiperwin.com/export/sites/win/events/materials/2019/downloads/MelbourneIHCD12March2019-4B_Everything_you_need_to_know_about_cyber-atta....pdf, p4.
23. https://avoidaclaim.com/2022/avoid-phishing-and-wire-fraud-scams-over-the-long-weekend/
24. CIS Password Policy Guide, https://learn.cisecurity.org/cis-password-policy-guide-passphrases-monitoring-and-more.
25. Verizon Data Breach Investigation Report 2022, www.verizon.com/business/resources/reports/2022/dbir/2022-data-breach-investigations-report-dbir.pdf, p12.
26. www.sra.org.uk/sra/news/press/risk-outlook-innovation-and-cybercrime/
27. 76 percent of breaches involve internal mistakes: www.pwc.co.uk/industries/law-firms/law-firm-survey-report-2021.pdf, p16.
28. www.practicepro.ca/wp-content/uploads/2017/07/EmployeeDepartureChecklist.pdf
29. American Bar Association, Law Practice Division, Legal Technology Survey Report 2021 Cybersecurity, www.americanbar.org/groups/law_practice/publications/techreport/2021/cybersecurity/, part 7.
30. www.sra.org.uk/globalassets/documents/sra/research/cyber-security-a-thematic-review.pdf?version=4a48a2, p.21.
31. www.isc2.org/-/media/ISC2/Research/Cyberthreat-Defense-Report/2021/CyberEdge-2021-CDR-Report-v10--ISC2-Edition.ashx, p.7.
32. www.itgovernance.co.uk/blog/data-breaches-and-cyber-attacks-quarterly-review-q1-2021
33. https://news.ambest.com/presscontent.aspx?refnum=30762&altsrc=9
34. www.coveware.com/blog/2022/7/27/fewer-ransomware-victims-pay-as-medium-ransom-falls-in-q2-2022
35. www.gov.uk/government/statistics/cyber-security-breaches-survey-2022/cyber-security-breaches-survey-2022
36. www.lawsociety.org.uk/topics/cybersecurity/how-we-can-help-you-in-the-fight-against-ransomware; https://ico.org.uk/about-the-ico/media-centre/news-and-blogs/2022/07/ico-and-ncsc-stand-together-against-ransomware-payments-being-made/
37. https://home.treasury.gov/news/press-releases/jy0364; www.fbi.gov/scams-and-safety/common-scams-and-crimes/ransomware; www.interpol.int/en/News-and-Events/News/2021/Joint-global-ransomware-operation-sees-arrests-and-criminal-network-dismantled; www.londoncrc.co.uk/report-cybercrime;

www.gendarmerie.interieur.gouv.fr/nos-conseils/pour-les-particuliers/me-proteger-sur-internet/rancongiciels-s-informer-pour-mieux-se-proteger; and www.bka.de/SharedDocs/Downloads/DE/Publikationen/JahresberichteUndLagebilder/Cybercrime/cybercrimeBundeslagebild2021.pdf;jsessionid=D3A64F5B-12F56AEE8CE30972C961BA2D.live612?__blob=publicationFile&v=5.

38. American Bar Association, Law Practice Division, Legal Technology Survey Report 2021 Cybersecurity, www.americanbar.org/groups/law_practice/publications/techreport/2021/cybersecurity/, part 4.
39. United States Government Accountability Office, Cyber Insurance: Insurers and Policyholders Face Challenges in an Evolving Market, May 2021, www.gao.gov/assets/gao-21-477.pdf, p2, 11.
40. https://assets.lloyds.com/assets/y5277-update-providing-clarity-for-lloyds-customers-on-coverage-for-cyber-exposures/1/Y5277%20Update%20%20Providing%20clarity%20for%20Lloyds%20customers%20on%20coverage%20for%20cyber%20exposures.pdf, Market Bulletin, Ref: Y5277 p1.
41. American Bar Association, Law Practice Division, Legal Technology Survey Report 2021 Cybersecurity, www.americanbar.org/groups/law_practice/publications/techreport/2021/cybersecurity/, part 2.
42. www.iso.org/isoiec-27001-information-security.html; www.iso.org/standard/44374.html.
43. www.nist.gov/cyberframework
44. www.cisecurity.org/controls
45. www.ncsc.gov.uk/cyberessentials/overview; https://getreadyforcyberessentials.iasme.co.uk/questions/
46. https://securityintelligence.com/posts/whats-new-2022-cost-of-a-data-breach-report/?_ga=2.85921808.849470340.1661823238-809024391.1661823238

Chapter 5: Criminal finances and investigations

By Anousheh Bromfield, senior associate, and Charles Kuhn, partner, Clyde & Co LLP

Introduction and types of financial crime

Financial crime is increasingly in the spotlight as governments, the media, and activist groups all recognize the detrimental effect of financial crime on wider society, public trust and confidence in the financial system, and economic development. This focus means that more than ever before businesses need to pay close attention to their internal processes to mitigate the risk of any exposure and to understand how the various regulators investigate potential breaches, and professional advisers need to be alert to these issues both in respect of their own obligations and responsibilities, and in order to assist their clients.

The term financial crime encompasses a variety of individual offences that can be separated into two broad categories defined according to the presence of a dishonest act or not. All result in, or have the intention of, obtaining or facilitating material benefit. The most common types of financial crime offences are fraud, money laundering, false accounting, terrorist financing, bribery and corruption, market abuse and insider dealing, and tax evasion.

Investigations

The offences are established by a range of legislation and are investigated and enforced by several different regulators or agencies including notably the National Crime Agency (NCA), Serious Fraud Office (SFO), HMRC, Prudential Regulatory Authority, Financial Conduct Authority (FCA), Insolvency Service, and Competition and Markets Authority. Each regulator or agency has its own powers, processes, and methods of investigation; however, there are several key areas common to each, which we will now discuss.

As a preliminary point, when a business (or individual) has notice of an investigation being commenced they will need to consider whether that triggers any reporting obligations to other regulators or the market and whether there are any implications arising from banking covenants.

Production orders

The SFO obtains its powers from Section 2 of the Criminal Justice Act 1987. Unlike most other agencies/regulators, the SFO can request information prior to an investigation being commenced. These section 2 powers enable the SFO to compel an individual or organization to provide it with information or documents that it believes are relevant to its investigation. This can be done in the form of document disclosures, written explanations or interviews (see below). The SFO can require the documents to be provided "forthwith"– a so-called "here and now" notice, generally interpreted as being "as soon as reasonably possible" – or at a specified time.[1]

The target of a section 2 notice (or other compelled notice) includes the company/individual under investigation, a company/individual considered to be a witness to the investigation, and the professional advisers of any such company/individual.

Failing to comply with a section 2 notice without "reasonable excuse" is itself an offence.[2] It is therefore critical to fully understand the scope of a section 2 notice, being mindful of date ranges, types of documents and any interpretative ambiguities over the nature or subject matter of the documents requested.

A section 2 notice cannot require the production of material subject to legal professional privilege (discussed further below).

It is important to bear in mind that the designation of an individual in receipt of a section 2 notice (whether that be a notice requiring documentation or interview) may change from witness to suspect. Such a change could also arise from a change in focus of the SFO; from, for example, agreeing a deferred prosecution agreement in respect of a corporate (and seeking information to be able to do so) to then, having achieved that goal, addressing individual culpability. It is therefore possible that someone interviewed under section 2 powers initially is then re-interviewed under caution as a suspect.

The FCA's evidence-gathering powers are derived under the Financial Services and Markets Act 2000 (FSMA). In similar vein to the SFO, they can be used to require firms and individuals to attend interviews and disclose documents and information to the FCA. A key way in which the FCA obtains information from firms is through a section 165 information request. A section 165 notice may be issued to assist the FCA with its supervisory and enforcement functions. Similar powers exist under section

122A with respect to individuals who discharge managerial responsibilities (or a person closely associated). There are also specific information-gathering powers under section 122B in respect of market abuse investigations. In addition, the FCA may exercise its powers to assist an investigation of an overseas authority (see, for example, section 169).

HMRC also has similar powers under Schedule 36 of the Finance Act 2008 as does the NCA (and other regulators, depending on the precise circumstances) under the Proceeds of Crime Act 2002.

Dawn raids

Another power in the regulators' arsenal is the dawn raid; a tool used by the SFO, HMRC, and FCA, amongst others. This is where the regulator, on the authority of a search warrant, carries out a search of premises, without prior notification.

Interviews

The regulators and agencies commonly conduct two types of interview – compelled interviews and interviews under caution. We will take the SFO and FCA as examples. The SFO will usually conduct compelled interviews (under its section 2 powers) during the investigative stage of the process and in respect of potential witnesses. Interviews under caution are reserved for suspects once a decision to charge has been made. The FCA will usually conduct compelled interviews for suspected misconduct cases (e.g. a breach of the FCA's own rules, including breaches of the principles for business, conduct rules, and perimeter offences) that do not amount to criminal offences. When criminal offences are being contemplated, including in respect of criminal market abuse or where an individual is otherwise considered to be a suspect, the interview will be under caution (on either a voluntary basis or following an arrest).

The main difference between a compelled interview compared to an interview under caution is that the individual does not have a right to silence and the protections against self-incrimination are not afforded to the individual. The compelled interview regime does build in safeguards in that the evidence provided by the individual cannot be directly used against them in criminal proceedings. However, evidence gathered as a result of information disclosed in the compelled interview is admissible. In the case of differing evidence in the criminal trial, the individual would risk an application for the interview to be adduced as a "previously inconsistent statement" pursuant to section 119 of the Criminal Justice Act 2003.

A failure to respond in a compelled interview by the FCA to a question could result in contempt of court pursuant to section 177 of FSMA. Other authorities have similar powers. In addition, if the individual was an approved person, they would face sanctions under the approved persons regime for not being open and transparent with their regulator, potentially resulting in fines and bans from the financial sector. Similarly, a failure to respond to a compelled interview by the SFO without "reasonable excuse" is itself a criminal offence.[3]

The remainder of this section will focus on compelled interviews.

Attending a compelled interview can be intimidating and concerning; the individual is often required to attend the regulator's offices, is given limited advance disclosure, and the interview may take place over several days and be conducted by more than one investigator.

However, there are some steps that can be taken to try to make the process less daunting. The first is having legal representation at the interview. The SFO does not guarantee that a person attending a compelled interview has the right to be legally represented at the interview. The lawyer must request permission to attend the interview and any agreement may be contingent on certain restrictions. A typical restriction, provided by way of undertaking, is that the individual's lawyer does not discuss the interview with the individual's employer/the company under investigation.

The FCA has similar powers enabling it to require a person to answer questions in an interview and, unlike the SFO, routinely allows interviewees to have legal representation during the interview.

To attempt to mitigate against the unknowns of a compelled interview and to take some ownership of the narrative, as well as providing a mechanism for allowing the interviewee to settle into the interview, it is often prudent to ask for permission for the interviewee to read out a prepared statement at the beginning of the interview. It goes without saying that even a compelled interview where the individual is not a suspect requires considerable preparation.

Privilege

The issue of privilege in an investigation is fraught with complexities and a detailed discussion of these is beyond the scope of this overview. However, there are several broad areas that merit mention.

The regulator's approach to legal professional privilege

The starting position is that compelled document requests do not require the production of any documents that benefit from legal professional privilege. What this means in practice is often the subject of debate between the relevant regulator and recipient of the document production notice. There are two types of legal professional privilege – legal advice privilege and litigation privilege. In most cases, litigation privilege is less likely to be relevant in the context of a regulatory investigation (as for litigation privilege to apply, the communications must be for the sole or dominant purpose of conducting litigation, which must be adversarial rather than investigative) and so we will focus on legal advice privilege. Legal advice privilege, which is of course a right of clients not lawyers, applies to communications between a lawyer and client made in connection with the giving or receiving of legal advice. It necessarily follows that not all communications between client and lawyer will be privileged.

Clearly, where a client is seeking legal advice or a lawyer is providing legal advice directly, those communications will benefit from legal advice privilege. However, the scope of the privilege is broader with the courts having held that it may also arise where the communications consist of facts in contexts where those communications are part of a "*continuum of communications*" between client and lawyer "*aimed at keeping both informed so that advice may be sought and given as required*".[4] Similarly, the court has held that where lawyers are tasked with investigating relevant information they must be able to relay their findings and any records of ensuing decision to their clients with the benefit of legal advice privilege.[5] There will also be certain documents that are not direct communications which came into existence for the dominant purpose of seeking or providing legal advice, for example, a solicitor's "working papers" or a briefing paper prepared by the client.[6]

Where the situation gets more complicated is where there are documents that cover several purposes or where communications involve multiple parties, not all of whom can be considered the "client". Care should always be taken to identify at the outset of any instruction who the client is, for example with respect to a corporate, and which individuals are tasked with seeking and receiving legal advice.

No privilege arises where a solicitor's assistance is sought in furtherance of crime or fraud or any similar conduct which is contrary to public policy, the interests of justice or good faith. The state of knowledge of the solicitor is irrelevant; the so-called crime/fraud or iniquity exception applies whether or not the solicitor is aware of the client's intent.

Recipients of compelled notices may take the decision to waive legal professional privilege in respect of certain documents or categories of documents. This is particularly the case with the SFO, which has publicly stated that it may ask corporates under investigation to do just that in certain circumstances. Any decision to waive privilege must be carefully considered given the serious consequences of doing so, particularly in the context of investigative and enforcement proceedings. In particular, once a privileged document has been provided to a regulator that regulator may, either by necessity or choice, share that document with other agencies (local or overseas), make that document or information contained within it public in the context of the proceedings, and may use that document as evidence against the disclosing party. Other parties may also seek to deploy the disclosed document in related proceedings.

Further, recipients of compelled notices and/or those under investigation should be alert to the (increasing) possibility of the regulator challenging the assertion of legal professional privilege.

Privilege in insolvency situations

Under the Insolvency Act 1986, the trustees in bankruptcy acquire ownership of all the bankrupt individuals' property (subject to certain exceptions that are irrelevant for present purposes). One may think that this transfer would include any privilege that had previously been held by the bankrupt individual. However, the court has held that this is not the case, limiting the transfer of privilege only to circumstances where the legal advice in question related to a particular piece of property which now formed part of the bankrupt estate held by the trustee.[7]

This is in contrast to the position in a corporate insolvency. In those circumstances, no assets are transferred; the liquidator or administrator takes over the company, including its assets and liabilities, and the benefit of any privileged legal advice the company has received.

Conflicts in privilege

In cross-border matters, consideration must be given to the privilege and professional secrecy obligations of all relevant jurisdictions. For example, contrary to the position under English law, in the EU, communications between a corporate client and its in-house lawyers do not benefit from privilege in the context of an investigation by an EU institution, such as the European Commission.[8]

When a regulator requests an organization, in relation to an investigation, to provide it with information that includes personal data, the organization needs to be careful to ensure that complying with the request does not breach its obligations under relevant privacy laws. This is particularly the case with cross-border issues/organizations that may be affected by the extra-territorial scope of certain privacy regulations (such as the European General Data Protection Regulation).

Similarly, where the information request is made of a lawyer, in addition to the application of legal professional privilege, the regulatory obligation of confidentiality (paragraph 2.5 of the SRA Code of Conduct for Solicitors must be considered, noting the express derogation (at paragraph 6.3) for disclosure required, permitted by law, or with client consent. The Proceeds of Crime Act 2002 (POCA) introduces a further concept (relevant only to money laundering disclosures) of "privileged circumstances".[9] This extends to tax advisers, auditors, accountants, and independent legal advisers in the regulated sector (see further below).

Representation

When faced with an investigation, in most circumstances, external counsel should be appointed. A decision will need to be taken as to whether the company and each relevant individual should instruct separate solicitors or whether, at least at the commencement of an investigation, one solicitor can represent all the relevant parties.

Two key considerations in making that decision are the application of privilege and the presence or risk of conflicts arising during the course of the investigation. In order to best protect all parties, the usual approach would be for each entity and/or individual to have separate legal representation. Depending on the potential for conflicts and level of interplay between the parties, a common interest privilege agreement is typically entered into to enable information and advice to be shared between the parties/their legal representatives without privilege being waived.

A further consideration is whether it is necessary to instruct counsel in various jurisdictions, either because of a cross-border element to the subject of the investigation (which may give rise to privilege considerations in several jurisdictions, for example) or because of multiple investigations.

Jurisdiction

As mentioned in the context of waiver of privilege, there is frequent cooperation between agencies/regulators, including cross-border cooperation. UK agencies/regulators such as the SFO commonly engage with their US counterparts at the United States Department of Justice (DOJ), the Commodity Futures Trading Commission (CFTC) and Securities and Exchange Commission (SEC), passing information and analysis between each other.

This cross-border cooperation, to some extent, extends the scope of an investigation and makes a distinction between, for example a UK company and its overseas subsidiary, less apparent for the purposes of an investigation. For example, where an organization may entirely legitimately withhold certain documents on the grounds that they are not within the jurisdiction and therefore not responsive to a compelled document request, the relevant regulator may simply seek the cooperation of its counterpart in that jurisdiction to obtain the documents. Nevertheless, it is important to consider jurisdiction at the outset and throughout the investigation to avoid, for example, bringing material into the jurisdiction unintentionally or unnecessarily.[10]

Furthermore, jurisdiction is a relevant consideration not only to the company itself but to the role of any individuals who may be subject to compelled requests (be that document requests or interviews). A decision may need to be taken whether to rely on a particular person, for example, being located outside of the jurisdiction to avoid being questioned, weighing up the potential prejudice of such an interview with the adverse inferences that could be drawn by the regulator in an individual failing to cooperate. It is noted that, in many cases, the regulator could make a request for mutual legal assistance from the third country, which could render any attempt to rely on being located outside of the jurisdiction fruitless.

Specific considerations for certain offences in law firms – (section 330 POCA)

Practical issues have resulted for those law firms with mixed regulated and non-regulated practices under POCA. By way of example, the question has arisen whether an individual in a law firm that carries out regulated activities can be liable for tipping off pursuant to section 330 of POCA if they disclosed to a client that another individual had made a relevant disclosure to the NCA. The scope of the regulated sector is deliberately tightly defined. As the Explanatory Notes make clear, the law as drafted "*ensures that people working in businesses which conduct both regulated and unregulated activities would only be caught by the failure to disclose offence at section 330* whilst actually carrying out *the regulated activities and not in the course of other non-regulated activities*"[11] (emphasis added).

The general provision of legal advice by solicitors and barristers are not regulated activities for the purposes of section 330 POCA. (See also the Strasbourg Court in *Michaud v. France* (2014) 59 EHRR 9 [at 74 and 97], which stated that duties on lawyers in the regulated sector will only arise in a context *unrelated to legal proceedings or advice*: "Lawyers were not affected in their activities linked to judicial proceedings or when consulted for 'legal advice.'")

This is also relevant to the money laundering reporting officer's (MLRO) disclosure obligations arising under POCA. Each circumstance potentially requiring a disclosure must be considered carefully and well documented to mitigate against the risk of personal liability arising on the MLRO.

Conclusion

Financial crime affects all professional sectors and industries and with ever-increasing sophisticated measures employed by perpetrators it is increasingly important for all businesses to be alert to the risks that affect their specific business and to implement effective processes and procedures to mitigate, identify, and deal with any potential issues that give rise to financial crime concerns. Those procedures need to include, inter alia, adequate training of all staff, protection for whistleblowers, processes for internal investigations, and reporting lines. Whereas, in the past, financial crime may have been treated as a faceless crime and been slightly ignored, as the real impact on societies is being publicly revealed, and with regulators and authorities taking more measures to enforce the legislation (including against those unwittingly caught up in criminal circumstances), now is the time for all businesses to act.

References

1 Sections 2(2) and 2(3) Criminal Justice Act 1987.
2 Section 2(13) Criminal Justice Act 1987.
3 *Ibid* 2.
4 Three Rivers (No 6); *Balabel v. Air India* (1988) 1 Ch 317.
5 *Property Alliance Group Limited v. The Royal Bank of Scotland Plc* (2015) EWHC 3187 (Ch).
6 *R (Jet2.com) v. CAA* (2020) EWCA Civ 35.
7 *Mikhail Shlosberg v. Avonwick Holdings Ltd & Ors* (2016) EWHC 416 (Ch).
8 *Akzo Nobel Chemicals Ltd v. European Commission* (2010) 5 CMLR 19.
9 See, for example, Section 330(6) of the Proceeds of Crime Act 2002.
10 *R (on the application of KBR, Inc) (Appellant) v. Director of the Serious Fraud Office (Respondent)* (2021) UKSC 2; *KBR Inc. R (On the Application Of) v. The Director of the Serious Fraud Office* (2018) EWHC 2368 (Admin).
11 Explanatory Notes to Proceeds of Crime Act 2002, "Schedule 9: Regulated Sector and supervisory authorities", §499.

Chapter 6: Anti-money laundering – are you doing enough to protect your firm?

By Brian Rogers, regulatory director, The Access Group

The money laundering landscape

Money laundering is a major international problem, with the United Nations[1] saying that two to five percent of world GDP ($800bn to $2tn) is subject to money laundering every year.

Like other countries, the UK has been targeted by money launderers, with many seeing London, dubbed the "London Laundromat", as a favorite location to carry out their crimes; the National Crime Agency[2] believes that over £100bn is laundered through the UK each year, with foreign investors being of particular concern.

Recent enforcement action has been taken against two UK banks with HSBC[3] fined £64m for "unacceptable failings" of anti-money laundering systems, and Natwest[4] fined £265m for allowing a customer to walk into its branches over a period of time and deposit millions of pounds in cash without asking any appropriate questions; some believe that large corporate entities now see such fines as just another business overhead because they are far less than the profits that can be made from such questionable transactions.

Law firm sanctions

Law firms have not gone unnoticed by regulators either, with one London firm[5] recently fined £232,500 for various breaches of the Money Laundering Regulations, including allowing its client account to be used as a banking facility, a lack of client due diligence, and failing to retain evidence to show what due diligence had been undertaken.

In 2021, a total of 13 firms were fined £800 each in addition to £600 costs for failing to complete an anti-money laundering (AML) declaration required by the Solicitors Regulation Authority (SRA);[6] another firm was fined £10,000 for various AML breaches including failing to train staff and a poor approach to risk assessments.[7]

In 2020, a firm was sanctioned for AML breaches and fined £14,000 plus £3,500 costs;[8] the breaches included not retaining appropriate identity documents, not applying an appropriate level of client due diligence for the risks posed, a failure to investigate clients' sources of funds, and ignoring clear AML red flags that had been identified in various regulatory publications that the firm should have read and acted upon.

SRA AML thematic reviews

Over the last few years, the SRA has been very active in its role as an AML sector regulator, with the introduction of a specific team dealing with AML compliance matters, undertaking a series of thematic reviews, and publishing numerous reports and guidance documents.

In 2019, the SRA[9] found that one in five firms were failing to meet their AML compliance obligations as they did not have a firm-wide risk assessment (FWRA), a document that is central to a firm's AML strategy and plans. During this review, 400 firms were assessed with 64 percent using poor quality risk assessment templates and 38 percent of firms' assessments dated within a short time before the SRA's deadline; this suggested that some firms may only have completed their assessments because they had been put under pressure from the SRA rather than completing them freely as part of their AML requirements.

In its *Three Pillars of Success* report published in November 2021, the SRA made various observations around three key areas related to AML compliance – namely authority, independence, and resources.

- *"Authority*
    - *All but one of the MLCOs and MLROs we spoke to held a position at or near the top of their firm's hierarchy.*
    - *18 out of 30 used their free access to all of the firm's management and business data to determine what the overall risk-based approach to money laundering would be.*
    - *They were able to choose and implement a wide range of methods to maintain fee earner knowledge and interest in AML.*

- *Independence*
    - *Few MLCOs and MLROs experienced resistance to AML measures from their colleagues, but around half experienced it from clients.*
    - *Despite this, clients are generally more aware of AML requirements and the reasons for them than in previous years.*

- *Two firms' MLCOs said that their decisions could theoretically be outvoted by the rest of the firm's management – we consider that they should automatically have the last word on AML matters.*

- *Resources*
  - *The majority of MLCOs and MLROs said that having enough time to carry out their duties was the most important resource.*
  - *Of the 54 MLCOs and MLROs we spoke to, the majority did not have any reduction in their fee-earning targets to take account of their extra responsibilities.*
  - *Only 48% of MLCOs and MLROs had a deputy to share the work and provide cover for them."*[10]

The SRA concluded that:

> *"Generally, AML officers tend to fulfil the two pillars of authority and independence well, being able to command the respect of their peers and capable of making clear-sighted and risk-based decisions.*
> *"The biggest challenge which AML officers discussed with us was resourcing, most acutely in relation to time – time to learn about the role, time to plan, time to check the firm's progress, time to reflect, and time to act in an emergency. All are significant parts of the role and need an appropriate investment. All other strategies – support, funding, training and so forth – are likely to be of limited use if the MLCO or MLRO do not have enough time to dedicate to their duties."*[11]

AML guidance

In addition to the UK's Proceeds of Crime Act and Money Laundering Regulations, law firms must act in line with guidance issued by other relevant authorities, for example, the Financial Action Task Force and the Legal Sector Affinity Group.

The Financial Action Task Force (FATF) is the global money laundering and terrorist financing watchdog. The inter-governmental body sets international standards that aim to prevent these illegal activities and the harm they cause to society. As a policy-making body, the FATF works to generate the necessary political will to bring about national legislative and regulatory reforms in these areas.

The Legal Sector Affinity Group (LSAG) is a group made up of the Law

Society and other legal professional body supervisors named in the Money Laundering Regulations; the group interprets the Regulations for the legal profession and provides appropriate guidance.

Although the LSAG guidance is not mandatory, firms that do not follow it will find it extremely hard to convince regulators that this was appropriate, so best practice is to follow it to the letter.

The LSAG guidance[12] is based around the high-level compliance principles shown below.

AML governance

Each firm that is covered by the Money Laundering Regulations must ensure its beneficial owners, officers, and managers are approved by the SRA, including the person(s) nominated to be its MLRO (responsible for the submission of suspicious activity reports (SARs)) and where appropriate its MLCO (responsible for compliance with the Money Laundering Regulations).

The AML policies, controls, and procedures (PCPs) must be approved by senior management, and all action and decisions must be evidenced in writing, even if it is just to say that nothing has been changed as a consequence of any review. Senior management must actively monitor, enforce, and manage compliance with all PCPs.

The appointment of an MLCO is subject to the size and nature of a firm, so some smaller firms could think they could get away with not appointing one; however, it is highly likely that only sole practitioners would be able to avoid such an obligation, because in effect they fulfil all compliance roles. The SRA has said that any firm (excluding sole practitioners) that decides not to appoint an MLCO will face an uphill struggle in justifying its position, so best practice is for all firms to appoint one.

Where a firm's Compliance Officer for Legal Practice (COLP) is not also the MLCO/MLRO they should be actively involved in ensuring their firm meets its AML obligations, otherwise they will not be able to meet their obligation under the SRA Code of Conduct for Firms (9.2b), which states:

> *"If you are a COLP you must take all reasonable steps to ensure compliance by your firm and its managers, employees or interest holders with the SRA's regulatory arrangements which apply to them."*[13]

Firm (practice)-wide risk assessment

Each firm must have an up-to-date written assessment that forms the foundations for its policies, controls, and procedures, and it must cover all the areas that are required by the SRA, including the firm's clients, geographical area served, products and services provided, transaction types, and delivery channels.

As noted by the SRA, it is this document that seems to cause many firms the most difficulty as its creation and the assessment of their firms' risk profiles require much thought by management teams and AML compliance officers.

The assessment must be periodically reviewed and, where appropriate, updated to reflect new/changed risks. Even if changes are not made the review should be noted; this is another area that seems to be overlooked by some firms as they either don't keep abreast of changes to the risks they face or don't act on the risks they become aware of and train staff accordingly.

Client/matter level risk assessment

Every new client and matter must be the subject of an AML risk assessment, especially if the matter is non-repetitive, and the outcomes used to assess the level of due diligence that is required on the client/matter.

Findings from file reviews show that some firms implement decent checklists to cover these assessments but then don't complete them, or don't complete them in full, or complete them but authorizing officers don't check them before authorizing the case handler to move forward with a matter.

Some firms handling multiple transactions for the same client can become blasé about the risks they could pose, so it is key to carry out appropriate assessments before work commences and throughout a matter.

AML policies, controls, and procedures

In order to meet their AML obligations, firms must have clearly documented policies, controls, and procedures, which are based around the findings contained in the firm-wide risk assessment; any reviews of and changes to the PCPs must be reflected back to this assessment.

Key areas for focus are:

- Client due diligence procedures – these must include:
  - The identification of the ownership and control structures of commercial entities – evidence shows that many companies being set up at Companies House bear the hallmarks of suspicious activity, and therefore firms need to use the enhanced search

facility to drill down into the detail when assessing the risks of company clients.

  - The identification and verification of individuals – the COVID-19 pandemic has led to new online ways of checking and verifying the identity of individuals, and although these are regarded as being safe, firms still need to take care, especially with deep fakes and other ways of trying to convince them that they are dealing with legitimate people.
  - Obtaining a clear understanding of a client's source of wealth and funds – with the introduction of open banking it is now much easier to check on sources of a client's funds for a transaction; however, bank transactions should be checked to make sure they make sense.
  - Reporting Companies House discrepancies – it is important that if discrepancies are found between the information obtained from clients and that held by Companies House, they are reported quickly, especially when so many companies are currently being set up in suspicious circumstances.
  - Higher risk clients / matters – firms must apply the correct level of due diligence to the risks that may be identified, for example, the client is not seen face-to-face, is a Politically Exposed Person (PEP), or is from a high-risk country.

- Suspicious Activity Reporting – it is essential that suspicious activity is dealt with quickly by making internal reports to a firm's MLRO, so they can consider whether a report should be made to the National Crime Agency and a defense against money laundering (DAML) obtained where appropriate; if such a report is necessary it is important that they are managed in line with the defined timescales and steps taken to avoid tipping off.
- Technology – with the increased use of technology to help identify clients and mitigate money laundering risks it is important that firms understand what the technology does and how they should interpret the data that is generated. For example, just because a report shows that a client has passed an online due diligence check on the whole doesn't mean the report shouldn't be interrogated to identify any areas where minor issues may have been found.
- Training – training plays a key part in reducing the risk of a firm getting caught up in money laundering activity, and it should be

provided to all relevant staff; best practice says that all staff, whether or not they work in a regulated area, should be given training. For example, some firms may think that a receptionist does not need training because they don't handle client work. However, what happens if a client drops off an envelope full of cash on the reception desk? Would they know what to do with it or whether they should accept it in the first place? Historically, there has been a view that update training need only be given every two years; however, with the increase in money laundering activity, firms should update staff on a more regular basis; this training could be in the form of update emails being sent to all staff about risks that have not been identified before or where the firm has entered into a high risk area of work for the first time.

- Internal controls – these controls cover the appointment of AML compliance officers, the establishment of an independent audit function, and the screening of staff. As the appointment of officers was discussed earlier the focus here will be on the other two controls, namely:
  - Independent audit function – the purpose of this function is to examine, evaluate, and make recommendations regarding the adequacy and effectiveness of a firm's AML and counter-terrorist financing policies, controls, and procedures. The person(s) carrying out the audit does not have to be external to the firm but must be independent of the function being reviewed; for example, if a senior partner doesn't hold any compliance officer roles they would be seen as independent.
  - The timing of audits should be assessed on a risk basis, but it is recommended that they take place at least annually, and take account of changes to a firm's risk profile, the work areas it covers, and whether there have been any changes to its structure.
- Record keeping – as with all aspects of compliance, it is very important that appropriate records are kept. These include client identification documents in compliance with the Money Laundering Regulations, audit reports, and decision notes; the SRA's view is that if evidence cannot be produced to show that something has been done/decided, then it didn't happen.

Conclusion

The pressure on firms to ensure they reduce the risk of involvement in money laundering activity is not going to go away, and therefore they must ensure they take appropriate steps to meet their compliance obligations and reduce the risk of being the subject of regulatory action and reputational damage.

References

1 Europol Data: www.europol.europa.eu/crime-areas-and-statistics/crime-areas/economic-crime/money-laundering.
2 www.nationalcrimeagency.gov.uk/news/national-economic-crime-centre-leads-push-to-identify-money-laundering-activity
3 www.fca.org.uk/news/press-releases/fca-fines-hsbc-bank-plc-deficient-transaction-monitoring-controls
4 www.fca.org.uk/news/press-releases/natwest-fined-264.8million-anti-money-laundering-failures
5 www.lawgazette.co.uk/news/mishcon-de-reya-fined-232500-over-numerous-aml-failings/5111049.article
6 www.todaysconveyancer.co.uk/seven-firms-fined-aml-failures/
7 www.legalfutures.co.uk/latest-news/profession-has-struggled-with-aml-rules-says-firm-fined-10000
8 www.legalfutures.co.uk/latest-news/firm-fined-14000-for-conveyancing-id-failures
9 Solicitors Regulation Authority, "Firm risk assessments", updated 25 November 2019, www.sra.org.uk/solicitors/guidance/firm-risk-assessments/.
10 Solicitors Regulation Authority, *Money Laundering Governance: The Three Pillars of Success*, 22 November 2021, www.sra.org.uk/sra/research-publications/money-laundering-governance-three-pillars-of-success/.
11 *Ibid.*
12 www.lawsociety.org.uk/en/topics/anti-money-laundering/anti-money-laundering-guidance
13 Solicitors Regulation Authority, Code of Conduct for Firms, 25 November 2019, www.sra.org.uk/solicitors/standards-regulations/code-conduct-firms/.

Chapter 7:
Professional indemnity insurance

By Rebecca Atkinson, director of risk and compliance, Howard Kennedy

The requirement to have professional indemnity insurance

The SRA Indemnity Insurance Rules (the Rules) require authorized firms and their principals to take out and maintain qualifying insurance with what is termed as a participating insurer.[1] If the firm is unable to obtain insurance it must cease practicing promptly and no later than the end of the cover provided.[2] The purpose of the insurance is to cover civil liability claims arising from the work conducted. The insurance will cover any losses successfully claimed and often will pay for the defense costs of defending claims against the firm.

The cover obtained must be adequate and appropriate in respect of the firm's practice, past and present. Further, the firm must ensure that clients have the benefit of the insurance required under the Rules and must not exclude or attempt to exclude liability below the minimum level of cover required by the Rules.[3]

Firms that are unable to obtain insurance must be given an extended indemnity period by their insurer from the previous indemnity year.

This cover extension is a 30-day extended indemnity period in which a firm can continue to practice and try to obtain qualifying insurance. It is therefore designed to keep the firm operating whilst it attempts to obtain other cover. After this time, firms will enter a cessation period of 60 days in which firms will be unable to accept new instructions and can only perform work in connection with existing work.[4]

A participating insurer is an insurer who has entered into an agreement with the SRA to provide insurance cover to law firms. Qualifying insurance means a policy that provides cover in accordance with the Minimum Terms and Conditions (MCT) as set out by the SRA.[5]

The Rules require that if a claimant asserts a claim against the firm and the claim relates to a matter under the terms of the policy (the MCT) then upon request by the claimant the law firm should provide the name of the insurer, policy number, and contact details of the insurer.[6]

Insurance is normally held for 12 months at a time and there is no longer a single renewal date, i.e. a single date by which all firms need to renew their insurance.

How much insurance cover to buy

All law firms need what is termed a "primary" layer of insurance. This is a compulsory amount of insurance cover. Sole practitioners and partnerships must have a minimum of £2m cover whilst other entities such as Limited Liability Partnerships or Alternative Business Structures must have a minimum cover amount of £3m.[7] Both these sums are per claim.

Many law firms buy more cover than the minimum amount required, taking into account the nature of their work.

Outcome 7.13 in the SRA Code of Conduct 2011 states that:

> *"You assess and purchase the level of professional indemnity insurance cover that is appropriate for your current and past practice, taking into account potential levels of claim by your clients and others and any alternative arrangements you or your client may make."*[8]

This Outcome has not fully translated to the 2019 Code for Firms – though there is a general requirement at paragraph 2.5 which sets out that you must "*identify, monitor and manage all material risks to your business, including those which may arise from your connected practices*".[9]

Below are some steps that firms may wish to undertake when deciding how much indemnity cover to buy.

Assessing your firm

The first step is to assess the firm. Some factors can include:

- The size of the firm;
- What types of work the firm does. Crime may be considered to be low risk but real estate high. Brokers can help firms here and often brokers and insurers will be able to provide firms with statistics on the types of work that give rise to the most claims;
- The firm's claim history – how large have claims been in the past;
- Whether the level of the cover is similar to other firms of a similar make-up and size. Again brokers can help here; and
- The firm's ability to meet uncovered claims.

Assessing firm risk

The level of cover that a firm may need depends on the firm's risk profile, which is derived from many factors. Questions firms can ask themselves may include:

- Does the firm conduct work in a high-risk area such as real estate or corporate? If so, how much of that work creates the firm's total revenue? A firm that derives five percent of its revenue from real estate is going to be lower risk than a firm that derives 50 percent.
- What are the values of the transactions that the firm handles? Are these values over and above the PI cover in place or contemplated?
- Is the firm coming up against opposition to the limitation of liability that the firm is placing on its retainers, i.e. maybe from banks who ask the firm to limit liability to value of the loan being provided?
- How much money does the firm hold in its client account at any one time? Remember, PI covers client monetary loss. Does the firm hold more in its client account than insurance cover held? If so, how can that risk be mitigated?

Taking the above into account, the ultimate question to ask is, if the firm were negligent on a matter, what is the maximum possible loss that the firm could cause and does that exceed the insurance cover? If yes, then more cover is needed.

What a circumstance is, when and how to notify possible claims to insurers, and who will handle the claim

It is important to notify insurers of matters that may give rise to a claim against the firm and that therefore in turn require payment from insurers or a sum to be noted against the firm's excess that will erode it (bringing the insurer closer to having to make a payment).

It is "circumstances" that should be notified to insurers. A circumstance is:

> *"An incident, occurrence, fact, matter, act or omission which may give rise to a claim in respect of civil liability."*[10]

"Circumstances" include not only an intimation of an intention to claim but also an awareness the firm or someone within it may have of a failing or doubt as to the effectiveness of performance where such failing might give rise to a claim.

In other words, firms should notify a circumstance to insurers where the firm is aware of a negligent act even if the client may be oblivious to the problem.

Practically speaking, the following might give rise to a cause to notify insurers.

- A client complains or indicates unhappiness with the firm's service. If the client is claiming a lack of service or losses that sound more a result of negligence, because they are claiming loss or damages, the firm needs to consider whether it is appropriate to notify the matter to insurers.
- A solicitor realizes they have given negligent advice, even if the client is not yet aware of the error. If the error has no impact, firms may decide to inform insurers anyway. Failing this, an internal record should be kept so that claims/notification/error trends can be spotted in the future.
- The client has not complained and you do not consider the firm has done anything wrong, but nonetheless there is a possibility that a claim will arise.

A firm's insurers and brokers will be able to guide a firm as to what amounts to a notification and most insurers want to see a cautious approach adopted and notifications made as a precaution if needed.

It is always open to insurers to reject a notification made to it, but this is unlikely to happen.

There is a misconception that more notifications to insurers will increase the premium but this is not the case. Claims against the firm for which payment is made increases the premium whereas precautionary notifications provide comfort that the firm spots when an issue arises and the firm is tackling the same.

Notifications should be made as soon as an issue arises and without delay. If the firm is considering its rectification options, the notification should be made to insurers in the meantime and a follow up provided to insurers.

The format of the notification is down to brokers and insurers to decide. Some will provide a form to be completed and some will be happy to receive an email setting out the detail. A form, however, can help the firm spot patterns and trends and a log should certainly be kept for this purpose.

In terms of who will handle a claim, that will depend on the arrangements between insurers and the firm. Some insurers provide a claims handling service and some firms may deal with the claim internally with the permission of insurers. Alternatively, external solicitors may be appointed to handle the claim with either insurers or the firm paying the costs thereof. Some insurers have a law firm panel for this purpose with negotiated hourly rates.

Should you rectify mistakes? Beware own interest conflict

Paragraph 3.5 of the Code for Firms under StaRs sets out:

> *"You are honest and open with clients if things go wrong, and if a client suffers loss or harm as a result you put matters right (if possible) and explain fully and promptly what has happened and the likely impact. If requested to do so by the SRA you investigate whether anyone may have a claim against you, provide the SRA with a report on the outcome of your investigation, and notify relevant persons that they may have such a claim, accordingly."*[11]

Firms that have a circumstance to notify must always seek the permission of insurers before admitting negligence to a client or other party. Failure to do this could result in insurers refusing cover (unlikely but possible) or the relationship between insurers and the firm becoming strained. Insurers do not like to feel that they are not part of the rectification of an error. Firms must balance their insurance position with the requirements of the Code and insurers are unlikely to stop a firm from informing the client of an error.

Firms must carefully consider whether they are able to rectify matters (i.e. "put matters right" as outlined in the above paragraph from the Code) and whether the firm has an own interest conflict (that is where the interests of the firm and the client come into conflict). This analysis is even more important in light of the Solicitors Disciplinary Tribunal (SDT) case of Howell-Jones [SDT case No. 11846-2018].

In that case, Howell-Jones (HJ) acted for a matrimonial client. After realizing that they might have under-settled their client's case they took Counsel's advice, who confirmed they had been negligent. They informed the client openly and frankly about their negligence and gave the client the choice of either taking the matter elsewhere and suing the firm or allowing the firm to rectify the matter by returning to court to seek an overturning of the settling order. HJ offered to write off fees, pay for the rectification work and pay any adverse costs order that might occur from the application they were offering to undertake.

The client agreed to their rectification offer and HJ made the application to court. However, things did not go according to plan. The judge refused to overturn the order and the client complained to the SRA.

The matter went before the SDT, which held that HJ should not have attempted to rectify the matter as there was an own-interest conflict. Whilst HJ advised the client he should take independent legal advice, they did not insist upon it. Presumably if they had insisted, HJ would have had to pay for that.

This is not a popular decision and subsequent SDT cases may undermine it. However, it does highlight that when faced with an issue which has resulted from negligence that is capable of rectification firms must carefully consider whether they should rectify or inform the client that rectification cannot be undertaken by the firm and they must seek legal advice elsewhere.

When firms do decide that they are able to rectify and there is no own-interest conflict or that can somehow be overcome, the firm must document its decision for future reference.

PI insurance renewal – what happens each year and top tips for renewal: how to present your firm well

Generally speaking, PI insurance is renewed every 12 months, though it is possible to have an insurance policy lasting 18 months.

The renewal process will differ from broker to broker and insurer to insurer but normally requires the completion of a proposal form, disclosing certain categories of information about the firm for brokers' and insurers' consideration. These categories may be as follows:

- Number of people the firm and how many are qualified lawyers;
- Practice areas and percentage of fees generated from those areas;
- Specific questions relating to those areas where there is a penchant for risk, for example additional questions on real estate areas may be asked;
- Turnover of the firm in the past year or more and budget for the coming year;
- Merger, bolt-on, or takeover plans;
- How risk management is handled in the firm to include supervision, claims handling, training and so on;
- A summary of complaints and claims and trends; and
- A summary of COLP and COFA reports to the SRA.

Brokers are likely to ask for the above information one to three months before renewal, depending on complexity and size of the firm (and perhaps how challenging the insurance market is in that year).

Often insurers will want to meet firms each year to discuss how the firm has performed over the past year in terms of turnover, market conditions, and claims. These meetings need to be prepared for and below are some suggestions for firms to consider.

- Seek help from the firm's broker – brokers are there to be utilized and will be able to guide firms on how to prepare for a renewal meeting as well as how to approach meetings with specific insurers.
- Prepare for any meeting well and give a good impression. Firms must be ready at the meeting to discuss anything disclosed in the proposal form or in addition to it.
- Be open and explain to prospective insurers everything they want to know about the firm in terms of clients and key clients, the work the firm does, the firm's vision and strategy, growth plans, firm culture and so on. Insurers look for long-term relationships and will want to insure those they can partner with for years to come.
- Be honest about issues and particularly claims. Be ready to explain to insurers what has happened and what steps have been taken to rectify and prevent further occurrence. It is best to provide straightforward answers and not avoid answering tough questions. Insurers will see through this.
- Be ready to talk about any regulatory issues. Insurers want to know about these too. If the firm has made breach reports to the SRA these need to be disclosed and discussed.
- Provide additional information beyond the renewal form where it is called for. If there is a big claim, firms should provide a summary of it along with an explanation of lessons learned. Also, if the firm has embarked on a training program or a project looking at the effectiveness of supervision in the firm, for example, these should be highlighted and will go down well with insurers.
- Discuss future risk and compliance plans – insurers want to know what firms have planned in terms of tackling issues or ensuring compliance, especially when they impact on the instances of notifications and claims. Giving insurers confidence in the firm's risk and compliance program can greatly increase the chances of a good premium price.

- Look at notification and claims schedules and any summaries provided as part of the renewal pack well in advance of the renewal meeting and be prepared to answer questions about them.

Possible PI insurance exclusions for sanctioned entities and certain types of work

Some insurers are placing more restrictions on the policies they are prepared to provide. One example is that of sanctions. Some insurers will not provide insurance cover in respect of a claim being brought by a US sanctioned entity. This is because the insurer is US-owned and to pay any claim out could mean they are falling foul of the US sanction imposed.

Insurers may also impose restrictions on covering certain types of high-risk work, such as acting in relation to buyer-funded real estate developments.

It is vital for firms to fully understand the cover that they have and ensure they are acting within their policy coverage. Remember too that not having minimum cover insurance is a regulatory breach as well as a huge risk for the firm.

A short note about cybercrime insurance

More firms are now taking separate cover for instances of cybercrime and the resulting losses. Cyber insurance can cover a whole range of consequences to a crime event, such as losses arising from business interruption, cyber extortion, data loss and data restoration, the cost of forensic investigators, public relations cost, regulatory defense and penalty costs, and money theft loss (though firms' professional indemnity insurance or crime insurance may cover this loss).

Law firms are being attacked day in and day out and are a prime target for cyber criminals. Firms must ensure their cybersecurity is the best it can be and it is strongly advised that firms consider taking out cyber insurance.

Limiting liability clauses

Indicative Behavior 1.8 of the 2011 SRA Code of Conduct set out the requirement that:

> *"If you seek to limit your liability to your client to a level above the minimum required by the SRA Indemnity Insurance Rules, ensuring that this limitation is in writing and is brought to the client's attention."*[12]

This has not found its way into the 2019 Codes. However, it is of course a matter of good practice that if a firm seeks to limit its liability it should be brought to the attention of the client. This can be done in the firm's engagement letter and reiterated in the firm's terms of business.

Limitations of liability only have a chance of standing up in court if they are reasonable and proportionate.

If a firm was acting on a transaction worth £150m and any negligence caused by the firm could amount to half that then a limitation of liability to £10m when the firm has £100m cover is probably not enough. It is important for the firm and its conducting lawyers to reflect on the work being done and the limitation being offered and adjust accordingly.

Sometimes clients (and sometimes banks who may not be the client but who are receiving the benefit of the firm's work) require unlimited liability. This is a judgement call for the firm to make, assessing the risk of losses caused being beyond the firm's insurance cover. If the firm is to offer unlimited liability, the firm needs to consider if additional checking of the work undertaken (beyond what is normal for the firm) should take place to mitigate the risk of negligence as far as possible.

Conclusion

The key to a good PI renewal is to prepare and present well to insurers as well as handle PI matters correctly throughout the insurance year. Firms who adopt good processes around notification and claims handling and who learn from their mistakes stand a good chance of achieving favorable insurance terms, including premium price.

References

1 Solicitors Regulation Authority, Indemnity Insurance Rules, 25 November 2019, www.sra.org.uk/solicitors/standards-regulations/indemnity-insurance-rules/, Rule 2.1.

2 *Ibid*, Rule 2.4.

3 *Ibid*, Rule 3.

4 *Ibid*, Rule 4.2.

5 *Ibid*, Annex 1: SRA Minimum Terms and Conditions of Professional Indemnity Insurance.

6 *Ibid* 1, Rule 9.2.

7 *Ibid* 5, paragraph 2.1.

8 Solicitors Regulation Authority, SRA Handbook, October 2011, www.sra.org.uk/solicitors/handbook/.

9 Solicitors Regulation Authority, Code of Conduct for Firms, 25 November 2019, www.sra.org.uk/solicitors/standards-regulations/code-conduct-firms/, paragraph 2.5.

10 Legal Services Board, BSB Minimum Terms of Entity Cover, www.legalservicesboard.org.uk/wp-content/uploads/2019/06/Annex-D-Minimum-terms-of-cover-for-entities.pdf, p8.

11 *Ibid* 9, paragraph 3.5.

12 *Ibid* 8.

Chapter 8:
Protecting partner assets

By Frank Maher, partner, Legal Risk LLP

Introduction

This chapter identifies some of the risks against which partners may assume they are protected, both while they are practicing and after retirement. Most of the time, professional indemnity insurance provides a safety net, but it is not possible to insure against everything that may go wrong in professional life, and it is therefore important to understand what the gaps in that safety net are.

The matters discussed here are addressed particularly at the primary policies for solicitors in England and Wales, which are required to comply with the Solicitors Regulation Authority (SRA) Minimum Terms and Conditions of Professional Indemnity Insurance (MTC).[1] Similar provisions will generally be found in other policies, whether primary cover under the compulsory schemes which apply in other jurisdictions and for other branches of the legal profession in the UK, or excess layer policies; exclusions in the latter may in some cases be significantly more onerous. The compulsory layer of primary cover under the MTC is £3m per claim including claimants' costs for limited liability partnerships (LLPs), limited companies, and Alternative Business Structures (ABSs, strictly "licensed bodies"), and £2m for sole practitioners and general partnerships.[2]

Although the wording of insurance policies varies, even for policies provided by the same insurer, and it therefore needs to be checked, there are some common exclusions that appear in probably all policies, and in so far as a primary policy may afford less cover than prescribed by the MTC, by clause 4.11 of the MTC, the provisions of the MTC prevail and the policy must be construed or rectified accordingly so as to comply with the MTC.

Attention also needs to be given to the question of what protection is in place once a lawyer has left a firm or retired. This in turn raises questions of how long cover is available for, and the time limits within which claims can be brought, and what happens in practice.

Many law firms seek to protect their members by incorporation, whether as LLPs or limited companies, but as we shall see, even this does not guarantee protection from personal liability.

Liability caps in firms' terms of business can provide considerable comfort against the risk of a catastrophic claim, but is that comfort misplaced in practice, and how might a claimant seek to exploit ways round them? We look at some of the areas of vulnerability to challenge.

The issues addressed here may also be relevant to law firm mergers and acquisitions, when considering what liabilities and risks, if any, are assumed by acquiring firms through indemnities, and those that are left behind with the sellers. This is not a complete list of exclusions – there are others, and it is always critical to read the policy.

Professional indemnity insurance and the exclusions

Liability outside the course of practice and the trading debt exclusion

The insurance provides cover against civil liability to the extent that it arises from private legal practice in connection with the insured firm's practice. This "civil liability" cover is wider than negligence and provides indemnity, for example, against the firm's and partners' vicarious liability for fraud of other partners or staff (but not of course one's own fraud or dishonesty). MTC policies also provide cover against an obligation on an insured firm and/or any insured to remedy a breach of the SRA Accounts Rules,[3] which is a valuable benefit.

But even civil liability cover is not unlimited. First, liability must arise in the course of practice; that refers to the delivery of services to clients, rather than the liabilities of the firm's own business. Policies also contain exclusions against debts, trading liabilities, and funding arrangements (generally referred to as the trading debt exclusion).

This is required in order to exclude the firm's wages bill and office rent from cover. However, the form of the exclusion permitted by the MTC extends to *"legal liability assumed or accepted by an insured or an insured firm under any contract or agreement for the supply to, or use by, the insured or insured firm of goods or services in the course of the insured firm's practice"* and any *"guarantee indemnity or undertaking by any particular insured in connection with the provision of finance, property, assistance, or other benefit or advantage directly or indirectly to that insured"*.[4] (We look at the exclusion for liability under any contract further below.)

A combination of the requirement for liability to arise in the course of practice and the trading debt exclusion also means that claims by a practice funder or disbursement funder are not covered. Two claims by law firm creditors against insurers for disbursement or practice funding have failed – a claim for nearly £600,000 in *Impact Funding Solutions Ltd v. AIG Europe Insurance Ltd*[5] in the Supreme Court and a claim for nearly £1.7m in *Doorway Capital Ltd v. American International Group UK Ltd.*[6]

The trading debt exclusion also means that if a client seeks repayment of costs they have paid where the service was of no use to them due to negligence or fraud, insurers may contend that that is not covered. Examples of this happening in practice include reimbursement of £1m fees to trust and estate clients following solicitor partner fraud, and repayment of approximately £500,000 costs of a personal injury case where the solicitor made significant mistakes in the retainer documents. But it is critical to look at the specific facts and policy wording.

Directors and officers

Directors' or officers' liability will also be excluded, save to the extent it arises from a breach of duty in the performance of (or failure to perform) legal work.[7] Those taking outside appointments as directors of clients, or sports clubs for example, should therefore ensure that the body concerned has appropriate directors and officers (D&O) insurance.

Those taking such appointments should also be clear that when acting in an executive capacity in such bodies, they are not providing legal advice – colleagues may assume that because they are lawyers, they are advising in their capacity as a member of the law firm. It is generally sensible to ensure that, if legal advice is required, it is provided by a colleague who is not a director in order to demark the boundaries between the appointee holding the executive position and the person providing legal advice.

Cyber, war, and terrorism

The cyber and war and terrorism exclusions are considered together for convenience and for reasons that will become apparent.

Cyber is a significant concern, with recent much publicized attacks on the Simplify conveyancing group[8] and two sets of barristers' chambers.[9] The widely reported NotPetya attack on DLA Piper, attributed by authorities to the Russian military, prevented 3,600 lawyers and their support staff from accessing their emails for six days.[10] There have been attacks on IT providers including Microsoft,[11] SolarWinds,[12] and Kaseya[13] in recent years. Attacks on providers of commonly used accounts, document management, or other IT systems, could affect large numbers of law firms at the same time.

A National Cyber Security Centre news item on 28 January 2022 urged organisations to bolster their cyber security resilience in response to the malicious cyber incidents in and around Ukraine.[14]

Cyber-attacks present the risk of data breaches, loss of data through ransomware attacks, and interruption to the provision of services while systems are restored (if they can be), which may in turn result in claims arising from missed time limits or other loss of opportunity.

The Cyber Claims Study 2021 published by cyber security provider NetDiligence[15] reported that professional service firms were the most targeted industry in 2021 – they hold sensitive data, perceived wealth, and, from the perspective of criminal hackers, the advantages of a one-to-many vector – the client base.

The extent to which a law firm's professional indemnity policies might also offer some protection against cyber claims – so-called silent cyber cover – has been under review across the whole insurance market and professional bodies have had to amend their rules for compulsory cover because the Prudential Regulation Authority[16] and Lloyd's of London[17] required that policies more clearly set out what is and is not covered in the event of a firm being subject to a cyber-attack or event.

The exclusion in the MTC received statutory approval from the Legal Services Board in November 2021.[18] The gist of the provision is that firms are covered for client claims but not for the firm's own losses; the distinction becomes more complicated when you ask whether there is cover for the cost of recovering client data to prevent a claim. The effect of the changes in practice will emerge when they are tested in anger but they may be rendered otiose by the next exclusion. Note too, that the exclusions in excess layer policies (and indeed firms' other insurance policies) may be far more onerous.

The war and terrorism exclusion may be significant going forwards as events in and around Ukraine unfold. It appears in nearly all insurance policies. Coverage disputes may arise in relation to war exclusions in both professional liability and cyber policies. Insurers have relied on war exclusions in response to cyber-attacks in some cases around the world, though the author is not presently aware of any decided cases in which they have succeeded.

Aggregation

Not strictly an exclusion, but it is critical to note that policies invariably contain an "aggregation clause" under which, in broad terms, multiple claims arising from similar causes or in the same matter or transaction may be subject to a single policy limit. The impact of this can be illustrated by reference to the Supreme Court decision in *AIG Europe Ltd v. Woodman*[19] where 214 claimants sued solicitors over losses in excess of £10m arising from failed investments in two schemes – one in Morocco and one in Turkey. It was held that the claims were subject to one £3m limit of cover for each scheme, leaving a substantial shortfall. Firms doing volume work, in particular, should be alert to this risk.

Retirement and professional indemnity insurance

Run-off cover and successor practice provisions

We turn now to the vexed question of protection in retirement or on leaving a firm. If the firm or a successor continues to provide cover, that may provide protection, but circumstances may change with restructuring or collapse of the firm, or change of regulator, for example where SRA-regulated solicitors are taken over by accountants with different insurance requirements, or solicitors move to regulation as licensed conveyancers. Or the firm might hit a problem continuing to buy its previous level of cover, perhaps due to adverse claims experience after the individual leaves.

If the firm ceases to exist, it may be able to buy run-off cover, which the SRA (and many other regulators) require. The MTC and some other compulsory schemes have some complex stings in the tail with successor practice provisions that need careful attention to detail before taking steps that may impact on cover, whether through merger or otherwise. The MTC require firms to take out six years' run-off cover,[20] which is provided automatically, but triggers an obligation to pay a substantial premium and there may be significant costs in relation to run-off cover for excess layer insurance, and beyond the six-year period on an ongoing basis.

In order to determine how long cover is needed for, it is necessary to consider the legal time limits for claims, and then look at what happens in practice. Note that cover is on a "claims made" basis, which means that claims are covered if either they are made during the policy period or, if circumstances giving rise to them are notified to insurers during the period of insurance, any time subsequently.

Time limits for claims

This is not the place for a comprehensive review of the law of limitation periods, for which reference should be made to the standard textbooks. Suffice to say that most applicable time limits are prescribed by the Limitation Act 1980.[21] The time limit in contract is six years from the breach, and in tort it is six years from when the cause of action accrued, which may be a later date than in contract as it requires proof of loss. Section 14A[22] provides a special time limit for negligence actions where facts relevant to the cause of action are not known at the date of accrual, which is three years from discovery of the facts on which the claim is based, with a 15-year longstop.

There are, however, situations where time does not run, including fraud, deliberate concealment, trusts where the beneficial interest has not vested, and persons under a disability, including infants and persons lacking mental capacity (as defined).

There is also the risk of a claim for contribution by another party jointly liable for the same damage under the Civil Liability (Contribution) Act 1978;[23] the time limit for such a claim, in outline, is two years from the date when the person claiming contribution is held liable or makes or agrees to make payment to a claimant; time can therefore run almost indefinitely.

Time limits in practice

While the time limits are the same for all professions, lawyers may be more exposed for longer periods in practice, for example, by acting for children on personal injury claims and in trust cases, where time may not even start running for many years, and in conveyancing work, where a title defect may not be discovered until sale many years later. They also take appointments as executors and trustees, which may carry liability for years.

The risk is illustrated by the recent case of *McClean & Others v. Thornhill*[24] where a claim was made by third parties against a barrister in relation to tax scheme advice in 2003, with the claim form issued only in 2018. The claim was successfully defended, but the costs of defending such claims may be substantial.

The report by actuaries Willis Towers Watson prepared for the SRA consultation, *Post six year run-off cover and the Solicitors Indemnity Fund*[25] (SIF), sets out SIF's claims experience – SIF provides cover for solicitors after the expiry of the compulsory six-year MTC run-off cover. (However, SIF is due to close to further claims on 30 September 2023; the SRA is planning to set up a replacement scheme, but no details are available at the time of writing.) The report contains tables showing statistics for different practice areas, and notes that *"the maximum reporting delay is 19 years,"*[26] but even this does not represent a final limit in practice.

Defensive practice

There are two key mechanisms to consider – incorporation, either as an LLP or limited company, and limiting liability contractually.

Incorporation

Nearly all property professionals and most accountants incorporate in the author's experience. Solicitors have been permitted to incorporate since 1992 (as limited companies, and LLPs since 2001), yet at the time of writing only 53 percent of SRA-regulated law firms are incorporated.[27]

There have been examples of claims against individual employees.[28] To provide protection, firms need to incorporate provision in their terms excluding personal liability of members and staff. This must be drawn to the attention of, and agreed by, clients. However, there are still limitations on this as a defense mechanism, because of personal appointments (for example, trustee or executor), and in view of the time lapses before claims are made, as mentioned earlier, pre-incorporation liabilities.

Limiting liability contractually

This is a large topic, space permitting only a brief overview. In briefest outline, liability caps must be fair and reasonable, either under the Unfair Contract Terms Act 1997[29] (in relation to business clients) or the Consumer Rights Act 2015[30] (for consumers). Note that the limit of insurance available includes claimants' costs, so liability should not blindly be limited to the limit of indemnity. Solicitors are not permitted to limit liability below the compulsory minimum insurance,[31] even though aggregation may mean there is a far smaller pot available to meet multiple similar or related claims, as explained above.

It is critical that a liability cap is agreed by the client in question. This can be a problem, for example, if there are terms with a corporate client but advice is provided to an individual manager. It is also important to avoid communicating with clients in terms that may demonstrate acceptance of personal liability, for example an email saying "I advise…".

Judges may be unwilling to accept that liability caps are reasonable unless insurance cannot be obtained.[32]

Trust corporations

While only an option for larger firms, setting up the firm's own trust corporation may provide a vehicle for personal appointments of trustees and executors, avoiding personal exposure.

Insurance options

Protection may be available within limits and at a cost. For example:

- Cyber policies may provide important emergency cover and assistance in the event of data breaches or ransomware attacks, but cover is becoming significantly more expensive and policies should be checked carefully for the precise wording of war and terrorism exclusions.
- Management liability or directors and officers policies may provide protection against liability arising from personal appointments.
- Asset protection policies may provide cover where a claim in excess of the firm's professional indemnity limit is pursued against the individual who provided advice.
- Additional run-off insurance may be available after the compulsory six-year MTC period has expired, and for sums in excess of the primary layer, but it may be expensive, hard to obtain, and availability will be dependent on claims experience.

Conclusion

Lawyers may be less protected by the firm's insurance than they realize. However, in the author's experience, uninsured personal liability is fortunately very rare in practice.

References

1 See Annex 1, Solicitors Regulation Authority, Indemnity Insurance Rules, 25 November 2019, www.sra.org.uk/solicitors/standards-regulations/indemnity-insurance-rules/.

2 *Ibid*, Rule 2.1.

3 Through the definition of "claim" in the SRA Glossary: www.sra.org.uk/solicitors/standards-regulations/glossary/.

4 See *Ibid* 1, Rule 6.6.

5 [2016] UKSC 57.

6 [2022] EWHC 182 (Comm).

7 See *Ibid* 1, Rule 6.9.

8 www.legalfutures.co.uk/latest-news/clients-desperation-grows-as-impact-of-simplify-cyber-attack-stretches-on

9 See *4 New Square v. Persons Unknown* (28 June 2021) and www.lawgazette.co.uk/news/wake-up-call-bar-council-warns-chambers-of-cyberattacks/5109310.article.

10 www.ncsc.gov.uk/pdfs/news/russian-military-almost-certainly-responsible-destructive-2017-cyber-attack.pdf; Barney Thompson, "DLA Piper still struggling with Petya cyber-attack", *Financial Times*, 6 July 2017, www.ft.com/content/1b5f863a-624c-11e7-91a7-502f7ee26895.

11 Gordon Corera, "China accused of cyber-attack on Microsoft Exchange servers", BBC News, 19 July 2021, www.bbc.co.uk/news/world-asia-china-57889981.

12 Kari Paul, "What you need to know about the biggest hack of the US government in years", *The Guardian*, 15 December 2020, www.theguardian.com/technology/2020/dec/15/orion-hack-solar-winds-explained-us-treasury-commerce-department.

13 Joseph Menn, "Kaseya ransomware attack sets off race to hack service providers – researchers", Reuters, 3 August 2021, www.reuters.com/technology/kaseya-ransomware-attack-sets-off-race-hack-service-providers-researchers-2021-08-03/.

14 www.ncsc.gov.uk/news/uk-organisations-encouraged-to-take-action-around-ukraine-situation

15 www.netdiligence.com/cyber-claims-studies/

16 Prudential Regulation Authority policy statement PS15/17, www.bankofengland.co.uk/prudential-regulation/publication/2016/cyber-insurance-underwriting-risk.

17 Lloyds Market Bulletin Y5258, published 4 July 2019 (Lloyds of London, 2019), www.assets.lloyds.com/assets/y5258-providing-clarity-for-lloyd-s-customers-on-coverage-for-cyber-exposures/1/Y5258%20-%20Providing%20clarity%20for%20Lloyd%E2%80%99s%20customers%20on%20coverage%20for%20cyber%20exposures.pdf.

18 See *Ibid* 1, Rule 6.12; www.legalservicesboard.org.uk/wp-content/uploads/2021/11/Decision-Notice-SRA-Cyber-security-FINAL.pdf.

19 [2017] UKSC 18.

20 See *Ibid* 1, Rule 5.3.

21 www.legislation.gov.uk/ukpga/1980/58/contents

22 www.legislation.gov.uk/ukpga/1980/58/section/14A

23 www.legislation.gov.uk/ukpga/1978/47/contents

24 [2022] EWHC 457 (Ch).

25 Solicitors Regulation Authority, *Post six-year run-off cover and the Solicitors Indemnity Fund*, 12 April 2022, www.sra.org.uk/sra/consultations/consultation-listing/solicitors-indemnity-fund/?s=c.

26 John Charles, Solicitors Regulation Authority PSYROC – *Analysis of options*, Willis Towers Watson, 19 November 2021, p73.

27 SRA statistics – Breakdown of solicitor firms: www.sra.org.uk/sra/research-report/regulated-community-statistics/data/solicitor_firms/.

28 See *Merrett v. Babb* (2001) EWCA Civ 214, involving an employed surveyor whose former employer was insolvent.

29 www.legislation.gov.uk/ukpga/1977/50/contents

30 www.legislation.gov.uk/ukpga/2015/15/contents/enacted

31 Solicitors Regulation Authority, Indemnity Insurance Rules, 25 November 2019: www.sra.org.uk/solicitors/standards-regulations/indemnity-insurance-rules/, Rule 3.2.

32 See for example the judgment of Turner J in *Lyons v. Fox Williams* LLP (2016) EWHC 2427 (QB) 2427 at [262], though the defendants won on liability and the decision was upheld on appeal.

Chapter 9:
SRA compliance

By Rebecca Atkinson, director of risk and compliance, Howard Kennedy

What is the SRA and when do you need to be authorized by it?

The Solicitors Regulation Authority (SRA) is responsible for the regulation of the professional conduct of solicitors, other authorized individuals, and law firms in England and Wales. Formed in 2007 by the Legal Services Act 2007, it is funded by the profession itself through the collection of an annual fee.

The purpose of the SRA is to protect the public by ensuring high standards are met by those they regulate and taking action when that standard is not being met. The SRA sets various rules and regulations including those enshrined within the Solicitors Standards and Regulations (StaRs), including the SRA Principles and Codes.[1]

A business needs to be authorized (meaning approved) by the SRA if it provides any of the following:

- *"Reserved legal activities for the public, unless your business is exempt from requiring authorization;*
- *Immigration services, unless your business is regulated by the Office of the Immigration Services Commissioner (OISC);*
- *Claims management services, unless your business is regulated by the Financial Conduct Authority (FCA);*
- *Regulated financial services activities, unless your business is regulated by the FCA."*[2]

Depending on the people involved and the work being done, firms may be able to choose whether to apply for authorization with the SRA or another approved regulator for legal services. An approved regulator is one permitted under the Legal Services Act 2007 (LSA) to regulate some or all reserved legal activities. A list of the approved regulators, and what they are permitted to regulate, can be found on the Legal Services Board's website.[3]

The vast majority of solicitors and firms will fall under the first point above in that they will be conducting reserved legal activities.

Reserved legal activities are set down in detail in section 12 and Schedule 2 to the LSA and can only be conducted by those authorized to do so.

These activities are:

- *"Rights of audience: the right to appear before and address a court, including the right to call and examine witnesses.*
- *Conduct of litigation:*
    - *The issuing of proceedings before any court in England and Wales;*
    - *The commencement, prosecution and defence of such proceedings; and*
    - *The performance of any ancillary functions in relation to such proceedings.*
- *Reserved instrument activities:*
    - *Preparing any instrument of transfer or charge for the purposes of the Land Registration Act 2002;*
    - *Making an application or lodging a document for registration under that Act; and*
    - *Preparing any other instrument relating to real or personal estate for the purposes of the law of England and Wales or instrument relating to court proceedings in England and Wales.*
- *Probate activities: preparing any probate papers for the purposes of the law of England and Wales or in relation to any proceedings in England and Wales. Probate papers means papers on which to found or oppose a grant of probate, or a grant of letters of administration.*
- *Administration of oaths: the exercise of the powers conferred on a commissioner for oaths by:*
    - *The Commissioners for Oaths Act 1889;*
    - *The Commissioners for Oaths Act 1891; and*
    - *Section 24 of the Stamp Duties Management Act 1891."*[4]

Note, notarial activities are regulated by the Master of the Faculties and not the SRA.

If a firm provides non-reserved legal activities, it does not need to be authorized. However, if the firm is an independent legal professional, trust, or company service provider and/or a tax adviser, as defined by the Money Laundering, Terrorist Financing and Transfer of Funds (Information on the Payer) Regulations 2017 (AML Regulations), firms are required to nominate a money laundering reporting officer, a money laundering compliance officer, and seek the SRA's approval for all beneficial owners, managers, and officers of the firm as defined by the AML Regulations.

Approvals under the AML Regulations are a statutory requirement and separate from approvals made under the SRA's own regulations.

To be authorized, firms need to be a sole practitioner practice, a legal services body such as a partnership, company, or limited liability partnership where all of the interest holders are legally qualified, or be a licensable body which is a body that has interest holders who are not qualified.

Once authorized, firms must also:

- *"Provide evidence that they can obtain the required level of qualifying professional indemnity insurance with a participating insurer;*
- *Nominate a compliance officer for legal practice (COLP) and a compliance officer for finance and administration (COFA) (together described as compliance officers);*
- *Identify all managers and owners of the body;*
- *Have at least one manager or employee, or procure the services of an individual, who has practised as a lawyer for at least three years;*
- *Seek all necessary role holder approvals under the SRA Authorization of Firms Rules; and*
- *Seek any approvals necessary under The Money Laundering, Terrorist Financing and Transfer of Funds (Information on the Payer) Regulations 2017 (MLR 2017).*[5]
- *Rule 9.3 of the SRA Authorization of Firms Rules allows the SRA to decide that it will not need to approve managers who are not involved in the following:*
- *The day to day or strategic management of the authorized body;*
- *Compliance by the authorized body with the SRA's regulatory arrangements; or*
- *The carrying on of reserved legal activities, or the provision of legal services in England and Wales."*[6]

The SRA will also not need to approve those managers and owners who are deemed to be approved to hold those roles under Rules 13.2 and 13.3 of the SRA Authorization of Firms Rules. Those rules set out specific criteria for when a person can be deemed fit and proper to hold their role. This includes certain individuals and firms authorized and regulated by the SRA, and certain previously approved managers and owners.

When considering applications for approval, the SRA will apply the SRA Assessment of Character and Suitability Rules.[7]

For further guidance, see the SRA's Guidance on firm authorization.[8]

How to get authorized

New firms that meet the criteria set out above need to apply for authorization with the SRA via its online portal, mySRA.

The SRA's authorization webpage sets out that applicants will need the following information:

"About the firm:

- *Professional indemnity insurance – quote or certificate;*
- *Firm structure details; and*
- *For incorporated bodies, the incorporation details.*

"About individuals:

- *Personal details, work history, professional regulation, and suitability to fulfil role;*
- *Certificates of Good Standing if regulated by another regulator; and*
- *Individuals who are not SRA-authorized need to register on mySRA before the firm completes the application."*[9]

An initial fee of £200 is taken and then once the approval has taken place the firm will need to pay the required regulatory fee. The SRA aims to make its decision within 90 days but it can take up to 180 days.

If the firm is already authorized but there are new role holders, an application for their approval needs to be made. Again, this is made through mySRA.

The annual reauthorization process

Each year a firm needs to reauthorize with the SRA and renew all their solicitors' practising certificates through a process known as bulk renewal. The application is completed online via mySRA – normally opens for completion on 1 October each year and has to be completed by 31 October. This date can vary slightly if the SRA has technical issues with mySRA (which has occurred in the past). The SRA will notify firms of the window within which they need to complete the process.

Below are the categories of information that the firm needs to have available when completing the reauthorization application (please note this list may change and so is not a replacement for reading the SRA website, which should be firm's first port of call):

- Largest, smallest and average client account balance for last accounting period;
- The firm's turnover and whether more than 20 percent comes from any single client, group of clients, or referral source;
- Areas of work that make your turnover, i.e. conveyancing, family, personal injury;
- Professional indemnity insurance details;
- Information about associations (such as introduction arrangements);
- Details about any arrangements, relationships or connections that might influence the running of the firm;
- Details about separate businesses clients are signposted to and the like;
- How many legally qualified and non-legally qualified fee earners the firm has;
- How many claims have been made in the last indemnity period and how many claims have been paid out in the last indemnity period, regardless of when the claim was made;
- Details about complaints that have gone through the firm's internal complaints process, what those complaints were about (i.e. delay, failure to advise, costs information) and which complaints went to Legal Ombudsman; and
- Details of solicitors for which a practising certificate (PC) will be granted (see below).

In terms of PC renewal, the firm will need to confirm on behalf of all solicitors practicing at the firm that the solicitor has met the continuing competency requirements.

The continuing competence regime replaced the continuing professional development (CPD) 16-hour-a-year requirement in November 2016. This regime requires solicitors to reflect on the quality of their practice and identify any learning and development needs (firms should consider whether it is a good idea to tie this in with appraisal time in the firm). With no minimum hour requirement this was a sea change for practitioners. The SRA is keen to understand whether the regime is working and may conduct a thematic review in the future, which could entail firm visits.

By ticking the continuing competence box (or allowing the box to remain ticked), the Authorized Signatory for the firm (the person who ultimately signs the application for reauthorization and PC renewal and is often the COLP or managing partner) is declaring on behalf of the solicitor "yes" to the following question: "Have you reflected on your practice and addressed any identified learning and development needs?". The Authorized Signatory in the firm therefore needs to be sure that the solicitors have completed their continuing competency reflection and plan.

Within the PC part of the application is the ability to apply for a reduced fee. Those who have had maternity/adoption leave or any equivalent leave (shared paternity leave would qualify) during a qualifying period will have the PC fee reduced.

All solicitors who need their PC renewed need to be "opted in" to the firm's bulk renewal via mySRA. A good time to make sure this opt in occurs is upon the solicitor joining the firm.

The SRA Standards and Regulations

This section briefly outlines the SRA Standards and Regulations (StaRs). The StaRs are made up of over 20 separate sets of rules and requirements. We will go through some of these at a high level here focusing on the Principles, Codes, accounts rules, and other rules such as those around price transparency.

SRA Principles

The current version of the SRA Principles came into effect on 25 November 2019 and is shorter than the prior version with some Principles having been removed.

The SRA Principles comprise the "*fundamental tenets of ethical behavior*"[10] that the SRA expects all those that it regulates to uphold. This includes all solicitors, partners in firms, employees, and firms themselves.

If the SRA Principles come into conflict with each other, then those Principles "*which safeguard the wider public interest (such as the rule of law and public confidence in a trustworthy solicitors' profession) take precedence over an individual client's interests".*[11]

The SRA Principles are that law firms and those within law firms act:

1. *"In a way that upholds the constitutional principle of the rule of law, and the proper administration of justice.*
2. *In a way that upholds public trust and confidence in the solicitors' profession and in legal services provided by authorized persons.*
3. *With independence.*
4. *With honesty.*
5. *With integrity.*
6. *In a way that encourages equality, diversity, and inclusion.*
7. *In the best interests of each client."*[12]

Principle 3 – to act with independence – has changed from its prior version (from 2011) which was worded "*not allow your independence to be compromised*".[13] The Principle therefore seems to be worded in a more positive way.

Principle 4 – to act with honesty – was a new addition in 2019 and this may be so that the SRA is able to use this Principle when disciplining firms and individuals as opposed to relying on the Principle of acting with integrity.

Integrity means the quality of being honest and having strong moral principles.

Principles that were removed from the 2011 iteration include:

- *"Provide a proper standard of service to your clients;*
- *Comply with your legal and regulatory obligations and deal with your regulators and ombudsmen in an open, timely and cooperative manner;*
- *Run your business or carry out your role in the business effectively and in accordance with proper governance and sound financial and risk management principles;*
- *Protect client money and assets."*[14]

They are not there anymore because they already exist in other parts of the SRA Codes of Conduct (see below). The Codes generally have been de-duplicated and aspects that are present in law such as money laundering regulation, data protection, and liens have been taken out of the Codes.

Just because these items are not in the SRA Principles or Codes does not therefore mean they can be forgotten. These aspects still exist but in the overall regulatory framework.

SRA Codes

The current Codes of Conduct came into force on 25 November 2019 and are much more streamlined than previous iterations. They have also been split into two Codes – one for Firms and one for Solicitors (full title Code of Conduct for Solicitors, Registered European Lawyers and Registered Foreign Lawyers). Non-solicitor employees are captured under the Code for Firms.

The Codes of Conduct describe the standards of professionalism that the SRA (and the public) expects of individuals (solicitors, registered European lawyers, and registered foreign lawyers) and firms authorized by the SRA to provide legal services.

The Codes apply to conduct and behavior relating to practice, and, as set out in the introduction to the Code for Solicitors, "*comprise a framework for ethical and competent practice which applies irrespective of a person's role or the environment or organization in which they work (subject to the Overseas Rules which apply to your practice overseas)*".[15] As set out in the introduction to the Code of Conduct for Firms, the aim of the Code is to "*create and maintain the right culture and environment for the delivery of competent and ethical legal services to clients. These apply in the context of your practice: the way you run your business and all your professional activities (subject, if you are a licensed body, to any terms of your licence).*"[16]

Solicitors must exercise their judgement in applying the standards and deciding on a course of action, bearing in mind their role and responsibilities, areas of practice, and the nature of their clients.

The SRA introduction to the Code for Solicitors goes on to confirm that solicitors are personally accountable for compliance with the Code and other regulatory requirements that apply to them and they must always be prepared to justify their decisions and actions. It is always good therefore to document actions and decisions.

Breaching the Codes can result in enforcement action by the SRA against individual solicitors, employees of the firm, or role holders (such as COLP or COFA) or against the firm itself: "*A failure or breach may be serious either in isolation or because it comprises a persistent or concerning pattern of behavior.*"[17]

Further, the Codes are underpinned by the SRA's Enforcement Strategy. That strategy explains the SRA's view about the issues it considers to be serious, and its approach to taking regulatory action in the public interest.

Each Code is split into sections as follows.

Code of Conduct for Solicitors:

1. *"Maintaining trust and acting fairly;*
2. *Dispute resolution and proceedings before courts, tribunals, and inquires;*
3. *Service and competence;*
4. *Client money and assets;*
5. *Referrals, introductions, and separate businesses; Other business requirements;*
6. *Conflicts of interest; Confidentiality and disclosure;*
7. *Cooperation and accountability;*
8. *Client identification; Complaints handling; Client information and publicity."*[18]

Code of Conduct for Firms:

1. *"Maintaining trust and acting fairly;*
2. *Compliance and business systems;*
3. *Cooperation and accountability;*
4. *Service and competence;*
5. *Client money and assets;*
6. *Conflicts of interest; Confidentiality and disclosure;*
7. *Applicable standards in the SRA Code of Conduct for Solicitors, RELs and RFLs;*
8. *Managers in SRA authorized firms;*
9. *Compliance officers."*[19]

As can be seen, there are many sections that are duplicated across the two Codes. However, they do not always follow the same numbering.

Each section sets out the rule to be followed. They are not explored in this chapter and readers should consider each Code found on the SRA website.

SRA Accounts Rules

In 2019, the SRA Accounts Rules were streamlined and now comprise of just 13 rules. The rules set out the SRA's requirements for when firms receive or deal with client monies including trust money or money held on behalf of third parties. The rules also apply to those within the firm such as solicitors, partners, and employees.

Firms are required to have systems and controls in place to ensure compliance with the Accounts Rules and the extent of those systems must be appropriate to the nature and volumes of client transactions dealt with and the amount of client money held or received.

The rule headings are as follows:

1. *"Application section (who the rules apply to);*
2. *Client money;*
3. *Client account;*
4. *Client money must be kept separate;*
5. *Withdrawals from client account;*
6. *Duty to correct breaches upon discovery;*
7. *Payment of interest;*
8. *Client accounting systems and controls;*
9. *Operation of joint accounts;*
10. *Operation of a client's own account;*
11. *Third party managed accounts;*
12. *Obtaining and delivery of accountants' reports;*
13. *Storage and retention of accounting records."*[20]

Worthy of exploration is Rule 3.3, known as the non-banking rule. This rule in its prior iteration as Rule 14.5 of the 2011 SRA Accounts Rules has been subject to much SRA disciplinary action.[21]

The rule itself sets out the following:

> *"You must not use a client account to provide banking facilities to clients or third parties. Payments into, and transfers or withdrawals from a client account must be in respect of the delivery by you of regulated services."*[22]

Regulated services is defined as the legal and other professional services that the firm/solicitor provides that are regulated by the SRA and includes, where appropriate, acting as a trustee or as the holder of a specified office or appointment.[23]

Effectively the rule means that firms/solicitors cannot make or receive payments on behalf of clients or any other party that do not relate to regulated services.

There are some clear and obvious examples of when this rule might be breached. For example, if a firm were acting on the sale of a residential property, the following payments will generally be fine to make:

- Payment to redeem the mortgage;
- Payment to the estate agent; and
- Payment for the surveyor.

However, in that same transaction it would not be permissible to make the following payments:

- For the client's children's school fees;
- Payment to a garage for the purchase of a car; and
- The client's gambling debt.

The reasons why the above payments are not acceptable to make are because they are not linked to regulated services, i.e. the residential property sale.

Firms may be asked by foreign individuals with a UK residence to pay their household bills for them, i.e. gas, electricity, water, council tax, cleaners. These payments must not be made from a firm's client account unless they relate to regulated services, which they are not likely to.

There are instances, however, where these types of payments are permissible because they relate to underlying work such as the administration of estates, trusts, or where the solicitor is acting as power of attorney.

Further, when a solicitor is acting as Power of Attorney, Trustee, or acting on a Trustee's instruction, any payments will generally not fall foul of the rules as long as it can be shown the payment relates to the underlying legal work or the payment forms part of normal regulated activities.

Not all scenarios are clear and when in doubt firms/solicitors should refer to the SRA Warning Notice.[24]

Other regulatory requirements

As mentioned above, there are over 20 sets of rules contained within the StaRs. Below is a list of some of the other key rules:

- SRA Authorization of Firms Rules;
- SRA Authorization of Individuals Regulations;
- SRA Financial Services (Scope) Rules and SRA Financial Services (Conduct of Business) Rules;
- SRA Overseas and Cross-border Practice Rules – these rules are split

into two parts. Part A are termed overseas rules and Part B cross-border practice rules;

- SRA Transparency Rules;
- SRA Indemnity Insurance Rules;
- Prescribed circumstances in which you can withdraw client money from client account to pay to charity of your choice; and
- Gathering, reporting, and publishing equality and diversity data – approximately every two years the SRA requires firms to gather, report, and publish equality and diversity (E&D) data. The SRA provides the specific questions that firms need to report on and in turn ask their people to answer. Once gathered, the data is submitted through the SRA's online portal, mySRA.

As well as gathering and submitting the data, firms must publish the data. Publishing here means making the data available to staff and anyone external. This can mean that firms choose to publish the data on their website. To that end, the SRA guidance[25] should be consulted.

Data published on a firm's website needs to be easy to find and easy to read with tables, diagrams, or graphics including a summary of what they show.

Firms should not publish data if to do so would identify individuals. This could happen for very small firms and therefore firms may find that they are unable to publish all of the data or the data at all. If that is the case, firms should document why they made this decision.

It is not compulsory for those in the firm to take part in any data gathering exercise and so people in the firm should not be told they must share their E&D data.

The SRA will communicate with firms when it wants the firm to gather, report, and publish E&D data.

SRA Enforcement Strategy

The SRA Principles and Codes provide solicitors and firms the standard required to be met and of which all solicitors and firms should be fully aware. Where there is any deviation from the standards these must be documented by solicitors and firms and both should be ready to justify their decision-making.

The SRA has a number of regulatory tools it may utilize to support compliance with its standards. These include:

- *"Conducting thematic reviews of areas of risk;*
- *Publishing a risk outlook highlighting priority risks;*[26]
- *Providing advice and support through the SRA Professional Ethics helpline and a range of toolkits and guidance; and*
- *SRA Innovate, a service which helps legal service providers to develop their business in new ways."*[27]

Every firm should consider the SRA's Enforcement Strategy, which sets out the SRA's approach to enforcement of breaches of the standards set, factors which the SRA considers make a scenario serious enough to warrant enforcement and who enforcement can be taken against.

The Strategy can be found on the SRA website and is subject to periodic update/change.

The COLP and COFA role and reporting requirements

Each firm is required to have a Compliance Officer for Legal Practice (COLP) and a Compliance Officer for Finance and Administration (COFA).

The obligations of the COLP are set out at paragraph 9.1 of the Code of Conduct for Firms. This sets out that as the COLP you must take all reasonable steps to:

a) *"Ensure compliance with the terms and conditions of your firm's authorization;*
b) *Ensure compliance by the firm and its managers, employees or interest holders with the SRA's regulatory arrangements which apply to them;*
c) *Ensure that the firm's managers and interest holders and those they employ or contract with do not cause or substantially contribute to a breach of the SRA's regulatory arrangements;*
d) *Ensure that a prompt report is made to the SRA of any facts or matters that you reasonably believe are capable of amounting to a serious breach of the terms and conditions of the firm's authorization, or the SRA's regulatory arrangements which apply to the firm, managers or employees; and*
e) *Notwithstanding sub-paragraph (d), you ensure that the SRA is informed promptly of any facts or matters that the COLP reasonably believes should be brought to its attention in order that it may investigate whether a serious breach of its regulatory arrangements has occurred or otherwise exercise its regulatory powers."*[28]

The obligations of the COFA are set out at paragraph 9.2 of the Code of Conduct for Firms. This sets out that the COFA must take all reasonable steps to:

a) *"Ensure that your firm and its managers and employees comply with any obligations imposed upon them under the SRA Accounts Rules;*
b) *Ensure that a prompt report is made to the SRA of any facts or matters that you reasonably believe are capable of amounting to a serious breach of the SRA Accounts Rules which apply to them;*
c) *Notwithstanding sub-paragraph (b), you ensure that the SRA is informed promptly of any facts or matters that you reasonably believe should be brought to its attention in order that it may investigate whether a serious breach of its regulatory arrangements has occurred or otherwise exercise its regulatory powers."*[29]

As can be seen from the above, the COFA role is solely concerned with the SRA Accounts Rules whereas the COLP role is concerned with all other regulatory arrangements. These can be the SRA Principles and Codes, any other rules or regulations within the StaRs, or other regulations or laws dealing with data protection, money laundering, tax evasion, and so on.

The reporting requirements are wider than their prior iteration, which set out that a report should be made when serious misconduct had been found (SRA Code of Conduct 2011, Outcome 10.4). This meant that many COLPs and COFAs would investigate potential breaches first and then only report if they found serious misconduct had taken place. The SRA did not consider this approach satisfactory and as such changed the rule so that if there appeared to be facts or matters which the COLP or COFA reasonably believe is capable of amounting to a serious breach, then a report should be made. This therefore suggests that a report prior to an internal investigation is appropriate.

The current rule also contains a "catch all" whereby, notwithstanding the decision whether to report or not, the COLP or COFA should bring to the SRA's attention anything that they reasonably believe the SRA should know about so that the SRA can decide whether to investigate.

When faced with a decision of whether to report or not, COLPs and COFAs should consider the SRA Enforcement Strategy, which sets out what factors the SRA considers make a breach serious and must document their decision-making process. COLPs and COFAs may also decide to take external legal advice.

Ethics and how to approach

Ethics sits at the heart of being a solicitor, and solicitors and those who work in law firms must behave in an ethical way at all times.

In the *Britannica* dictionary, ethics is described as:

> *"Ethics, also called moral philosophy, the discipline concerned with what is morally good and bad and morally right and wrong. The term is also applied to any system or theory of moral values or principles."*[30]

In the Cambridge dictionary it is defined as:

> *"A system of accepted beliefs that control behavior, especially such a system based on morals."*[31]

As set out above, the SRA Principles comprise the fundamental tenets of ethical behavior that the SRA expects all those that it regulates to uphold, and if the Principles come into conflict with each other, those that safeguard wider public interest take precedence over an individual client's interests.

In terms of navigating ethical conundrums, the following steps may help:

- Understand the dilemma – understand the facts and problem;
- Consider what Principles or Code rules apply;
- If any of the Principles conflict, consider which one takes precedence;
- Consider what is in the best interests of the client;
- Consider any commercial considerations; and
- Based on the above considerations, decide what steps to take.

SRA warning notices and guidance

The SRA publishes what it terms as warning notices. These are notices that set out the SRA's stance on a particular activity and against which a solicitor or firm will be judged. They do not form part of the StaRs but solicitors and firms are expected to be aware of the warning notices and act as the notices advise.

The warning notices can be located by navigating to the SRA's guidance page[32] and either viewing them within the separate areas for specific subjects or by selecting "All topics" at the bottom and applying a filter for warning notices on the right hand side.

Examples of warning notices are:

- Improper use of client account as a banking facility: www.sra.org.uk/solicitors/guidance/improper-client-account-banking-facility/.
- Use of non-disclosure agreements: www.sra.org.uk/solicitors/guidance/non-disclosure-agreements-ndas/.
- Investment schemes including conveyancing: www.sra.org.uk/solicitors/guidance/investment-schemes-including-conveyancing/.
- Holiday sickness claims: www.sra.org.uk/solicitors/guidance/holiday- sickness-claims/.
- Tax avoidance, your duties: www.sra.org.uk/solicitors/guidance/tax-avoidance-duties/.
- Offensive communications: www.sra.org.uk/solicitors/guidance/offensive-communications/.
- Money laundering and terrorist financing suspicious activity reports: www.sra.org.uk/solicitors/guidance/money-laundering-terrorist-financing-suspicious-activity-reports/.
- Compliance with the money laundering regulations – firm risk assessment: www.sra.org.uk/solicitors/guidance/compliance-money-laundering-regulations-firm-risk-assessment/.
- Money laundering and terrorist financing: www.sra.org.uk/solicitors/guidance/money-laundering-terrorist-financing/.

The SRA also provides numerous guidance pieces.[33] These are not mandatory to follow but can offer insight into how the SRA interprets the StaRs.

Those who wish to undertake certain legal activities need to consider the requirement for SRA authorization. Once authorized, firms and solicitors need to fully understand the regulatory framework and the SRA's expectations as set out in its Enforcement Strategy and warning notices.

References

1 Solicitors Regulation Authority, Standards and Regulations, 25 November 2019, www.sra.org.uk/solicitors/standards-regulations/.

2 Solicitors Regulation Authority, Guidance, 'Firm authorisation', 25 November 2019, www.sra.org.uk/solicitors/guidance/firm-authorisation/.

3 https://legalservicesboard.org.uk/about-us/approved-regulators

4 *Ibid* 2.

5 *Ibid*.
6 Solicitors Regulation Authority, Authorisation of Firms Rules, 25 November 2019, www.sra.org.uk/solicitors/standards-regulations/authorisation-firms-rules/, Rule 9.3.
7 Solicitors Regulation Authority, Assessment of Character and Suitability Rules, 25 November 2019, www.sra.org.uk/solicitors/standards-regulations/assessment-character-suitability-rules/.
8 www.sra.org.uk/solicitors/guidance/firm-authorisation/
9 Solicitors Regulation Authority, 'Apply for authorisation of a new firm', 11 May 2022, www.sra.org.uk/solicitors/firm-based-authorisation/authorisation-recognition/.
10 Solicitors Regulation Authority, Principles, 25 November 2019, www.sra.org.uk/solicitors/standards-regulations/principles/.
11 *Ibid*.
12 *Ibid*.
13 Solicitors Regulation Authority, SRA Handbook, 2011, www.sra.org.uk/solicitors/handbook/handbookprinciples/part2/rule1/, Principle 3.
14 *Ibid*, Principles 5, 7, 8 and 10.
15 Solicitors Regulation Authority, Code of Conduct for Solicitors, RELs and RFLs, 25 November 2019, www.sra.org.uk/solicitors/standards-regulations/code-conduct-solicitors/, Introduction.
16 Solicitors Regulation Authority, Code of Conduct for Firms, 25 November 2019, www.sra.org.uk/solicitors/standards-regulations/code-conduct-firms/, Introduction.
17 *Ibid* 15 and 16.
18 Solicitors Regulation Authority, Code of Conduct for Solicitors, RELs and RFLs, 25 November 2019, www.sra.org.uk/solicitors/standards-regulations/code-conduct-solicitors/.
19 Solicitors Regulation Authority, Code of Conduct for Firms, 25 November 2019, www.sra.org.uk/solicitors/standards-regulations/code-conduct-firms/.
20 Solicitors Regulation Authority, Accounts Rules, 25 November 2019, www.sra.org.uk/solicitors/standards-regulations/accounts-rules/.
21 *Fuglers LLP v. SRA* (2014) EWHC 179 (Admin) and *Patel, Premji Naram Patel v. Solicitors' Regulation Authority* (2012) EWHC 3373 (Admin) are examples.
22 *Ibid* 20, Rule 3.3.
23 *Ibid* 20, Glossary terms.
24 www.sra.org.uk/solicitors/guidance/improper-client-account-banking-facility/
25 www.sra.org.uk/solicitors/resources/diversity-toolkit/your-data/
26 www.sra.org.uk/sra/research-publications/risk-outlook-202122/
27 Solicitors Regulation Authority, Enforcement Strategy, 7 February 2019, www.sra.org.uk/sra/corporate-strategy/sra-enforcement-strategy/.
28 *Ibid* 19, paragraph 9.1.
29 *Ibid*, paragraph 9.2.

30 www.britannica.com/topic/ethics-philosophy
31 https://dictionary.cambridge.org/dictionary/english/ethic
32 www.sra.org.uk/solicitors/guidance/
33 *Ibid.*

Chapter 10:
Mitigating risk through your client journeys and practices

By Peter Noyce, head of legal sector, Menzies LLP

An ideal situation for any business is for it to generate additional profit whilst removing risk. This will undoubtedly increase its value given that profit increasing and risk reducing – which in turn would increase any multiple applicable – must see capital value increasing.

This chapter looks at the concept of taking risk out of your business, and shall initially explain how this can be linked to the client journey within your practice. This starts with your take on processes and continues all the way through to the receipt by the client of your fee note and the appropriate closing down of the client file. Putting a little meat on the bones of that client journey follows.

Take on process

This is the best point to be educating your clients in not only how they will be dealt with by your firm but also how they should behave during the process. They will be allocated persons within your practice that have the necessary specialism, experience, and capabilities to deal with their particular transaction. The right people doing the right work is a risk mitigator. In its most basic form you would not have a conveyancer dealing with client's probate; not only may revenue opportunities be missed but this also increases the risk that the assignment could and probably would go wrong. This is an early opportunity to take risk out of your process, and therefore out of your law firm as a whole.

The take on process should also be very well laid out within your practice manual to ensure that all fee earners follow the appropriate AML and engagement processes so that you're not leaving yourself open to these risks.[1] There should be regular reviews of adherence to this by appropriately senior people within the practice and results fed back in a timely fashion.

Throughout the transaction

Professional services always like to think that they keep their clients fully informed throughout their transaction or assignment. This not only ensures great communication with and provides reassurance to the client, but also enables you to give appropriate messaging when things are not going as smoothly as desired. As regards this messaging, there may be scope to increase your fees, but communication is also essential to ensure that the client is aware of changing and evolving risks to them and fully informed in this respect. That approach reduces the possibility of future claims against the firm. The ability to stop complaints and claims coming in (at source) will be uppermost in the strategy of your internal risk team; increasing professional indemnity premiums are one of the biggest risks to any law firm's viability at present, so reducing the likelihood of claims is very helpful.

Financial measurements can be early indicators of risk too as there are many aspects of the transactional process where fees can be collected and work in progress controlled. These elements are not simply an accountant talking lock-up but pointing out that many issues and red flags can arise when work in progress is building up, or when fees are not being paid. The uncontrollable build-up of work in progress may well suggest that the ownership of the case in question is not quite what it should be and perhaps the fees are outstanding for a reason, which could be far from satisfactory client service.

This links to further examples of how you can take risk out of your business by simply having appropriate prompts within your case management system to ensure that those build-ups of work in progress or outstanding fees are flagged early to senior management so that potential problems can be nipped in the bud.

Completion

As we progress through and reach completion of a transaction, this is often a period of (hopefully controlled) activity where deadlines are met and you have a fully satisfied client. If that is the situation, great! However, this is not always the case and again this is where your risk management needs to be part of the firm's overall culture. In this situation, a culture should be developed that encourages fee earners and indeed all client-facing staff to be able to ask for help when things get out of their comfort zone, or workload issues mean that client service is not what it should be. Having this kind of open and transparent culture reduces the firm's overall risk.

The aforementioned deadlines at, around, or even after completion need to be appropriately diarized – having processes in place for file closedown should ensure that none of these are missed. The SRA has for a number of years now been very hot on residual balances remaining on client ledgers long after work has been finished, as specifically referenced in the new (shorter) Accounts Rules published by the SRA in November 2019.[2] This is not simply because it is the client's money and should be returned, but also because it can be indicative of file closedown processes not working properly, which can lead to problems in regards to deadlines being missed, outstanding fees, and a breakdown in effective client communication.

Financial disciplines and controls should also be part of the toolkit

Combined with the strategies above for removing risk in relation to client service, it is also worth considering some of the good financial disciplines that can assist risk management.

- **Lock-up management** – these can be excellent key performance indicators, not just for the financial aspects of your business but also for highlighting problems that are building up within certain portfolios. It is worth considering this not just for the firm as a whole but also by department and by individual and to emphasize the importance of open and transparent communication lines on these matters.
- **Cash flow management** – law firms very rarely fail due to a lack of profitability but more often because of a lack of cash. This is where three-way forecasting is crucial as this shows the interaction of not just the profit and loss and balance sheet but also a cash flow forecast. This will identify cash flow issues and pinch points arising well ahead of time and can assist management in ensuring the firm rides these out rather than them affecting the law firm's ability to trade effectively. Having appropriate liquidity measures will assist by comparing the firm's ability to pay its creditors versus the amount of cash and near cash it has over a short-term period. Firms that habitually lean on their banking and lending facilities are indicative of risky businesses that are not well-managed financially or otherwise.

Other non-lock up matters to consider would be:

- Net Promoter Score: The link between client satisfaction and risk should never be ignored or underestimated, so using client surveys during and after work will be a useful indicator of risks inherent within your teams. They can also be a fee-generator by highlighting additional services, so have a dual purpose and benefit.

- **Salary to fees ratio:** Accountants, or the owners of law firms themselves for that matter, do not normally moan about their clients making too much profit out of their staff, but having firm-wide or individual team metrics that indicate a stretched staffing structure will not provide medium- or long-term excellent client care. Therefore, any resourcing issues flagged up outside set parameters can be indicative of either under-resourced teams or staff with too little to do; the latter can cause people to take on work they should not be doing, which also creates risk.
- **Departmental performance:** There needs to be a balance between strict financial indicators of performance and those that indicate excellent collaboration with other departments, particularly as regards feeding work. This ensures the most experienced and so suitable individuals undertake the work and the client is provided with a full service and full solution. Again, all positives in reducing risk.
- **Client complaints overall and by department and breaches register:** Whilst firms may not want to see any complaints, there are advantages to maintaining a well-populated record. The former is delusional in any law firm and the latter can be a sign of an open and transparent culture. Any record of complaints and internal breaches is key to understanding where there are gaps and development needs in teams and identifying trends that indicate shortcomings in performance that need addressing. All of these provide early warning signals of risk and an opportunity to take that risk out of the business, but only if the culture allows the recording in the first place.
- **Succession:** When looking at the risk profile of a firm, consider the quality of not just the fee earners and partners and the future proofing of these roles, but also that of the back-office, finance, and support teams. Due to the high level of regulation, the legal sector will always require specialist back-office support. An example of this is the firm's finance team – not only will the provision of timely and reliable management information always be important but having the expertise to deal with clients' money and the relevant knowledge is also paramount. Do not ignore succession in your finance team when considering that important element of any firm's organizational future.

This is all the more important since the SRA shortened the Accounts Rules and made them less prescriptive, as the historical knowledge and understanding of the previous detailed Rules will decline over time. Whilst this may be countered by the use of well-resourced and trained external providers, any recruitment will need to be tailored to an appropriate handover period to avoid that knowledge being lost.

- **Attitude to cyber risk:** This is an area that keeps many law firm owners and managers awake at night, and one to take seriously. The key point here is that a cyber or fraud event is normally down to human error. That may be an individual or the firm as a whole not having a well-thought-through strategy but again the risk can be reduced, as with most areas of risk, by ensuring this is on the management agenda on a regular basis. Ensuring your own IT department is not marking its own homework by having independent assessments is always a good starting point.
- **Staff engagement:** Finally, keep your staff onside. Several of the above points talk about your team doing the right thing, be that following internal processes and controls from take-on of clients, to communication with clients and completion of matters in an effective and compliant manner. These behaviors must be lived each day by the partners and the leadership team, otherwise the whole risk mitigation policy is undermined and attracts risk into the practice rather than driving it out.

Conclusion

Taking on some risk is good for business, but in the highly regulated legal sector, not understanding the existing risks and not having appropriate internal systems and controls in place to mitigate your identified risks means you are falling at the first hurdle. With relevant controls in place, you and your teams can take much of that risk out of the business. As highlighted above, this provides the foundation for success in risk mitigation and should be continually measured by satisfied clients of the right type, staff knowing what is expected of them, a culture of openness and respect, and growth in both profits and the value of the practice. That aim is too risky to ignore.

References

1 See chapter six for more guidance on anti-money laundering.

2 Solicitors Regulation Authority, Accounts Rules, 25 November 2019, www.sra.org.uk/solicitors/standards-regulations/accounts-rules/, Rule 2.5.

Chapter 11: Outside counsel guidelines

By Noah Fiedler, shareholder and co-leader of the Attorney Risk Management Practice Group, Barron & Newburger, P.C.

Client outside counsel guidelines (OCGs) have existed for nearly 20 years. Over the past decade, corporate, public sector, and financial institution clients have exerted tighter control over outside counsel engagements through the increased use of OCGs.

Comprehensive outside counsel guidelines become standard

Traditional lawyer regulation assumes that clients – of all sizes – require protection from their attorneys, who held all the power in the relationship. Until about a decade ago, lawyers typically had the upper hand in the attorney–client relationship. A client who wanted high quality legal service would pay what the law firm asked and permit the firm to determine staffing and related administrative issues.

The past ten years have seen larger institutional and corporate clients alter that playing field significantly, based mainly on the scope and value of their purchase of legal services. Outside counsel guidelines that now control many if not most of the administrative and even substantive aspects of the attorney–client relationship have become the norm for institutional clients.

As more and more organizations hired in-house counsel and grew their legal departments, demand for outside counsel dropped. Statistical and data-driven review of outside counsel's performance led to further decreases in outside counsel spending. As corporate cost-reduction efforts grew, so did the control and oversight of all purchasing decisions, even legal relationships, by procurement departments.

Today's standard OCGs encompass all elements of the attorney–client relationship. This includes the definition of a conflict of interest, data security requirements, approved vendors, and billing protocols, to name a few. Many clients now demand that the uniformity that applies to their other vendors also applies to their lawyers, often including indemnity agreements.

Most OCG provisions deal with administrative issues, and make it easier for large and sophisticated clients to manage their business. These provisions must be identified, analyzed, and catalogued as discussed below, in order to ensure that business runs smoothly between the firm and the client.

Setting aside the more innocuous provisions, a number of common OCG provisions have raised concerns for the legal industry, particularly those relating to conflicts and indemnity, as well as confidentiality and information security. These provisions can create ethical and civil liability for a firm where there otherwise would be none.

Law firms have with some success resisted the application of certain portions of OCGs that require indemnity agreements in excess of insurance coverage, or define conflicts of interest more broadly than does case law or regulations. However, OCGs are here to stay, and law firms now find themselves in the position of learning to identify, analyze, negotiate, accept, monitor, and abide by client OCG requirements. Failure to do so can lead to disaster for the firm. The most common and troubling guidelines are set forth below.

Indemnity provisions

It is standard for OCGs to contain indemnity provisions that obligate the firm to hold the client harmless against a variety of losses that otherwise would not be the firm's responsibility under any regulation or tort law. Such provisions, left unchallenged, can have serious consequences for law firms.

In the original language of some indemnity provisions, the law firm agrees to guarantee the representation's outcome, even if there is no error or omission by the firm. Another variation of this type of provision imposes a heightened standard of care beyond the commonly accepted "reasonable lawyer" standard applicable to professional negligence. Other provisions may require the firm to indemnify the client against any injury arising from the lawyers' services without regard to whether the services were competent, within the standard of care, or even whether the firm caused the injury. That is, these provisions seek to hold the firm liable for outcomes arising from non-negligent work on the part of the firm.

Similarly, many provisions require that the law firm indemnify the client against injury caused by third party providers that may be engaged in connection with the firm's legal services, regardless of who selected the provider, or whether the firm had the ability to supervise the provider.

Agreeing to such provision can have serious consequences for a firm's ability to seek coverage under one or more of its insurance policies. Professional liability insurance is designed to protect a firm (and its clients) against claims arising from negligence in the provision of services to a client.

Lacking the trigger of a breach of the standard of care, or an error, contractual indemnity promises may not fall within the law firm's insurance coverage, leaving the firm to pay for injuries out of its own pocket. Indemnification agreements (contractual liability) are most often excluded from the coverage of professional negligence policies. Given sufficient sums at stake in the representation, an uninsured loss could destroy the firm.

From the client's perspective, such a loss is uncollectible, and therefore also problematic. As will be seen later, this is a good reason many clients will negotiate the terms of indemnification provisions.

Defining conflicts of interest

Another common OCG provision changes the commonly-understood definitions of "conflict of interest". Many of the OCG definitions and requirements create serious ethical issues, and often require violations of other ethical duties such as confidentiality, diligence, and competence, as well as a lawyer's fiduciary duty.

There are three primary ways that OCGs create conflicts of interest where none would otherwise exist:

1. Expanding the definition of "the client" beyond existing law;
2. Limiting the pool of clients from whom the law firm may accept work; and
3. Expanding the definition of "interest" and "positional" conflicts.

Expanding the definition of the lawyer's client

In this regard, the most common provisions inflate the definition of "client" to include client-constituent or -affiliated organizations. These provisions obviously create problems in conflicts screening and the likelihood of being conflicted out of a later representation.

The language of these provisions is contrary to ABA Ethics Opinion 95-390 (*"A lawyer who represents a corporate client is not by that fact alone necessarily barred from a representation that is adverse to a corporate affiliate of that client in an unrelated matter"*).[1] Note that the Opinion also provides that a lawyer can have an "understanding" with the client that adversity with corporate affiliates will be avoided.

Such a provision is also inconsistent with Model Rule 1.7, Comment 34, which provides that a "*lawyer who represents a corporation or other organization does not, by virtue of that representation, necessarily represent any constituent or affiliated organization, such as a parent or subsidiary*".[2] In addition, courts recognize that the existence of an attorney–client relationship with one corporate affiliate does not create an attorney–client relationship with all corporate affiliates.[3]

Expansion of the "client" definition causes administrative problems for law firms. Unilateral corporate action by buying or selling subsidiaries, among other things, will change the identity of the "client" and the law firm will never know. Even with highly sophisticated conflicts avoidance systems, law firms can and will fall into disqualifying conflicts.

Expressly limiting the lawyer's universe of potential clients

These provisions define the representation of a client's competitor to be a conflict of interest, despite the rules of professional conduct that reject that idea. Comment 6 to Rule 1.7 of the Model Rules states that "*simultaneous representation in unrelated matters of clients whose interests are only economically adverse, such as representation of competing economic enterprises in unrelated litigation, does not ordinarily constitute a conflict of interest and thus may not require consent of the respective clients*".[4] Before entering into an engagement, law firms must carefully balance the benefits and risks of agreeing to such a proposition.

Redefining "positional" conflicts

Ordinarily a lawyer is permitted, and even encouraged, to take inconsistent legal positions at different times on behalf of different clients. Advocating a legal position in the representation of one client that might be adverse to the interests of a client represented by the same lawyer in an unrelated matter does not create a conflict of interest under the rules.[5]

Some OCG provisions seek to prevent this historically typical advocacy by expanding the current definitions of interest or positional conflicts. These provisions are problematic for lawyers, sometimes requiring the violation of ethical and fiduciary duties of confidentiality and loyalty to other clients. These provisions must be identified and at the very least amended to permit lawyers to abide by rules and duties that govern the profession. Failure to do so risks both civil and disciplinary liability.

Managing the risk of OCGs

Understand the content and scope of current and future OCGs

Firms must fully identify, review, and understand current and future contractual requirements with clients. Only then can the most potentially damaging be negotiated, and only then can procedures be introduced to monitor compliance and avoid potential problems. OCGs appear in a variety of forms, and are often sent only to the partner wishing to introduce the business. Sometimes they take the form of a client-generated engagement letter, a request for proposal, or management guidelines sent only after the engagement has formally begun.

Firms should take steps to ensure that whatever the format of the OCGs, the requirements are reviewed by general counsel, or the firm's central risk management program. If a firm has not reviewed each and every OCG to which it has already agreed, it should do so immediately.

Next, firms should establish procedures in the intake process providing for mandatory review of new OCG requirements. No OCG should be agreed to without review by a designated member of firm management. The firm should also request that, if clients wish to enforce OCGs, those provisions must be provided before the representation commences.

As part of the OCG screening process, partners and firm personnel should be educated on the issues and risks associated with OCGs. These include the necessity of central review of OCGs, potential liability, and the possibility that OCGs can surreptitiously creep into the engagement (for example, in documents sent after the engagement has already commenced).

While these procedures may not eliminate an unintentionally-agreed-to OCG, they should reduce that possibility and enable better control by the firm.

Negotiate OCGs

Many firms have successfully negotiated the complete removal of problematic provisions. Often, clients do not meaningfully appreciate the consequences of a specific requirement on the firm, or of the possible harm caused to the client itself. At the very least, amending the language to make the arrangement acceptable to both parties is an attainable goal.

For instance, indemnity provisions can be limited to losses "to the extent that they are covered by the firm's malpractice insurance policy", or using language that voids the indemnification agreement if it invalidates the firm's professional liability insurance. Many times such discussions with the client will end when the client is satisfied that the firm has sufficient insurance coverage (including general, cyber, and professional negligence) to respond to potential claims.

If a client refuses to amend its demanded indemnification provision, firms should exercise caution. Clients who refuse to negotiate a provision are the most likely to later seek to enforce it. Keep in mind a client's reputation for litigation and past actions when weighing the decision to proceed with the engagement. Firms should also consult with their insurance carriers if faced with highly desirable business that brings with it potentially unacceptable OCG provisions.

There is authority to assist counsel in negotiating unacceptable OCG provisions. Model Rule 5.6, "Restrictions on Right to Practice",[6] appears to be the rule most relevant to overly restrictive OCGs. That Rule has been the subject of five ABA Formal Ethics Opinions: ABA Comm. on Ethics & Prof'l Responsibility, Formal Op. 06-444 (2006); ABA Comm. on Ethics & Prof'l Responsibility, Formal Op. 00-417 (2000); ABA Comm. on Ethics & Prof'l Responsibility, Formal Op. 95-390 (1995); ABA Comm. on Ethics & Prof'l Responsibility, Formal Op. 94-381 (1994); and ABA Comm. on Ethics & Prof'l Responsibility, Formal Op. 93-371 (1993).

ABA Formal Op. 94-381 considers two questions. First, may corporate in-house counsel offer, and may outside counsel accept, representation of the corporation contingent on an agreement by outside counsel never to represent at any point in the future a party adverse to the corporation. Second, may corporate in-house counsel offer, and may a lawyer accept, in-house employment contingent on such an agreement.

According to the Opinion, the proposed restriction would prevent representation where the Rules would not, because it would *"prohibit the lawyers involved from representing others in any matter adverse to the corporation, even if that matter were unrelated to any representation of the corporation in which the lawyers had been involved"*.[7] The Opinion concludes that the agreements would violate Rule 5.6 because *"an agreement denying the lawyer the opportunity to represent any interest adverse to a former client is an overbroad and impermissible restriction on the right to practice"*.[8]

OCGs are here to stay

OCGs are not going anywhere, so lawyers must learn to live with them. Exercising appropriate care and preparation, firms will effectively identify, negotiate, and comply with OCGs in order to avoid potential liability and to maintain and promote solid client relationships.

The author gratefully acknowledges the support and assistance of Cassidy Chivers and Anthony Davis.

References

1 ABA Comm. on Ethics & Prof'l Responsibility, Formal Op. 95-390 (1995).
2 ABA Model Rules of Prof'l Conduct R. 1.7 cmt. [34].
3 See e.g. GSI Commerce Solutions, *Inc. v. BabyCenter*, LLC, 618 F.3d 204, 210 (2d Cir. 2010).
4 ABA Model Rules of Prof'l Conduct R. 1.7 cmt. [6].
5 See e.g. ABA Model Rules of Prof'l Conduct R. 1.7 cmt. [24].
6 ABA Model Rules of Prof'l Conduct R. 5.6.
7 ABA Comm. on Ethics & Prof'l Responsibility, Formal Op. 94-381.
8 *Ibid.*

Chapter 12: Conflicts of interest and confidentiality duties – effective risk management

By Tracey Calvert, founder and director, Oakalls Consultancy Limited

The risks associated with dealing with conflicts of interest and confidentiality duties incorrectly must not be underestimated by law firms. Not only can this have adverse regulatory consequences, but breaches of duties in these areas can lead to reputational loss, damaged client relationships, and professional indemnity implications. It is essential that law firm risk management extends to ensuring that there are suitable policies and procedures, systems, and controls to ensure the correct response.

Chapter six of the SRA Code of Conduct for Solicitors, Registered European Lawyers, and Registered Foreign Lawyers and chapter six of the SRA Code of Conduct for Firms describe the regulatory and professional duties that apply to conflicts of interests, confidentiality, and disclosure requirements. The fact that these requirements are identically stated in each Code means that the SRA expects everyone within the firm, whether they are legally qualified or not, whether they are providing client or business services, to understand and comply with the duties.

The starting point for risk management of these topics is by ensuring that there is the correct understanding of what is meant when using these terms and the outcomes that the SRA expects us to achieve. Here we are helped by the fact that this information is clearly stated in the two Codes and also the SRA Glossary.

Own interest conflict

The SRA tells us that an own interest conflict "*means any situation where your duty to act in the best interests of any client in relation to a matter conflicts, or there is a significant risk that it may conflict, with your own interests in relation to that or a related matter*".[1]

Our duty in such circumstances is simple: "*You do not act if there is an own interest conflict or a significant risk of such a conflict.*"[2]

Conflicts of interests when acting for clients

The conflict that arises when acting for more than one client on joint instructions, or otherwise in circumstances where multiple clients are instructing an individual or the firm in the same or a related matter, is described by the SRA as a conflict of interest.[3] Practitioners, however, tend to use the term client conflict to distinguish this from own interest conflict.

This means *"a situation where your separate duties to act in the best interests of two or more clients in the same or a related matter conflict"*.[4]

The outcome that must be achieved when these circumstances are present is less absolute than with own interest conflict:

- *"You do not act in relation to a matter or particular aspect of it if you have a conflict of interest or a significant risk of such a conflict in relation to that matter or aspect of it, unless:*
  - *the clients have a substantially common interest in relation to the matter or the aspect of it, as appropriate; or*
  - *the clients are competing for the same objective,*

and the conditions below are met, namely that:
  - *all the clients have given informed consent, given or evidenced in writing, to you acting;*
  - *where appropriate, you put in place effective safeguards to protect your clients' confidential information; and*
  - *you are satisfied it is reasonable for you to act for all the clients."*[5]

In other words, the starting point is that where a conflict of this type is identified, then instructions cannot be accepted or continued unless one of two exceptions can be applied to the circumstances. These exceptions are known as the "substantially common interest" exception (i.e. a situation *"where there is a clear common purpose between the clients and a strong consensus on how it is to be achieved"*)[6] and the "competing for the same objective" exception (i.e. a situation in which *"two or more clients are competing for an 'objective' which, if attained by one client, will make that 'objective' unattainable to the other client or clients, and 'objective' means an asset, contract, or business opportunity which two or more clients are seeking to acquire or recover through a liquidation (or some other form of insolvency process) or by means of an auction or tender process or a bid or offer, but not a public takeover"*).[7] These exceptions include three conditions that must be satisfied in all circumstances. Given that an inherent conflict has been identified then deciding to make use of an exception is a riskier strategy than deciding not to act further.

Confidentiality and disclosure

Confidentiality is a professional principle listed in the Legal Services Act 2007, which states at section (1)(3)(e) that *"the affairs of clients should be kept confidential"*.[8]

That the duty of confidentiality is a fundamental professional obligation – both at common law and in ethical requirements – cannot be disputed. All solicitors, and everyone else employed in the law firm, own responsibilities connected with their acquisition of confidential information from clients who seek legal services. This duty is explained in the SRA Codes as follows: *"You keep the affairs of current and former clients confidential unless disclosure is required or permitted by law or the client consents."*[9]

In practice, this means that all members of the firm must ensure that they do nothing that places them in breach of this duty. Breach triggers are many and varied; overheard conversations, unauthorized sharing of information with third parties; inappropriate gossip; working away from the office and enabling unauthorized access to confidential information; communications sent to the wrong recipients; data breaches; cyber fraud; careless storage and destruction of client documents, and so on. Latterly, risks associated with remote and/or hybrid styles of providing legal services, accelerated because of COVID-19, have also triggered confidentiality issues.

In practice also, fee earners must consider the possibility that a conflict might arise between this duty of confidentiality owed to all past and present clients (including deceased clients), and the impact that acquired knowledge may have on their ability to act in the best interests of current clients and make full disclosure of material information to them.

This disclosure duty is described in the SRA Codes:

> *"Where you are acting for a client on a matter, you make the client aware of all information material to the matter of which you have knowledge, except when:*
>
> *a) the disclosure of the information is prohibited by legal restrictions imposed in the interests of national security or the prevention of crime;*
>
> *b) your client gives informed consent, given or evidenced in writing, to the information not being disclosed to them;*
>
> *c) you have reason to believe that serious physical or mental injury will be caused to your client or another if the information is disclosed; or*

> d) *the information is contained in a privileged document that you have knowledge of only because it has been mistakenly disclosed."*[10]

The duty to disclose is not absolute and can be altered in certain scenarios. These are all described in the SRA Codes. The most common reason for needing to vary the duty of disclosure arises where this would be satisfied only by revealing information to which the duty of confidentiality attaches and the client to whom this duty is owed does not give consent to such disclosure. The duty of confidentiality takes precedence over the duty of disclosure. Such a situation would mean that the current client could not be represented unless the duty of disclosure had been varied as described in the Codes.

Where the clients in question have adverse interests, the SRA Codes stipulate that you must not act for the client to whom disclosure is owed unless either effective measures have been taken which result in no real risk of disclosure of the confidential information or, alternatively, the client to whom confidentiality is owed gives informed consent (given or evidenced in writing) to you acting, including to any measure taken to protect their information.[11]

Risk management

The SRA Handbook[12] was in force between 2011 and 2019 and contained specific outcomes that required firms to have compliance systems designed to manage the risks associated with conflicts of interest and the conflicts that arise in connection with confidentiality and disclosure. Additionally, in terms of conflicts of interest, there was non-mandatory guidance (the so-called Indicative Behaviors included in the Handbook) of the SRA's requirements that suggested staff should be given training on this subject.

We currently work with the SRA Standards and Regulations and there is nothing like-for-like with the specific outcomes mentioned above. Instead, however, we are told in chapter two of the SRA Code of Conduct for Firms that the authorized firm must have compliance and business systems that include the following:

> *"You have effective governance structures, arrangements, systems and controls in place that ensure:*
>
> a) *you comply with all the SRA's regulatory arrangements, as well as with other regulatory and legislative requirements, which apply to you;*
>
> b) *your managers and employees comply with the SRA's regulatory arrangements which apply to them;*

"You keep and maintain records to demonstrate compliance with your obligations under the SRA's regulatory arrangements.

"You identify, monitor and manage all material risks to your business."[13]

This is directional but lacks prescriptive or illustrative content. This style is intentional and demonstrates what the SRA expects of individuals and authorized law firms. We must identify the risks of breaches that are present because of our own working environment. These will be risks because of clients, because of the understanding of regulatory duties, and the experience of work colleagues, service types, delivery channels, and so on.

The SRA will want to be satisfied that firms are acting appropriately and managing their own risks in order to achieve the stipulated outcomes. Therefore, all managers and owners, the Compliance Officer for Legal Practice (the COLP), any colleagues with risk and compliance responsibilities, heads of departments, and supervisors will need to ensure that there are demonstrably effective systems and controls in place that assist with safe decision-making.

The SRA will consider disciplinary action against individuals and firms where they consider that there has been a breach of these regulatory duties as such misbehavior strikes at the core of professionalism and how we treat our clients. Recent examples of high profile enforcement action include the following:

- Partners in a law firm were fined £10,000 each, and each ordered to pay costs of £25,000 for acting in the sale of a business in which they had a financial interest (i.e. an own interest conflict).[14]
- A solicitor agreed to remove himself from the solicitor's roll in 2017 after admitting that he had shared confidential information many years previously without obtaining his client's consent or without relying on any legal permission.[15]

Risk compliance objectives

In terms of conflicts of interest, the firm's managers and the firm's COLP will want to have confidence that:

- Conflicts searches are both performed and analyzed by fee earners. This analysis is not an administrative exercise and fee earners will want to be confident that they can justify any decisions made about own interest or client-based conflicts;

- Own interest characteristics and situations are identified and, where necessary, fed into conflicts searches data;
- The absolute prohibition on acting in an own interest scenario is not flouted under any circumstances;
- The client conflict regime is understood, and the exceptions are used with great care and in a transparent and documented manner; and
- Colleagues understand what a high-risk scenario is, and involve the COLP in (or otherwise make) decisions when these are identified.

With confidentiality and disclosure duties, the firm's managers and the firm's COLP will want to have confidence that:

- Everyone understands the need for personal accountability in respect of confidentiality duties;
- Relevant colleagues understand the need to manage risks associated with disclosure obligations; and
- Any information barriers erected are done so under the strict oversight of the COLP.

Risk management pinch points

It must be understood that getting these topics correct is non-negotiable, yet there are misunderstandings that may create obstacles to achieving the correct objective. These must be acknowledged and factored into the firm's risk management response.

For example, with conflicts of interests the following points must be noted:

- The SRA's requirement is that we consider not only actual conflicts but also whether there is a significant risk of a conflict arising.
- The conflict decision is a live decision. In other words, we are required to continually reflect on our analysis and ensure that nothing has changed our original decisions (such as might occur with a change in client or change in instructions).
- Asking a client for consent to act is not allowed when an own interest conflict is present.
- Asking clients for consent to act is allowed when client conflict is identified but only when using one of the two exceptions (the substantially common interest or the competing for the same objective

exceptions) and subject to strict compliance with all the conditions attached to these exceptions.

- We are asked to consider conflicts of interest in respect of current clients only.
- It is not a conflict of interest to act against the interests of a former client.
- Beware the risks attached to the use of general files. We are expected to make conflicts searches and perform an analysis exercise with each new matter irrespective of file opening protocols.
- An information barrier is not the mechanism with which to avoid a conflict of interest. It cannot be used as a means of acting for two or more clients where a conflict of interest exists.
- Risk management must be applied to circumstances such as fee earners joining the firm and mergers etc.

With confidentiality and disclosure, the following points must be managed:

- The duty of confidentiality which is attached to information about client matters is only overridden by informed client permission or where the law prevails.
- The duty of confidentiality continues despite the end of the retainer and even the death of the client. It is a duty owed to a client even after the solicitor or other employee leaves your firm.
- Confidentiality duties are owed only to the client and not to third parties even where they are closely connected with the retainer (e.g. a director providing instructions on behalf of a company client is not owed a duty of confidentiality but the company client is owed this).
- Disclosure duties apply to current clients only.
- Duties of disclosure can be varied if this is an issue because of confidentiality owed to another current or former client, but the client who is agreeing to non-disclosure must give informed consent evidenced in writing and there is the expectation that it is reasonable to continue acting.
- Information barriers are a high-risk strategy. Any inappropriate use, accidental disclosure of confidential information, or client misunderstandings are likely to lead to reputational damage, adverse publicity, complaints, and even legal action against the firm.

Compliance solutions

The right solutions will be dependent on such factors as the size of the firm, how it provides services, staff dynamics and so on. The aim is to ensure that whatever solutions are put into practice, the result is effective in managing the risks of a breach of these important regulatory duties. What is determined to be effective will be decided through thorough analysis of the risk factors that may be present within the firm.

Broadly, it will be prudent to have documented policies to explain what the regulatory duties are and to explain what the firm expects from managers and employees to ensure a consistent response. For example, with any conflicts policy, the firm can decide whether it wishes to prohibit certain behaviors (for example, a prohibition on acting for both seller and buyer in all residential transactions is often included in such policies to completely eliminate the risk of acting in a conflict scenario) or to ensure that certain decisions are made by designated individuals such as the COLP (for example, perhaps for the COLP to decide whether it is appropriate to act for both seller and buyer, or whether to rely on the substantially common interest or competing for the same objective exceptions).

A confidentiality and disclosure policy can also be used in a similar way. It can include the firm's internal criteria for acting when confidentiality and disclosure duties are conflicting, provide for decision-making protocol for high risk scenarios, include strategies for managing the risks associated with asking for client consent to override confidentiality duties, and, very importantly, to control the use of information barriers. This policy can also be used to explain expectations when individuals are providing legal services away from the office.

Ancillary policies will provide additional compliance strength. An effective supervisory policy will include the need for oversight of compliance with regulatory duties and identify any training needs. An internal reporting procedure will enable colleagues to report breaches promptly and in a form that provides the managers and the COLP with relevant information with which to decide next steps. An "Own Interest Register" can be useful to document all such matters for the purpose of firmwide conflict analysis. A remote working policy can include the firm's expectations about the management of confidential information outside the office. A social media policy can highlight confidentiality risks associated with the use of social media for both professional and personal purposes. IT and data protection policies will consider legal risks that extend the firm's obligations in respect of the duty to protect information. A learning and development policy will ensure that the firm has the added reassurance that comes with training solutions that address lack of appropriate knowledge.

The bigger picture

Breach of these duties not only creates regulatory concerns and the need to consider the SRA relationship and the possibility that a serious breach needs to be reported promptly. We have already discussed the additional reputational damage caused by the wrong decisions and the legal remedies available should an aggrieved client or former client consider that the firm should not be acting.

In addition, and with conflicts, regulatory duties may be extended by commercial agreements and contractual agreements entered into with clients not to act against their interests or perhaps not to act for their competitors. A breach of confidentiality might also indicate a data protection lapse with the need to consider whether a disclosure must be made to the Information Commissioner Officer under the data protection legislation.

For all these many reasons, it is essential that the firm takes a robust attitude to risk management of these topics.

References

1 Solicitors Regulation Authority, SRA Standards and Regulations, www.sra.org.uk/solicitors/standards-regulations/code-conduct-solicitors/, Glossary terms.

2 Solicitors Regulation Authority, Code of Conduct for Solicitors, RELs and RFLs, 25 November 2019, www.sra.org.uk/solicitors/standards-regulations/code-conduct-solicitors/, paragraph 6.1 and repeated in SRA Code of Conduct for Firms, 25 November 2019, www.sra.org.uk/solicitors/standards-regulations/code-conduct-firms/, paragraph 6.1.

3 Solicitors Regulation Authority, "Conflicts of interest", 29 October 2019, www.sra.org.uk/solicitors/guidance/conflicts-interest/.

4 *Ibid.*

5 Solicitors Regulation Authority, Code of Conduct for Solicitors, RELs and RFLs, 25 November 2019, www.sra.org.uk/solicitors/standards-regulations/code-conduct-solicitors/, paragraph 6.2. and repeated in SRA Code of Conduct for Firms, 25 November 2019, www.sra.org.uk/solicitors/standards-regulations/code-conduct-firms/, paragraph 6.2.

6 Solicitors Regulation Authority, SRA Standards and Regulations, www.sra.org.uk/solicitors/standards-regulations/code-conduct-solicitors/, Glossary terms.

7 *Ibid.*

8 www.legislation.gov.uk/ukpga/2007/29/contents

9 Solicitors Regulation Authority, Code of Conduct for Solicitors, RELs and RFLs, 25 November 2019, www.sra.org.uk/solicitors/standards-regulations/code-conduct-solicitors/, paragraph 6.3 and repeated in SRA Code of Conduct for Firms,

25 November 2019, www.sra.org.uk/solicitors/standards-regulations/code-conduct-firms/, paragraph 6.3.

10 Solicitors Regulation Authority, Code of Conduct for Solicitors, RELs and RFLs, 25 November 2019, www.sra.org.uk/solicitors/standards-regulations/code-conduct-solicitors/, paragraph 6.4. and repeated in SRA Code of Conduct for Firms, 25 November 2019, www.sra.org.uk/solicitors/standards-regulations/code-conduct-firms/, paragraph 6.4.

11 Solicitors Regulation Authority, Code of Conduct for Solicitors, RELs and RFLs, 25 November 2019, www.sra.org.uk/solicitors/standards-regulations/code-conduct-solicitors/, paragraph 6.5, and repeated in SRA Code of Conduct for Firms, 25 November 2019, www.sra.org.uk/solicitors/standards-regulations/code-conduct-firms/, paragraph 6.5.

12 Solicitors Regulation Authority, SRA Handbook, October 2011, www.sra.org.uk/solicitors/handbook/.

13 Solicitors Regulation Authority, Code of Conduct for Firms, 25 November 2019, www.sra.org.uk/solicitors/standards-regulations/code-conduct-firms, paragraphs 2.1, 2.2, and 2.5.

14 *SRA v. Evans and Whiteley*, SDT 11907-2018, www.solicitorstribunal.org.uk/sites/default/files-sdt/11907.2018.Evans_.Whiteley.pdf.

15 www.lawgazette.co.uk/news/retired-solicitor-ends-career-after-historic-breach-of-client-confidentiality/5061780.article

Chapter 13: Complaints

By Rebecca Atkinson, director of risk and compliance, Howard Kennedy

The requirements regarding complaints

Paragraphs 8.2 to 8.5 of the Solicitors Regulation Authority (SRA) Code of Conduct for Solicitors, Registered European Lawyers and Registered Foreign Lawyers (Code for Solicitors) sets out the requirements in relation to complaints handling.[1] The Code for Firms sets out at paragraph 7.1 that these same requirements apply to firms also.[2]

Paragraph 8.2 of the Code for Solicitors sets out that solicitors should ensure that they establish and maintain or participate in a procedure for handling complaints in relation to the services that they provide.

Paragraph 8.3 sets out that solicitors should ensure that clients are informed in writing at the time of engagement about their right to complain to the solicitor/firm about their services and charges, how to complain, and to whom and of the right they have to make a complaint to the Legal Ombudsman, and when they can make such a complaint.

Paragraph 8.4 sets out that solicitors should ensure that when clients have made a complaint, if this has not been resolved to the client's satisfaction within eight weeks of the complaint being made, the client is informed in writing of their right to complain to the Legal Ombudsman, the timeframe for doing so, and full details of how to contact the Legal Ombudsman. Further, where the firm's internal complaints procedure has been exhausted and the solicitor or firm cannot settle the complaint, the name and website address of an alternative dispute resolution (ADR) approved body that would be competent to deal with the complaint and whether the firm agrees to use the scheme operated by that body should be provided to the client in writing.

Finally, paragraph 8.5 sets out that complaints must be dealt with promptly, fairly, and free of charge.

In addition to the above, Rule 2.1 of the SRA Transparency Rules[3] sets out that law firms and solicitors must publish their complaints-handling procedure on their website. This procedure must include details about how and when a complaint can be made to the Legal Ombudsman and to the SRA. This requirement therefore goes beyond informing clients about how to complain about service only (to the Legal Ombudsman) but also how to complain about matters of conduct to the SRA.

What should the complaints handling process be and who should undertake complaint handling in the firm?

Each firm is able to determine its own procedure. However, what is important is that wherever possible the complaint is reviewed by an independent person so as to provide a fresh review of matters. Some firms may choose to ask the conducting fee earner to draft the reply to the complaint and place this in the name of a senior person, with that senior person not reviewing the complaint, file, or discussing the same with the conducting fee earner. This is a dangerous method of complaint resolving and, if the service was poor, the conducting fee earner may not be prepared to admit as such and further the fee earner may draft the reply defensively.

If a firm is very small and there is no one else in the firm who would be able to review the complaint, an external consultant could be engaged to investigate the complaint or a reciprocal arrangement entered into with a separate firm to investigate the complaint of the other with appropriate non-disclosure agreements in place (note that sending client data outside of the firm for this purpose should also be covered off in the firm's terms of business). If neither of these options are available then the conducting fee earner should respond to the complaint.

The documented complaints process should set out whom to make the complaint to, what will happen when a complaint is made, and in what timescale. For example, the process could say that the complaint is to be made to the supervising partner, the head of the department, the complaints handling partner, or the Compliance Officer for Legal Practice (COLP). It is a good idea for the process to set out that all concerns should be raised with the conducting fee earner in the first instance to see if early resolution can take place.

In terms of timescales, the process could say that once a complaint has been made the person to whom the complaint is made will acknowledge the complaint within, say, three working days and will review the matter and respond substantively within, say, ten working days of the complaint being made.

Below is some suggested text that firms might like to adopt:

Our Complaints Policy

We pride ourselves on our client care and professional approach to our work.

Whilst we rarely receive complaints, it is important to have procedures in place to help you in the unlikely event of your wishing to make a complaint.

The following procedure sets out the way in which we handle complaints, and help you to decide the best approach to take. When something goes wrong, we would like you to tell us about it so that we can address it.

Our Complaints Procedure

The person with overall responsibility for managing complaints is [insert name and any details of supervision or who assists this person].

To help us understand your complaint we ask that you set out your concerns in writing.

If you want to raise a complaint under this procedure please email [insert name and email address]. Alternatively, you can write to the lawyer with conduct of your matter or the supervising partner and request your complaint be forwarded to [insert name].

What will happen next?

We will send to you an acknowledgement of your complaint within three working days of receipt and enclose a copy of this procedure. We will at that stage decide who is best placed to respond to your complaint. We will also record your complaint in our central register. [NB it is important to record complaints, outcomes and learn from them.]

We will then investigate your complaint. This may involve inviting you to a meeting to discuss your concerns.

We will send you a reply to your complaint within ten working days of receipt. If we are unable to respond to you within that time, we will inform you. The majority of matters are resolved at this stage.

If your complaint is not resolved to your satisfaction within eight weeks of it having been made to us, you have the right to complain to the Legal Ombudsman. Any complaint to the Legal Ombudsman must usually be made within six years from the act or omission complained of or within three years from when you should have reasonably known of the cause for complaint.

Further, you must raise your complaint with the Legal Ombudsman within six months of our written response to your complaint. We hope that this will not be necessary but the Legal Ombudsman can be contacted by telephone on 0300 555 0333, by email at enquiries@legalombudsman.org.uk or by post at Legal Ombudsman, PO Box 6806, Wolverhampton WV1 9WJ. We will remind you of this right to complain to the Legal Ombudsman at the conclusion of our complaints process.

Where we are unable to resolve your complaint, you also have the option of contacting an alternative complaints body competent to deal with complaints about legal services should both you and our firm wish to use such a scheme.

We will inform you at the end of the complaints procedure whether we agree to the use of an alternative complaints body.

We are of course always happy to receive comments on our service and to hear how we can help improve the service we provide. Any complaint is always taken very seriously and if you do find cause for complaint you can be assured that it will be investigated thoroughly.

How to effectively handle complaints

Technically, a complaint can be any expression of dissatisfaction, whether oral or written, which alleges that the person complaining has suffered financial loss, distress, inconvenience, or other detriment.

To that end, complaints can be made informally initially and may be made to the conducting fee earner, which can be resolved easily without any formal process being followed.

Firms may choose to only record and concentrate on those complaints that are made formally through the firm's complaints procedure. Firms may wish, however, to try and capture expressions of dissatisfaction and their reasons even though they have not been raised in a formal way so that wider issue trends can be spotted and action taken to tackle them. The capture could happen via line management discussions with fee earners or through a file review process instead of requesting that every expression of dissatisfaction is recorded centrally.

If the complaint is not minor in nature and an independent review is needed then the client should be invited to raise their complaint under the complaints procedure. If the client does not wish to do so the firm may choose to handle the complaint via that procedure in any event.

Clients are able to complain about any aspect of the service that they receive. This could be any of the following:

- Delay;
- Failure to advise;
- Incorrect advice;
- Failure to update;
- Lack of progress;
- Conduct; and/or
- Costs information or level of costs.

Note that during the SRA annual reauthorization process for the firm, the firm will need to report on the complaints received in each of these categories alongside whether the complaint was resolved and/or went to the Legal Ombudsman.

Below are some top tips to effectively handle complaints.

Have a clear external complaints procedure and internal process

Whatever your process is, it needs to be clear and easy to understand and follow. Further, all those in the firm need to understand where to find the procedure and when to highlight it to clients. The process should also be on the firm's website and in the firm's terms of business or engagement letter or both.

Think carefully whether it is appropriate for the fee-earner being complained about to draft the complaint response

As set out above, the formal complaints process in the firm should be an independent one. As the fee earner understands the matter and the complaint more readily, it is tempting to ask the fee earner to draft the reply to come from a separately named person with the latter not reviewing the matter or complaint. Consider if this is appropriate. Firms should consider if instead the conducting fee earner should produce an internal memo to assist the independent reviewer with the complaint investigation.

Make sure the complaint is understood

Some complaints are clear and some are not. Some clients are unable to set out what they are complaining about clearly and, where appropriate, reasonable adjustments should be made for those who need assistance in articulating their complaint.

It is perfectly reasonable to ask a client to clarify their complaint and even to rephrase it for them in a way that makes sense to respond to. It is best to try to get to the nub of the complaint so that the heart of the issues can be addressed. It is a good idea at the beginning of the complaints process to repeat back to the client what their complaints are and ask them to confirm the firm's understanding is correct before the investigation begins.

Consolidate where possible

Clients can repeat their complaint in multiple different ways but the complaint may actually boil down to a couple of areas. Firms should be able to consolidate complaints where it is appropriate to do so. If, for example, the client has raised 50 complaints, these can legitimately be grouped together if that would be a reasonable way of investigating the complaint. The Legal Ombudsman does this and so can firms.

Front load the complaint

When responding to a complaint, make the response as full as possible, backing it up with evidence, such as copy letters or emails, attendance notes, time recording etc. This means that if the client wishes to pursue the matter with the Legal Ombudsman, the firm can provide its response and accompanying evidence to the Ombudsman. Often, the Legal Ombudsman will not have seen the complaint response. If the firm makes their complaint response full first time around, this will cut down the time needed to respond to the Legal Ombudsman.

Keep a record of your complaint responses and associated documentation

While the client has six months from the date of the firm's final response to the complaint to go to the Legal Ombudsman, the Ombudsman often takes a year or more to start investigating a complaint. The Ombudsman also allows clients to suspend complaints and re-start them many months after suspension. This means that firms need to retain good records for many months – if not years – after they have responded to a complaint.

Be conciliatory and try and resolve the complaint, even if unfounded

The purpose of the complaints-handling process is to resolve the complaint. Firms should adopt a conciliatory tone and, where necessary, apologize to the client for any poor service. Where necessary, an offer of compensation or a write-off of fees should be made and if it is made and the offer is a reasonable one, the Legal Ombudsman has the ability to decline to investigate the complaint. It is therefore worth making an offer where it is warranted.

Complaints made by non-clients

Firms are obliged to utilize their complaints process for complaints made by those to whom they have provided a service, i.e. clients. The exception to this is beneficiaries in probate matters, especially where the executors are the solicitors at the firm providing the service. This is because the beneficiaries are benefitting from the firm's service. The Legal Ombudsman will accept complaints from beneficiaries and so should the firm.

Complaints can be made by a client's opposing party or a person on the other side of a transaction. When this happens the firm should consider if it is appropriate to respond to the complaint at all, whether the complainant is represented, and a response should be given to their representation and whether it is appropriate to engage directly with the non-client complainant.

It may not be appropriate to respond in length to a complaint about a firm's handling of a litigation matter for their client, for example, but it may be appropriate to address the complaint in a short/brief way and signpost the complainant to the SRA to raise a complaint of conduct. When responding, the firm needs to also consider what is in the best interests of their client.

How to handle online reviews – good or bad

In July 2021, the SRA published its view on customer reviews:

> *"Proactively publishing information on key indicators of service quality, for example customer reviews, not only helps the public when they are looking for a legal services provider but should also help your firm win more business."*[4]

Further, the SRA says that finding information on the quality of solicitors can be challenging and that it is *"looking to help make more information of this type readily available within the legal sector, whether it is published directly by law firm themselves, or hosted by third parties such as comparison websites"*.[5]

The SRA has published guidance on how to engage with online reviews,[6] which sets out the following key points:

- Do not disclose confidential or privileged material when responding.
- Be careful to maintain professionalism and act in accordance with the SRA Standards and Regulations.
- If a defamatory review has been given, firms can take legal action but

they may wish to take an alternative approach. Being heavy handed with a client could be a deterrent.

- Thank a client for a positive review.
- If the review is negative – always respond (be careful though in making any admissions as this could cause difficulty with insurance cover).
- Do not get personal or defensive – no matter how hard that may be!
- Remember that negative reviews can be good for your business,[7] because people can be skeptical of businesses with only positive reviews.
- If a firm thinks a review is fake, the firm should try and check the authenticity. Firms may decide to respond in a neutral way by replying *"We have not been able to verify this review is from a genuine client"*.[8]
- Respond quickly.

The use of online reviews is being promoted by the SRA and therefore firms need to be able to spot the review and consider how to respond. Some of the websites where a review can be left include Trustpilot,[9] The Law Superstore,[10] Review Solicitors,[11] Legal Utopia,[12] Really Moving,[13] REVIEWS.io,[14] Solicitor.info,[15] Chawker,[16] and Search4legal.[17]

The Legal Ombudsman Scheme Rules, publication, and case fee

The Legal Ombudsman has been in existence since 2010 and will consider complaints made about the service provided by solicitors and firms. The Ombudsman operates under a set of Scheme Rules[18] that set out how the Ombudsman investigates complaints, who can complain, and the timescales by which a complaint must be raised.

Key aspects of the Scheme Rules are as follows:

- The Rules set out who can complain to the Ombudsman, which includes the following:
  - *"[A]n individual;*
  - *[A] business or enterprise that was a micro-enterprise (European Union definition) when it referred the complaint to the [law firm];*
  - *[A] charity that had an annual income net of tax of less than £1m when it referred the complaint to the [law firm];*

- *[A] club/association/organization, the affairs of which are managed by its members /a committee/a committee of its members, that had an annual income net of tax of less than £1m when it referred the complaint to the [law firm];*
- *[A] trustee of a trust that had an asset value of less than £1m when it referred the complaint to the [law firm]; and/or*
- *[A] personal representative or beneficiary of the estate of a person who, before he/she died, had not referred the complaint to the Legal Ombudsman.*"[19]

- The Rules set out what the complainant can complain about and this includes an act or omission that does not have to relate to reserved legal activities (under the Legal Services Act 2007) but that the complaint must relate to the services provided.
- Law firms must inform clients about the ability to complain to the Legal Ombudsman and the timescales (six years from the act or omission complained of or within three years from when the complainant should have reasonably known of the cause for complaint; further, the complaint must be raised with the Legal Ombudsman within six months of the firm's final written response to the complaint) at the time of engagement and at the end of the firm's internal complaints process.
- The Ombudsman can extend the time limit.
- The Rules set out the grounds for dismissing or discontinuing the complaint with reasons being that the complaint has no reasonable prospects of success, no loss suffered or likely to be suffered, the firm has already offered reasonable redress for the complaint, the complaint has been made before, the complaint relates to the use of discretion under a will or trust, and other reasons.
- The Rules set out that the Ombudsman can refer the complaint to court if there is a legal question. It is not clear if this has ever been done.
- The Rules set out the remedy that the Ombudsman can request the law firm to provide. This can be an apology, pay compensation for loss, pay interest on that compensation, pay compensation for inconvenience/distress caused, put right (or pay to be put right) any error or omission, to pay for costs incurred in pursing the complaint, and limit fees. The limitation of fees payable is not capped but awards for compensation or putting matters right is limited to £50,000.

In February 2022, the Legal Ombudsman consulted on amending its Scheme Rules and is seeking to reduce the time limits for a complaint to be raised to one year from date of act or omission, amongst other potential changes.[20] These changes will reduce the number of complaints that the Ombudsman will accept to investigate. As of July 2022, no changes have been made.

The Legal Ombudsman publishes data on its website[21] about the complaints where a final decision has been made by an Ombudsman. The information published is limited and includes firm name, area of law, date of decision, remedy and amount, complaint reasons, whether poor service was found, and whether the internal complaints handling was reasonable. The data is published for the past 12 months and is updated quarterly.

All complaints that the Legal Ombudsman investigates incur a £400 case fee unless there are reasons for the fee to be waived. The decision to waive a case fee will depend on the outcome of the investigation. For example, if the Ombudsman finds that a firm has not provided a poor service, or that the firm has already made a reasonable offer before the Ombudsman became involved, it will waive the case fee unless it believes that the firm had not properly dealt with the complaint internally.

Further guidance

The Law Society and Legal Ombudsman provide guidance in respect of complaints handling and these should be consulted. These are:

- Law Society Practice Note: "Handling complaints".[22]
- Law Society Practice Note: "What to do when a complaint goes to the Legal Ombudsman".[23]
- Legal Ombudsman: "Preventing complaints" guidance.[24]
- Legal Ombudsman: "Good complaints handling" guidance.[25]

References

1 Solicitors Regulation Authority, Code of Conduct for Solicitors, RELs and RFLs, 25 November 2019, www.sra.org.uk/solicitors/standards-regulations/code-conduct-solicitors/.

2 Solicitors Regulation Authority, Code of Conduct for Firms, 25 November 2019, www.sra.org.uk/solicitors/standards-regulations/code-conduct-firms/.

3 Solicitors Regulation Authority, Transparency Rules, 25 November 2019, www.sra.org.uk/solicitors/standards-regulations/transparency-rules/.

4 www.sra.org.uk/solicitors/resources/transparency/customer-reviews/

5 *Ibid.*

6 www.sra.org.uk/solicitors/resources/transparency/customer-reviews/engaging-online-reviews/

7 *Ibid.*

8 *Ibid.*

9 www.uk.trustpilot.com

10 www.thelawsuperstore.co.uk

11 www.reviewsolicitors.co.uk

12 https://legalutopia.co.uk

13 www.reallymoving.com

14 www.reviews.io

15 www.solicitor.info

16 www.chawker.com

17 www.search4legal.co.uk

18 www.legalombudsman.org.uk/information-centre/corporate-publications/scheme-rules/

19 *Ibid*, Rule 2.1(a)-(f).

20 www.legalombudsman.org.uk/media/nahpyypc/olc-scheme-rules-consultation-feb-2022.pdf

21 www.legalombudsman.org.uk/information-centre/data-centre/ombudsman-decision-data/?provider=MW%20Solicitors&page=1

22 www.lawsociety.org.uk/topics/client-care/handling-complaints

23 www.lawsociety.org.uk/en/topics/client-care/what-to-do-when-a-complaint-goes-to-the-legal-ombudsman

24 www.legalombudsman.org.uk/information-centre/learning-resources/preventing-complaints/

25 www.legalombudsman.org.uk/information-centre/learning-resources/good-complaints-handling/

Chapter 14: Effective supervision in remote and hybrid teams

By Jamie Butler, executive coach and facilitator and founder, Jamie Butler Coaching Limited

Why is good supervision important?

A firm's obligation to train and develop its lawyers continues beyond admission to maintain competence appropriate to the practice area and level of responsibility. Much of this takes place on-the-job through the effective delegation and supervision of client work by those lawyers with greater experience. Good supervision therefore ensures the quality of client service and provides valuable opportunities to develop skills and competencies. The relationship with our supervisor or manager also impacts our job satisfaction, motivation, and broader wellbeing.

The Solicitors Regulation Authority (SRA) sets out its core regulatory requirements in relation to supervision in both the SRA Code of Conduct for Solicitors, RELs and RFLs, and the SRA Code of Conduct for Firms. These requirements include to:

- *[R]emain accountable for compliance with the SRA's regulatory arrangements where your work is carried out through others;*[1]
- *[E]nsure your managers and employees are competent to carry out their role and keep their professional knowledge and skills, as well as their understanding of their legal, ethical and regulatory obligations, up to date;*[2] *and*
- *[H]ave an effective system for supervising clients' matters.*[3]

Our experiences of the recent COVID-19 pandemic have confirmed that good supervision is even more critical as many lawyers have been managing junior team members, including trainee solicitors, from a distance. Now that some form of hybrid or remote working arrangement is a permanent reality for many firms, it remains key to build on these experiences to maximize the engagement, inclusion, and wellbeing of our teams.

Risks, challenges, and opportunities of remote supervision

Some organizations had been using remote working as a strategic tool for many years to improve performance and productivity. However, COVID-19 clearly prompted opportunities to do more. For the majority of firms and individuals, key benefits include the reduced commute, scope to be more productive, and improved work–life balance. These often result in increased commitment to the firm, created by the flexibility and trust offered by supervisors and managers.

Conversely, risks and challenges include the blurring of work and personal life, reduced access to learning and development opportunities, and a potential negative impact on team engagement, cohesion, or culture. Regarding supervision, many have commented on the reduced availability of on-the-job learning, observing others, and learning by osmosis, although many firms have embraced virtual formats for training and development, e.g. elearning, webinars, interactive online workshops, and one-to-one coaching or supervision (using Zoom, Teams, or other platforms).

We have recently seen the first "COVID Cohort" of trainees qualify as solicitors, who have completed their entire training periods during the pandemic. Whilst some argue that they have missed out on in-person supervision, mentoring, and other development opportunities (impacting their confidence and future contribution), in many cases the sector has responded well. Nevertheless, as we return to the office and hybrid ways of working, the development of trainees and junior lawyers remains a top priority.

Core skills and characteristics of an effective remote supervisor

Firms have recognized that the role of the supervisor, manager, or team leader has been critical in encouraging the benefits of remote working but also helping to respond to the challenges. This has prompted reflection on what it means to be an effective remote supervisor:

- Keeping in touch regularly;
- Responding in a timely way;
- Asking how people are – leading with empathy and compassion;
- Clarity around communication and "getting things done";
- Asking for help and delegating;
- Giving regular feedback – both positive and constructive;
- Dealing with any problems or conflict quickly and by phone/video – not email;

- Managing for results and productivity;
- Encouraging team spirit; and
- Reinforcing positive messages.

A key theme has been to focus on the human side of our relationships, not just getting tasks done. Managers have shared their home-schooling "war stories" or the challenges of living, eating, and working around the kitchen table. We have tried to relate on a personal level first, then jump into the work. This has reinforced the need to lead with empathy and compassion and adopt more of a coaching style to our approach (see below).

Setting "ground rules" to establish responsibility and build trust

Our effectiveness as remote managers rests largely on how we communicate, both in terms of our clarity but also the processes and procedures we adopt. Many will have set ground rules already (and they are working well); however, if not, there may be an opportunity to re-group and consider some of the following areas:

- Communicate to build responsibility and trust;
- How best to contact each other;
- Response times for calls and emails;
- Share calendars and use "status" symbols (e.g. active, away, do not disturb);
- Plan and structure the day – as if in the office;
- Daily touch-points, updates, or "huddles";
- Engage in calls and video-cons – don't multi-task;
- If in doubt, over-communicate (to repeat, reinforce, or clarify) – with your junior/team, with your own manager, and with clients/others; and
- "Check in", don't "check up".

The best approach is to discuss these areas as a group rather than impose them – give your team responsibility to come up with ideas so that you own the rules collectively and trust that everyone will play by them. Have open discussions about how best to contact one another and expected response times given the nature of your work and clients. Most importantly, role-model what you agree, e.g. always try to respond in a timely manner and if you can't deal with something now, say when – this helps others prioritize and not wait around for your response.

We have seen huge benefits of daily or regular updates, if only a brief ten-minute call at the start or end of each day to keep everyone on-track, visible, and engaged. These also provide opportunities for team members to raise questions or concerns. However, always remember your tone and intention – a "check in" says so much more about your level of trust and support than a "check up", which often leads to micromanagement and distrust.

Communicating for effectiveness and productivity

More than ever before, the pandemic has prompted us to match task to tech – to really think about what technology we use and how we use it, depending on the task or conversation at hand.

Many of us default to email because we often (wrongly) believe that it is the quickest approach. However, it has been encouraging to see lawyers challenge this habit and have more conversations by phone, Zoom, or other video platforms, particularly when there is a need to humanize the communication and leverage the benefits of seeing non-verbal signals and body language. Without the scope to observe non-verbal communication, there is more potential for confused understanding or inferred meaning and we often miss an opportunity to pick up when something may be wrong or a team member needs support. Eye contact is particularly important to show interest and empathy and to read other people's body language and the signs that they may be struggling.

The basic message is to use as much face-to-face communication as possible, which explains the increased popularity of Zoom – and its share price! If you do need to use email, then take greater care with your language and expression; often quick, reduced emails can result in confusion or offence.

In terms of supervision, a Zoom call often works best if delegating a new task or project as the supervisor can provide detailed information and a platform to answer any questions. Similarly, if a longer conversation is required, perhaps to provide feedback or address a more sensitive issue, then speaking by phone or Zoom is advised.

Maximizing engagement, inclusion, and wellbeing

It is positive that the topic of wellbeing has been elevated in importance during the pandemic to keep in mind the impact of remote working on our broader health, happiness, and resilience. An employer's duty of care extends to those working from home so it is critical to check in on the health and wellbeing of our team members to ensure that they remain engaged and feel part of the team. Unfortunately, a lot has been written about the impact of COVID-19 and remote working on stress, burnout, and broader wellbeing;[4] a key part of a supervisor's role is therefore to balance wellbeing with the commercial drivers of productivity and profit.

Much of this links to points raised above, particularly optimizing our communications to facilitate performance, reduce isolation, build relationships, and enhance cohesion. But even more so, this demands positive role-modelling – where realistic and relative to our role and workload, supervisors should encourage their teams to switch off and help them demarcate the blurring lines between home and work.

Whilst accepting the benefits discussed above, we should also beware "Zoom fatigue". Our brains work harder on screen to interpret what people say and we need to pay more attention to pick up on some of the non-verbal signs mentioned earlier. For many, there is little or no time to rest between calls, seeing our own camera image may create additional stress, and silence on a call can feel like a pressure to contribute. Therefore, whilst there are benefits to having cameras on during Teams or Zoom calls, sometimes we need to look away or switch our cameras off because something else may be happening in the background. Supervisors can encourage face-to-face contact but trust individuals if this is not always possible or comfortable. Be open to challenging if you always need Zoom and suggest phone or a "walk and talk" meeting instead (where you catch up with a colleague by phone and both get some exercise and fresh air).

Supervisors and managers have also experimented in other ways to maintain engagement and inclusion:

- Consider logging into Zoom or Teams with your junior for a couple of hours each week where you can both chat or ask questions, as if in the office – some call this "virtual office hours". Whilst you can both work on your own tasks, it provides an opportunity to lift your heads, take a break, or ask a question. The junior can also ask for input or support as they would do if physically in the office.
- Help your juniors work out what is most effective and productive for them. At the start of lockdown, many found it very easy for work to expand to fill a longer working day without the commute. Tasks that should have taken a morning were easily spilling into mid-afternoon. Be more transparent about blocking out time in your calendar for detailed work without interruptions or set up calls or Zooms for

catch-ups around the "natural" 11am or 3pm break times when you may crave some social interaction. You might also alter your work environment to give yourself a break or change of scene. Share with your juniors what works for you and this will give them confidence to work out an approach for themselves too.

- Increase scope for taking regular breaks, particularly if you spend much of the day on screen. Adopt the "Pomodoro Technique"[5] – set a timer for 50 (or 25) minutes and focus on your task or dial into a meeting for the allotted time; get up for ten (or five) minutes for a break, stretch, drink, some fresh air, or a chat to someone else at home; then return to your desk and set the timer again. Whilst not rocket science, you need to be disciplined to make it a habit, otherwise you just rush from task to task or meeting to meeting.
- Encourage "camera-free Fridays" with voice-only meetings or calls – the idea is to create a more relaxed transition into the weekend by putting less pressure on teams to be on camera and redressing the risk of "Zoom fatigue" (see above).

Hybrid working – developing approaches

Most people agree that the "working from home experiment" has been largely positive and revealed how productive and effective we can be so that remote, flexible, or hybrid working becomes the norm in non-crisis times. Equally, as highlighted in some of the challenges referred to above, we have recognized the benefits of being able to collaborate, innovate, network, socialize and bond with colleagues in person.

This explains why hybrid working appears to be the favored approach for many law firms, to combine the autonomy and independence of working remotely with the benefits of in-person collaboration. Whilst working policies will vary between firms, many are encouraging a 60/40 split between the office and home and all seem to recognize the benefits of having new starters and trainees in the office for a larger proportion of the week than other team members (to help them settle in, get to know people in person, and understand the firm's physical resources and facilities).

As mentioned, firms will need a mechanism for encouraging transparency around where people are and this prompts the need for detailed guidance around the work-from-home set-up, including taking regular breaks and maintaining catch-ups and check-ins with team members, regardless of location.

For many firms, hybrid working is operating on a pilot basis, often reviewed monthly and taking into account feedback from team members, management, and clients.

It is important for supervisors and their teams to reflect on what hybrid means for them as an organization in terms of both the opportunities and challenges. Experience to date will identify what is most relevant and present for the team; however, there are a number of potential areas to consider.

Hybrid working and supervision – opportunities and challenges

- Recognize when "in-person" communication, supervision, and development is likely to be most beneficial, e.g. scheduling "overlap" days for supervisors and juniors to be in the office at the same time, holding weekly team meetings in person where possible, and encouraging learning and development to take place face-to-face where attendees can also network and share ideas beyond the pure content of the session.
- Facilitate effective "hybrid meetings" that pose particular challenges, given the need to include all attendees regardless of whether they are physically in the room or joining remotely via Teams or Zoom. Structure meetings clearly and be mindful of engagement and participation across all attendees.
- Maintain fairness and inclusion – potentially the greatest challenge – irrespective of location, e.g. around providing work opportunities, learning and development, mentoring, and sponsorship. The fear is that those physically in the office will receive preferential treatment; however, all team members should be afforded the same opportunities, particularly as they will impact the progression, promotion, and retention of employees.
- Keep wellbeing front-of-mind, particularly a recognition that a return to commuting and potentially greater distractions in the office are likely to pose negative effects.
- Consider how hybrid working can improve team and office culture, particularly where many have felt that this has been lacking or where teams have become tired of the Zoom quiz or virtual happy hours.

Any type of change will take time and whilst much is being discussed about hybrid working, none of us really know what the future may bring.

Many argue that hybrid is more complex than remote working since we no longer experience the same level playing field. The key is to try new ideas, test what works, make tweaks, keep experimenting, and share learnings and good practice.

"Supervisor as coach" skills – managing from a distance

As an executive coach, it has been encouraging to see many firms move away from a traditional or hierarchical leadership model to something much more distributed and collaborative.

You have a choice to make about how to supervise and show up for your team

We have observed the changing face of leadership and management during the pandemic and most people agree that the best leaders and managers have used coaching skills to maintain engagement, motivation, and a sense of wellbeing in their teams. Whilst some firms were already encouraging a coaching management style, the pandemic and shift to remote working has offered a positive, effective, and welcome alternative to the traditional "command and control" approach. This requires us to ask more and tell less; "pull" more ideas and solutions from the team rather than "push" our own requirements or ways of working on them; and recognize empathy as the core emotional intelligence skill to help supervisors create and maintain trust and rapport.

If successful, over time firms will create a management and supervision model where responsibility is shared amongst a team. This will result in a clear understanding of what is required to both survive and thrive, as well as a supportive yet challenging environment where we empower team members to be engaged and take responsibility for their actions and goals, and where we appreciate the importance of wellbeing to manage human anxieties and adapt to change.

We have a great opportunity to create new, flexible, and sustainable ways of working and your contribution as a supervisor will play a central role.

References

1. Solicitors Regulation Authority, Code of Conduct for Firms, 25 November 2019, www.sra.org.uk/solicitors/standards-regulations/code-conduct-firms/, paragraph 2.3.
2. *Ibid*, paragraph 4.3.
3. *Ibid*, paragraph 4.4. See also paragraphs 3.5 and 3.6 of the SRA Code of Conduct for Solicitors, RELs and RFLs.

4. For a practical review and guide to supporting mental health, see www.cipd.co.uk/knowledge/culture/well-being/supporting-mental-health-workplace-return?msclkid=6e014dd7c14611ecbb679cb89ecdefb7.
5. www.forbes.com/sites/bryancollinseurope/2020/03/03/the-pomodoro-technique/

Chapter 15:

Lateral hiring in law firms – risks and reward

By Ruth Bonino, professional support lawyer, and Chris Holme, partner, Clyde & Co LLP

Introduction

Companies that carry out due diligence in the context of lateral hires point to research that suggests that about 48 percent of lateral hires have departed their new firm within five years of joining.[1] A contributing factor to this may well be a failure by firms to carry out proper due diligence. However, the potential reward of carrying out what may be considered a "full" due diligence process needs to be balanced against (and properly take into account and cater for) the risks for firms and individuals.

This chapter considers how firms can navigate lateral hiring recruitment to seek to make sure the "right person" has been hired, whilst being aware of (and avoiding) the risks of ethical, legal, and regulatory breaches (particularly in terms of confidential client information).

Basic legal, ethical, and regulatory obligations of partners in UK law firms

Legal duties

Law firms proposing to recruit a lateral hire need to be mindful of the partner's obligations and duties owed to their current firm. The extent of these obligations of course depends on the obligations they are bound by under their partnership or LLP members agreement, but there are consistent duties that are very likely to apply.

Obligations partners owe their current firm may include:

- A duty to act in the best interests of the firm – this will include the partner doing their best to promote the business of the firm. Of course, this will not prevent a partner from leaving to join a competitor in accordance with the relevant notice provisions but in considering leaving, partners need to be mindful that their own interests do not conflict with the interests of the current firm.

- A general duty to disclose to their firm information that is material to the firm's business – this includes information about any activity that could damage the interests of the current firm, for example another law firm considering competing or moving into a particular area of business.

The partner will of course also have wide-ranging confidentiality obligations and restrictive covenants that apply post leaving their current firm.

A partner's confidentiality obligations will prevent the partner from disclosing confidential firm and client information to third parties, which includes recruiters and other law firms.

The partner's duties of confidentiality owed to their current firm and clients will potentially give rise to risks for the hiring firm. Such risks could include a partner breaching confidentiality obligations during the recruitment process and disclosing, albeit inadvertently, information in a business plan or lateral hire questionnaire. Partners should take care to include non-confidential information only, and to preserve confidentiality through the process.

Whether certain information is confidential, and the extent of a partner's confidentiality obligations is not always obvious or straightforward in certain middle and grey cases. For example, the mere fact that information is not in the public domain or that it's only generated as a result of a client engagement might not render the information confidential per se. Ultimately, however, hiring firms (and partners) will want to avoid the need to have technical debates about such information, and will likely want to stay within circumstances whereby they are only receiving (and providing) information that is clearly not confidential.

Hiring firms therefore also need to be careful in relation to the information that they ask for and receive, and also what they do with information that they receive. Those involved in recruitment exercises should be aware of the various duties owed by partners to help avoid issues arising, and to manage the risks involved in recruitment and due diligence processes.

Regulatory/ethical duties

The Solicitors Regulatory Authority (SRA) has set out a number of rules (SRA Principles) that UK qualified solicitors must abide by. The SRA Principles that are potentially relevant in the context of lateral hiring are:

- *"Principle 2 – You must act in a way that upholds public trust and confidence in the solicitors' profession and the legal services provided by authorized persons;*
- *Principle 4 – You must act with honesty;*
- *Principle 5 – You must act with integrity; and*
- *Principle 7 – You must act in the best interests of each client."*[2]

The SRA Codes of Conduct for Individuals and for Firms (Code) are also relevant:

- Clause 6.3 (for individuals and for firms) – "*You must keep the affairs of current and former clients confidential unless disclosure is required or permitted by law or the client consents.*"[3]
- Clause 8.1 (for firms) – "*If you are a manager, you are responsible for your firm's compliance with the Code and that responsibility is joint and several if you share management responsibility with other managers of the firm.*"[4]

Further to this, it is apparent that the SRA can and does investigate issues around lateral hiring processes in certain circumstances, and there have been some reported prosecutions in the Solicitor's Disciplinary Tribunal (see below). Whilst there is little in the way of guidance on lateral hiring and the application of the principles specifically, those involved in recruitment (and partners considering moving) should refresh and remind themselves of the SRA Principles and Code (as always) and check that they are complying with them.

Setting the scene

So who are the key stakeholders in the lateral hire process and what is the context in which the legal and regulatory rules should be considered?

- **The candidate/lateral hire:** The partner being recruited will be involved in providing information to the hiring firm, and most probably to a recruitment consultant. The partner will be bound by their confidentiality obligations as set out in the previous section, and of course also by regulatory duties.
- **The legacy firm:** If a partner leaves, the legacy firm needs to consider which client matters are continued and looked after, and who will

supervise and carry out the work. The legacy firm is entitled to enforce any restrictive covenants preventing the departing partner from taking particular clients with them, but where the legacy firm is no longer able to service the client's needs, it needs to consider the position carefully, and may well have to let the client go elsewhere (including taking a commercial view that restrictive covenants which would otherwise bite are waived in particular circumstances).

- **The hiring firm:** The new firm obviously has to comply with its own regulatory obligations and should also be cognizant of not inadvertently procuring confidential information from the prospective hire. In any event, following any hire, the hiring firm needs to consider onboarding carefully, such as in relation to post-hiring processes of cultural integration and training.
- **Non-lawyers involved in the recruitment process:** HR professionals, recruitment teams, and others in support departments (for instance, in finance) will likely be closely involved in the due diligence process. These individuals are also subject to SRA Principles, and a safeguard to their firm complying with its own obligations. They therefore need to be aware of what those obligations involve.

The due diligence process – how to avoid overstepping the mark

At its most basic, the due diligence process is about making sure the potential lateral hire is the right person for the role, that they have the skills the hiring firm believes they have, and that they are capable of building the practice needed. The information that the candidate themselves is actually able to provide is key evidence and data with which to make the assessments required.

The key risk area to consider is that certain information that may be useful in making these assessments may be information that should not be provided. For instance, client details, client rates, historical billings for clients etc., are all confidential (and client) information. The information that is requested therefore needs to be considered carefully.

As part of this, due diligence questionnaires or lateral hire questionnaires (or other forms that individuals are asked to fill in) need to be given careful consideration in relation to the information they are requesting. Those who interview and procure information also need to be trained as to what they are permitted to obtain. With careful thought, consideration, and preparation, it is perfectly possible to run a recruitment process without overstepping the mark. That said, with absent thinking and a lack of consideration, it is also perfectly possible (and easy) to overstep the mark.

A few practical points the hiring firm may want to consider by way of example are:

- The candidate is able to refer to information that is already in the public domain. This could include transactions that have been published in press releases or reported cases emerging out of litigation work where the individual is credited with leading teams/managing the litigation or transaction. Legal directories often list clients of individuals that could be referred to as they are already in the public domain (with, it is presumed, client consent).
- Rather than referring to a client by name, the candidate might be able to refer to clients generically, e.g. an international bank.
- The hiring firm should only give the candidate the information they need to, remembering the individual to whom that information is disclosed is a partner of, and owes duties to, another firm.
- The hiring firm should remind the candidate that they are expected to comply with both their legal obligations to their current firm (in particular, confidentiality obligations) and their regulatory obligations at all times through the process.

Pre-employment vetting

Be aware that background checks differ in different jurisdictions

The hiring firm will wish to carry out various background checks; these will of course include immigration (right to work) checks and regulatory approvals, and may also include social media, psychometric tests, and other tests or checks. It is very important to confirm in advance that the particular checks to be carried out are lawful in that jurisdiction – for instance, in Germany there are specific rules about what information can be taken from social media accounts.

Be aware of data protection issues

Pre-employment vetting, including asking for opinions about the candidate (whether to third parties or within the hiring firm's partner cohort) should be carried out with data protection laws in mind. Again, these will differ depending on the jurisdiction. In the UK, the hiring firm needs to comply with the Data Protection Act 2018 and the UK GDPR; in summary this means that generally these checks should only be carried out if necessary and proportionate. The candidate should also be informed that vetting is taking place through a privacy notice which should capture partner recruitment in the same way as it does employee recruitment. When the hiring firm sends out an email asking its partners for information on a potential hire, it should consider the implications of storing the replies which may contain personal information, such as opinions about the candidate. Aside from the hiring firm's GDPR obligations around storage of personal information, data which is processed regarding a third party (in this case a partner who may or may not be hired) could potentially come within any data subject access request (DSAR) subsequently made.

Be careful not to miss the real basics

This might include checking whether the candidate has the qualifications required to be a partner and practicing lawyer, and the right to work in the jurisdiction concerned.

Conflict checks – how to avoid breaching confidentiality obligations

The hiring firm will want to undertake conflict checks to ensure that any clients or client matters which the candidate would bring with them would not be subject to conflicts (whether legal or commercial). Of course, in line with previous sections in this chapter, a firm needs to be comfortable that the information being provided is done so in accordance with confidentiality and regulatory obligations. Is it confidential? Does the current firm know it is being provided? Does the client know, and do they consent, to it being provided? At a practical level, hiring firms need to manage and carefully consider confidentiality obligations in any conflict checks which are carried out.

Integration issues

Confidential information

Once the candidate has made the decision to leave their legacy firm and join the hiring firm as a new partner, they might serve a notice period. During that time, the legacy firm will want to ensure that it's not just confidential client information that is protected, but also other propriety information such as knowhow and precedents. Departing partners should be reminded not to take such information.

Where there is concern that information might have been taken, a partner could be asked for confirmations, and to return any information. Further steps could be taken as appropriate in the circumstances.

To avoid any issues arising, as noted above, hiring firms should remind the candidate when going through the recruitment process that they should not provide any confidential information, whether that is knowhow and precedents or client confidential information, which has not been authorized by the legacy firm/the client (as appropriate).

Value of restrictive covenants

The value of restrictive covenants in lateral hire moves varies depending on jurisdiction. In the US, for example, restrictive covenants are very rare, but they are more common in Europe, the Middle East and Asia Pacific, and very common in the UK. Restrictive covenants are designed to protect the legacy firm's business after the partner has joined the new firm. In the UK, restrictive covenants that prevent the partner from competing, say, within a certain radius of the firm, are more commonly seen in smaller firms and perhaps more rarely in larger firms. Far more common are restrictive covenants that seek to preclude the partner from soliciting or dealing with particular clients, albeit that their enforcement requires both careful legal and commercial consideration.

Exaggeration by lateral hires

Exaggerated claims in CVs or other documentation during the recruitment process should obviously be avoided.

Embellishing or exaggerating in CVs came into sharp focus in 2021, when a former city law firm partner was struck off the roll of solicitors by the Solicitor's Disciplinary Tribunal.[5] In that case, the Tribunal found that the solicitor had made exaggerated claims relating to billing figures during one lateral move, which were then repeated two years' later during a second lateral move. The Tribunal found that the SRA's allegation of dishonesty was proven against that individual. The harm caused by this particular misconduct was entirely foreseeable. The hiring firm had incurred significant expense in the recruitment exercise in which misleading documents were supplied, and the harm to the profession caused by an experienced and successful solicitor dishonestly providing misleading information in order to secure personal advancement was very serious.

In addition to regulatory breach, the hiring firm may well want to consider the option of expelling the lateral hire from the firm in circumstances where they have provided information that they knew was incorrect, and it was done for personal gain.

Key rules of the road

To conclude, here are some key rules of the road for a successful lateral hiring process:

- Ensure there is a full process in place from the start when considering lateral hiring, from first approach (whether through a recruitment agency or directly) right through to onboarding and the integration process.
- Ensure that everyone involved, including members of the HR and recruitment teams, understands the legal, ethical and regulatory risks behind the process which they manage.
- Explain the full process to the candidate.
- Don't assume basics are covered – make sure the candidate has the appropriate documentation, including the relevant right to work and a practicing certificate, depending on the jurisdiction.
- Once the lateral hire is onboard, make sure that they understand the hiring firm's policies and procedures such as money laundering, bribery, and "know your client" procedures, and that they receive the appropriate training for managing risks within the firm.

References

1 Decipher investigative intelligence conduct due diligence helping law firms with their lateral hiring process, https://decipherglobal.com/what-we-do/.

2 Solicitors Regulation Authority, Principles, 25 November 2019, www.sra.org.uk/solicitors/standards-regulations/principles/.

3 Solicitors Regulation Authority, Code of Conduct for Solicitors, RELs and RFLs, 25 November 2019, www.sra.org.uk/solicitors/standards-regulations/code-conduct-solicitors/.

4 Solicitors Regulation Authority, Code of Conduct for Firms, 25 November 2019, www.sra.org.uk/solicitors/standards-regulations/code-conduct-firms/.

5 *Solicitors Regulatory Authority v. Tracey Ann Sheenan* Case No. 11944-2019, www.solicitorstribunal.org.uk/sites/default/files-sdt/11944.2019.Sheehan%20%282%29.pdf.

Chapter 16:
Culture matters – a new era for law firm risk management

By Jessica Clay, partner, Iain Miller, partner, and Lucinda Soon, professional support lawyer, Kingsley Napley

Regulatory risk management in law firms has traditionally focused on ensuring appropriate and adequate systems, processes, and controls are in place and that they operate effectively. This requirement was first formulated in the Solicitors Regulation Authority's (SRA) Code of Conduct 2007 under Rule 5, which placed a duty on firms to evidence such arrangements, encompassing *"all systems, procedures, processes, and methods of organization"*.[1] Chapter seven of the SRA Handbook 2011 positioned these arrangements as mandatory outcomes. Firms were required to *"have a clear and effective governance structure and reporting lines"*[2] (Outcome 7.1) and *"effective systems and controls in place"*[3] (Outcome 7.2). These remain core duties, set out as standards, within paragraph 2.1 of the SRA Code of Conduct for Firms (Code for Firms),[4] effective from November 2019, and their importance is emphasized in various places within the current SRA Standards and Regulations, not only in the Code for Firms, but also in the SRA Enforcement Strategy:

> *"We will usually take action against a firm alone, or in addition to taking action against an individual, where there is a breach of the code of conduct for firms or of our other requirements. For example... when the events demonstrate a failure which relates to the culture, systems, supervision arrangements or processes for which the firm, as a whole, should be held accountable."*[5]

The requirement for firms to have adequate systems and controls in place to identify, monitor, and manage risk is therefore well established. However, it has become increasingly apparent to both the SRA and those involved in law firm risk management that the effective operation of business systems and governance arrangements relies on the collective understanding and behaviors of people within a firm to comply with those arrangements; simply having a gold standard set of processes, policies, and procedures is not enough if they are not followed and understood implicitly. This raises the question of the effectiveness of risk management, and the role that law firm culture has to play within this context.

Several high profile prosecutions brought by the SRA, notably *Solicitors Regulation Authority v. James and Others* (2018) EWHC 3058 (Admin), demonstrate the damaging consequences of poor workplace culture on solicitors' mental health and the ensuing regulatory risks that can arise.[6] Notably, these cases generated significant criticism towards the SRA for pursuing allegations solely against the individuals concerned, despite their conduct taking place within a law firm culture that was acknowledged to be toxic and unsupportive.[7] In parallel to rising mental health concerns, the SRA has also received increased reports of bullying and harassment in legal workplaces, sparked by the #Metoo movement. Between 2017 and 2018, the SRA received 70 complaints about sexual harassment in the workplace, many of which related to law firm working environments.[8] Reports have continued in subsequent years.[9] Against this backdrop, there have been several developments over recent years that demonstrate not only the SRA's increased focus on ethical culture, but also its endeavors to extend its gaze in the direction of the firms and entities it regulates.

Ethical culture under the spotlight

A year after the High Court delivered its judgment in the case of *Solicitors Regulation Authority v. James and others*, the SRA published its new Standards and Regulations 2019. While the timing is not remarkable – in that work had been underway for some time to overhaul the SRA Handbook 2011 – the temporal context within which the Standards and Regulations were born is noteworthy. This was a time when issues pertaining to poor workplace culture had not only started to surface, but were also being met with growing disconcertion across the profession. It is therefore unsurprising that several references are made to ethical culture within the Standards and Regulations. The introduction preceding the Code for Firms expresses that the standards contained therein *"aim to create and maintain the right culture and environment for the delivery of competent and ethical legal services to clients"*.[10] This message is reinforced within the SRA Enforcement Strategy, which stipulates the SRA's aim to *"promote a culture in which ethical values and behaviors are embedded"*.[11] The explicit inclusion of culture is significant. While the SRA offered little guidance to firms at the time the Standards and Regulations came into force in November 2019, in respect of what a good culture might comprise, it marked an important starting point.

Then, in the summer of 2021, the SRA launched its thematic review on workplace culture. The review analyzed responses to a survey of more than 200 solicitors working in law firms, together with follow-up interviews with participants willing to discuss their answers in more detail and in-depth interviews with 12 law firms of varying sizes. The output of the thematic review was a report published in February 2022,[12] along with new guidance to firms on the workplace environment and risks of failing to protect and support colleagues.[13]

The purpose of the guidance is made clear; to set out *"the main standards that apply to law firms and those responsible for their culture and the systems in place within them"*.[14] The guidance also offers clarity in relation to the SRA's expectations in relation to systems and controls, supervision and competence, and fairness and inclusion. Firms are reminded of their obligation under paragraph 2 of the Code for Firms: *"A failure by firms to put in place and effectively implement systems to support and protect staff will increase the risk that individuals or firms breach one or more of our other regulatory requirements."*

Firms are equally reminded of the requirement under paragraph 4, to ensure proper systems are in place to supervise clients' matters and regularly monitor and assess employees' workloads, capacity, and competence. The SRA also states it expects firms to have in place *"systems and culture so that staff can confidently raise concerns and be supported if they are experiencing problems"*. This expectation on firms also aligns with subsequent guidance published by the SRA specifically on sexual misconduct ('SRA Guidance: Sexual Misconduct', 1 September 2022), which states that the SRA expect *"firms to foster a culture of zero tolerance of sexual misconduct, where staff feel that they can speak up freely and report matters to their firm and to us"*.

Finally, the guidance on workplace environment reinforces the fundamental ethical tenets contained within the SRA Principles, notably Principle 6 and the duty on firms to act in a way that encourages equality, diversity, and inclusion, and sets out its expectation on firms *"to treat all of their employees fairly and with dignity"*. This is stated to include creating an environment that is inclusive and free from discrimination, bullying, harassment, or victimization. Notably, in respect of this expectation, the SRA guidance refers to Principle 6 and paragraph 1.2 of the Code for Firms, which imposes an obligation on firms not to abuse their position by taking unfair advantage of clients or others.[15] Indeed, there is currently no more explicit an obligation in the SRA Codes of Conduct than these requirements. This leads us onto the most recent development in the SRA's endeavors to regulate ethical workplace culture.

Within a month of the SRA publishing its suite of resources and new guidance on workplace culture, it launched a consultation on proposed changes to its rules and Codes of Conduct to address issues relating to wellbeing and unfair treatment at work.[16] Specifically, the addition of a new provision is proposed in respect of both Codes in the following terms:

Code for Individuals: "*You treat colleagues fairly and with respect. You do not bully or harass them or discriminate unfairly against them. You challenge behavior that does not meet this standard.*"[17]

Code for Firms: "*You treat those who work for and with you fairly and with respect, and do not bully or harass them or discriminate unfairly against them. You require your managers and employees to meet this standard, and you challenge behavior that does not meet this standard.*"[18]

The link to culture was made clear by the SRA's General Counsel, Juliet Oliver, when the consultation was launched:

> "*A poor workplace culture can not only affect wellbeing, with all the distress and concern that brings, but also ethical behavior, competence, and ultimately the standard of service received by clients. It's timely that, further to our recent thematic review and guidance, we consult on new rules that explicitly spell out what we expect from the firms and individuals we regulate.*"[19]

Despite the underlying intention of the SRA Standards and Regulations to remove rules and increase flexibility on those whom it regulates,[20] the proposed rule change cuts against the grain by placing an additional express obligation on the regulated community. Such a decision is unlikely to have been made lightly, and demonstrates a clear intention by the SRA to regulate the workplace and work-based relationships. Its current approach to do this has been limited to reliance upon the SRA Principles, which are wide ranging and cover similar territory at a higher level. These include an obligation to act "*in a way that encourages equality, diversity and inclusion*" (Principle 6) and to "*act in a way that upholds public trust and confidence in the solicitors' profession and in legal services provided by authorized persons*" (Principle 2).[21] However, the dangers of this approach are evident from the Divisional Court's decision in *Beckwith v. Solicitors Regulation Authority* (2020) EWHC 3231 (Admin). In that case the Court was of the view that any breach of a Principle had to be anchored in a provision of the Code itself. The proposed new rules will effectively address the lacuna the SRA faced following *Beckwith*.

The rule change will require the approval of the Legal Services Board, so the changes will not come into force until the end of 2022, at the earliest.

However, it seems unlikely that any response will cause the SRA to fundamentally shift its approach. As and when the changes are implemented, they will represent a harder-edged enforcement approach to law firm ethical culture than the SRA is able to adopt within its current regulatory framework. Indeed, the SRA acknowledges its current Codes of Conduct *"do not include an explicit requirement to treat people fairly at work, requiring us to rely on [the] wider Principles and Standards"*.[22] The additional rules will thus strengthen the SRA's ability to regulate and enforce against poor ethical culture within its regulated community. However, they are also anticipated to raise several challenges, as explored below.

Assessments of unfair treatment

The scope of the proposed new rules – to treat colleagues and employees fairly and with respect and not to bully, or harass them, or discriminate unfairly against them – is wide. Not only is it wide, it concerns behaviors that by their nature involve often complex emotional and subjective elements. Feelings of being treated unfairly and without respect may vary widely depending on person and context. While there will be serious and unambiguous circumstances concerning bullying, harassment, and discrimination, where behaviors may easily and objectively be viewed to breach the new rules, there are likely to be more circumstances where, on an objective assessment, the outcome is not so clear-cut. This raises the question of how the SRA will assess reports it receives concerning these behaviors and the evidence it will seek. Its guidance on workplace environments points towards possible factors it will consider, including:

- *"[A] pattern of the abuse of authority by senior staff that has been left unchecked by the firm*
- *[A] complaint of discrimination, victimisation or harassment not dealt with by the firm in a prompt and fair manner*
- *[C]omplaints of bullying raised with the firm over a period of time involving a number of staff and inadequate action taken by the firm as a result; or evidence that the incidents had not been brought to light sooner because of the firm's culture and/or inadequate reporting and disciplinary procedure*
- *[A] firm pressurising staff to withdraw their complaints*
- *[I]neffective systems and controls, including failure to supervise or support staff, leading to serious competence or performance issues or delivery failures*
- *[T]he imposition of wholly unreasonable workloads or targets."*[23]

However, the position is less clear where there is no evidence of abuse of authority or of bullying, discrimination, or harassment, but where an employee considers they have nonetheless been treated unfairly or without respect. This may arise with the imposition of "wholly unreasonable workloads or targets". However, this situation presents difficulties for law firms where, save for objectively onerous targets being imposed, perception is always subjective. For instance, one employee may consider their workload to be wholly unreasonable while another may perceive the same workload to be reasonable. Whether a person feels unfairly treated or disrespected will depend on their perception of the situation, which will in turn be influenced by their personal situation and circumstances and potentially other factors including contextual ones, such as how they perceive relationships at work and the support they receive, or do not receive.

Concurrent employment claims

Another challenge concerns the overlap between the proposed new rules and claims falling within the remit of the Employment Tribunal, including those relating to the Equality Act 2010. Where bullying, harassment, and discrimination at work relates to, or arises because of, a protected characteristic under this Act, an unlawful discrimination claim may be pursued. Where this is the case, a breach of the Equality Act 2010 will likely be of sufficient seriousness to automatically result in a breach of the SRA's new rules. Notably, even before these rules come into effect, such a contravention would bring into play a breach of Principle 2, to act in a way that upholds public trust and confidence in the solicitors' profession and in the provision of legal services. However, the new rules raise several questions in terms of how they will operate alongside employment claims.

First, it is unclear how the SRA will consider situations that involve parallel employment proceedings; for example, whether it would commence an investigation while proceedings are ongoing. This would be in line with the SRA's general approach in relation to parallel investigations:

> *"[O]ur work will continue unless there is a real risk of prejudice to the regulated person or to other proceedings… There is no double jeopardy arising from parallel proceedings (Ashraf v. General Dental Council [2014] EWHC 2618 (Admin)). This is because the character and purpose of civil, criminal and regulatory proceedings are different."*[24]

Thus, where a matter reported to the SRA involves ongoing civil or criminal proceedings, the SRA decides whether to stay its proceedings based on a number of factors, including the need to take immediate action to prevent harm to clients or others, and the stage of any parallel proceedings – whether they are only contemplated, ongoing, or near conclusion. It is probable the SRA will adopt a similar approach in respect of potential breaches of the new rules; however, this is likely to result in a lot more reports being received by the SRA, alleging unfair treatment at work, and this will require greater internal resource and may result in more investigations being undertaken.

Following on from this, a second issue arises that concerns the reporting of such matters to the SRA. Currently, the SRA is less likely to be concerned about proceedings that are being defended before the Employment Tribunal, where the findings are yet to be determined. However, under the proposed new rules, ongoing employment claims for unfair treatment and discrimination would require prompt reporting to the SRA under the reporting obligations set out in the Codes of Conduct, regardless of whether such proceedings result in an adverse finding.[25]

Thirdly, the new rules may inadvertently lead to the SRA adopting a quasi-employment claims role, whereby claimants may be able to choose not to pursue claims before the Employment Tribunal (instead, seeking to bring the matter to the SRA's attention) to avoid the costs associated with such action or where they have been unfairly treated but not in relation to a protected characteristic under the Equality Act 2010. The remedies available to claimants will of course differ, and the potential of SRA prosecution will not provide a claimant with damages for their unfair treatment; however, it might be viewed as an easier, no-cost route to right the wrong they have experienced.

Where the SRA draws the line between reports that warrant regulatory intervention and those that may be more appropriately resolved via civil means alone will need to be carefully considered. This will necessarily involve future guidance to the profession setting out the factors the SRA will take into account in making its decision to ensure its actions are proportionate, reasonable, and consistent.

Challenging behavior that does not meet the standard

The new rules will also impose a positive obligation on both individuals and firms to *"challenge behavior that does not meet this standard"*. In theory, this requirement makes good sense. However, difficulties arise in the interpretation of this obligation and how it would apply in real life scenarios. For example, if a junior solicitor witnesses what they perceive to be inappropriate behavior by a partner towards a junior colleague during an after-work event, they would be obligated under the proposed new rule to challenge that behavior. This raises questions as to what challenging the behavior would necessarily entail and if in such a situation, a junior solicitor would have the confidence to do so. What if the situation, as the solicitor perceives it from afar, is not as it appears, is mistaken, or is consensual between the relevant individuals? What steps should the solicitor take to satisfy themselves that this is behavior that requires challenging? If the behavior is indeed inappropriate, a solicitor who witnesses it and does nothing to challenge it would, under the new rules, be breaching their obligations under the Code.

From a firm's perspective, the new rules will place a heavier burden to not only have relevant policies, processes, and controls in place to prevent unethical behaviors, but to also challenge the behaviors of managers and employees that do not meet the expected standards. This may involve taking a harder line against certain individuals or groups of individuals, who have previously been able to bypass processes because of their seniority or level of profitability. Ensuring ethical values are demonstrated, and unethical ones are challenged, across the board may require a deep cultural shift, one that must be supported and rigorously upheld and followed by the senior leaders.

Personal and professional boundaries

Finally, the proposed new rules raise prevailing issues in respect of the SRA's regulatory reach into matters within an individual's private life. Indeed, the SRA's consultation document makes specific reference to the new rules having a wide remit:

> *"Our proposal is that the obligation should go beyond staff in a formal employment relationship, to include others with whom solicitors and firms regularly work closely, such as contractors, consultants, barristers and experts who may be instructed by the firm. This is reflected in the use of the term 'colleagues' in the draft standard.*
> *"Although the obligation is principally intended to cover behavior at work (whether in an office or remotely), in our view it would also cover behavior outside the workplace or direct delivery of legal services as well. This is where behavior is in the context of a relationship between colleagues rather than a purely personal relationship."*[26]

The SRA is not covert in its rationale behind these paragraphs, referencing the case of *Beckwith v. Solicitors Regulation Authority* (2020) EWHC 3231

(Admin) in which the Divisional Court confirmed that the public would expect members of the profession to treat junior colleagues with respect. While in that case, allegations could not be proved in the absence of a breach of a specific rule in the Code, the proposed new rules would provide the SRA with the hook it would need if such a case arises in the future. What remains less clear is how wide the impact will be in relation to other situations where, for example, inappropriate communications and social media use in one's personal life are alleged to constitute unfair and disrespectful treatment to colleagues, being all persons employed or instructed by the firm. The new rules therefore significantly extend the SRA's reach into the private lives of its regulated community.

Conclusion

It seems unlikely that responses to the consultation will fundamentally shift the SRA's intention to introduce greater requirements on individuals and firms to treat colleagues fairly and with respect. While these ethical tenets of behavior are enshrined within the overarching SRA Principles, the new rules will emphasize further that such behaviors will not be tolerated. Clearly, little disagreement to the new requirements can be made substantively; there can never be any justification for treating colleagues unfairly or disrespectfully, nor should anyone be subjected to bullying, harassment, or discrimination at work. The change that awaits lies in the practical shift that law firms and those involved in law firm risk management must now make towards ensuring culture is managed effectively, alongside systems, processes, and controls.

As a bare minimum, firms should ensure policies are in place, which are reviewed and updated periodically, to guide employees on expected behaviors at work and the reporting mechanisms to challenge inappropriate and unethical behaviors they witness. Monitoring compliance with these policies and procedures will be the greater challenge and will likely require an assessment of the culture of the firm to remove any barriers that exist which might prevent open and honest communications. Encouraging an openness to challenge unethical behaviors at work has certainly taken on a new imperative and this will require a systemic shift in approach. A firm's culture is often reflected in the behaviors of senior people, and it is the senior members of firms who will need to not only talk the talk but also walk the walk for cultural change to take place and to remain effective. In addition to investing in firm-wide training on the obligations under the new standards and the reporting requirements that apply alongside it, reviewing key performance indicators and seeking to reward those who display ethical behaviors will also help to create a culture where the new standards are more likely to be met.

References

1 Solicitors Regulation Authority, Code of Conduct, 2007, Rule 5.
2 Solicitors Regulation Authority, Code of Conduct, 2011, www.sra.org.uk/solicitors/handbook/code/, Chapter 7, Outcome 7.1.
3 Solicitors Regulation Authority, Code of Conduct 2011, www.sra.org.uk/solicitors/handbook/code/, Chapter 7, Outcome 7.2.
4 Solicitors Regulation Authority, Code of Conduct for Firms, 25 November 2019, www.sra.org.uk/solicitors/standards-regulations/code-conduct-firms/, paragraph 2.1.
5 Solicitors Regulation Authority, Enforcement Strategy, (first published: February 2019; updated: January 2022), www.sra.org.uk/sra/corporate-strategy/sra-enforcement-strategy/, Section 3.
6 See also: *Solicitors Regulation Authority v. De Vita, Platt & Scott* (SDT 11696-2017).
7 See for example: Letter from the Law Society, Junior Lawyers Division, to the CEO of the SRA concerning recent decisions of the SDT regarding junior lawyers, 13 February 2019, www.communities.lawsociety.org.uk/Uploads/n/s/k/JLD-letter-to-SRA-13-Feb-2019.pdf.
8 SRA Report: Upholding Professional Standards, www.sra.org.uk/sra/research-publications/upholding-professional-standards-2017-2018/.
9 SRA Report: Upholding Professional Standards, www.sra.org.uk/sra/research-publications/2018-19-review/upholding-professional-standards/; www.sra.org.uk/globalassets/documents/annual-reports/upholding-professional-standards.pdf.
10 Solicitors Regulation Authority, Code of Conduct for Firms, 25 November 2019, www.sra.org.uk/solicitors/standards-regulations/code-conduct-firms/.
11 *Ibid* 5, Section 1.1.
12 SRA Workplace Culture Thematic Review, 7 February 2022, www.sra.org.uk/sra/research-publications/workplace-culture-thematic-review/.
13 SRA Guidance: Workplace environment: risks of failing to protect and support colleagues, 7 February 2022, www.sra.org.uk/solicitors/guidance/workplace-environment/.
14 *Ibid*.
15 *Ibid* 4, paragraph 1.2.
16 SRA Consultation: Rule changes on health and wellbeing at work, 4 March 2022, www.sra.org.uk/sra/consultations/consultation-listing/health-wellbeing-profession/.
17 *Ibid*.
18 *Ibid*.
19 SRA News Release: New rules on health and wellbeing would help protect clients and the public, 4 March 2022, www.sra.org.uk/sra/news/press/wellbeing-consultation/.

20 See chapter 17 for more on this.

21 Solicitors Regulation Authority, SRA Principles, 25 November 2019, www.sra.org.uk/solicitors/standards-regulations/principles/.

22 *Ibid* 16.

23 *Ibid* 13.

24 SRA Guidance: Parallel Investigations, updated 25 November 2019, www.sra.org.uk/solicitors/guidance/investigations-parallel/.

25 Solicitors Regulation Authority, Code of Conduct for Solicitors, RELs and RFLs, 2019, www.sra.org.uk/solicitors/standards-regulations/code-conduct-solicitors/, paragraphs 7.7 and 7.8; Solicitors Regulation Authority, Code of Conduct for Firms, 2019, www.sra.org.uk/solicitors/standards-regulations/code-conduct-firms/, paragraphs 3.9 and 3.10.

26 *Ibid* 16.

Chapter 17:
Innovation and the opportunities in flexible regulation

By Jonathon Bray, director, Jonathon Bray Limited

"Humans are allergic to change. They love to say, 'We've always done it this way'."
Grace Hopper[1]

"Ships in harbor are safe, but that is not what ships are built for."
John A. Shedd[2]

This chapter explores the commercial opportunities for law firms and individual lawyers presented by principles-based regulation (PBR) and steps towards deregulation of the legal profession; increased market forces encouraged by, amongst others, the Legal Services Board and Competition and Markets Authority; liberalization of the profession under the Legal Services Act 2007; and increased anti-money laundering burdens on firms.

It is not intended to be a guide to innovation. That is not something you can learn too much about in a regulatory text. Instead, this chapter aims to give a broad overview of a regulatory framework which, increasingly, gives lawyers and law firms the space in which to be innovators.

Regulation-led Innovation

For well over a decade, the Solicitors Regulation Authority (SRA) has pursued and embraced a form of principles-based regulation (PBR). PBR drops most black and white written rules in favor of more ambiguous, and yet inherently flexible, outcomes.

Some see this as adding complexity and ambiguity to regulation, making compliance with the rules much more complex. To others, the freedom presents an opportunity for the regulated to pursue business activities in a way that suits them, rather than having to adhere to strict prescriptive rules.

The SRA explicitly extols the flexibility virtues of PBR, encouraging firms to innovate and to improve client service. In fact, as a regulator, the

SRA takes the traditional concept of PBR much more seriously. It takes a proactive approach to innovation in the legal sector. This is driven in no small part by the fact that the SRA sits underneath the Legal Services Board (LSB), which is responsible for driving implementation of the Legal Services Act 2007. More on that later.

One of the SRA's core strategic priorities for 2020-2023 is to "*actively support the adoption of legal technology and other innovation that helps to meet the needs of the public, business community, regulated entities and the economy*".[3] This elevates innovation to the same level as maintaining professional standards of solicitors.

In 2021, the regulator published a report produced by the University of Oxford (Technology and Innovation in Legal Services), finding that "*Legal services providers see technology and innovation as a way to improve the quality and efficiency of service delivery, and to satisfy unmet legal needs*".[4]

It has also set up a "regulatory sandbox" called SRA Innovate. Under this scheme, law firms, and those thinking about entering the legal services market, are able to go to the regulator with new and non-traditional business models. If the SRA deems that the proposals meet its definition of innovation and have the potential to benefit the public, the candidate will be allowed to test out the proposal in a live, but tightly controlled, environment. Those that make it out the other side of the sandbox potentially find themselves with a real USP.

A further example is the SRA's recent "unbundling" pilot, which is being run through the SRA Innovate scheme to address the "*substantial unmet legal need among individual consumers and small businesses*".[5] Unbundling refers to breaking down a full legal service into its constituent parts, with lawyers providing clients with one or more parts of the service whilst expressly excluding others. For the client, this has the potential benefit that they get legal help where it's needed, whilst able to self-serve where a DIY approach may well suffice. There are clear regulatory (not to mention insurance) risks, but the SRA is plainly keen to encourage firms to think about whether unbundling is a route that could benefit their clients and indeed open up new markets.

CMA report

The SRA's active approach to innovation has its roots in a 2016 investigation into legal services by the Competition and Markets Authority,[6] which found that a large proportion of potential clients preferred to instruct a non-regulated business over a profession. The CMA concluded that this was due to the market not operating as it should. Either legal services were so expensive that they were inaccessible to individuals and small businesses, or there was a perception that they were.

This led to the SRA Transparency Rules, which have been mirrored by other legal regulators. The Transparency Rules require firms (in a distinctly non-PBR manner) to publicize prescribed information about price, service levels, and regulatory protection.[7]

The SRA wants firms to go beyond the floor of transparency compliance and make legal services more accessible to individuals and small businesses. The regulator included "access to legal services"[8] as a key risk to the profession in its annual Risk Outlook document, placing this category of risk on a par with theft of client money, cyber security, and money laundering. The rationale being that:

> *"Around 35 percent of people with a legal need try to resolve it on their own without any legal or professional help. And, 50 percent of small businesses try to resolve their legal needs alone."*[9]

This same thinking has also led the SRA to make regulatory data available to third party price comparison engines as a way to improve access to legal services.

Deregulation-led innovation

The past decade has seen a distinct move towards deregulation in the SRA environment. Take, for example, the removal of what was formerly known as the "separate business rule", which effectively prohibited practicing lawyers from participating in other professional businesses and unregulated legal services. With the rule relaxed, solicitors find that they can now own and operate businesses that sit alongside their regulated legal activities, such as unregulated will writing, fiduciary services, accountancy and the like. The SRA appears to have struck the right balance. Regulation does not restrain a solicitor's trade outside of the main SRA remit, and client protections are still present under the Codes of Conduct; referrals must be in the client's best interests and the solicitor's interest in those external businesses must be made explicit.

We can also see an element of deregulation under the 2019 Codes of Conduct themselves – now under the banner of SRA Standards and Regulations (StaRs).[10]

Since 2019, solicitors have been able to practice as solicitors in unregulated law firms. Before this was permitted, solicitors could not directly provide legal services to the public outside the law firm (or sole practice) environment. The situation meant that all sorts of awkward and cumbersome structures were put in place in unregulated businesses to allow qualified solicitors to provide advice to the public. For example, in-house solicitors could advise non-lawyers on the law and its practical application, that legal advice being passed on to the end client, but the lawyers were not allowed to directly advise clients.

Under the new rules, solicitors with a practicing certificate can practice in unregulated businesses. They can hold themselves out as solicitors, they don't need cumbersome and expensive professional indemnity insurance, and clients get the benefit of a solicitor's quality advice. At the same time, clients have the confidence that the solicitor acting for them is regulated in their own individual capacity just as any other practicing solicitor.

The limit to this flexibility is that non-regulated law firms are not permitted to provide any of the "reserved activities" under the Legal Services Act 2007,[11] namely rights of audience, conduct of litigation, reserved instrument activities, probate activities, and administering oaths. However, that still leaves significant areas of the law that do not technically need to be provided through a fully regulated law firm. Commercial law, will writing, estate administration, employment, and pre-litigation can fall into the category.

Some law firms have chosen to take this a step further by hiving off parts of their practice into the unregulated environment. For example, a firm that specializes in probate could hive off all of the non-reserved activities (will writing, LPA drafting, and estate administration, for example) into an unregulated entity with a lower cost base, whilst retaining the reserved work (obtaining the grant of probate and property work) under the SRA regime.

And let's not forget the role of "freelance" self-employed solicitors. Again stemming from the SRA Standards and Regulations, this new breed of sole trader is able to act largely outside of the SRA framework (again, only really regulated in a personal capacity) whilst being able to provide all of the reserved activities. There are of course practical limitations, notably the availability of insurance, but it does potentially open up new ways for solicitors to organize themselves, such as the Chambers-style collection of freelancers all sharing the overhead of a common back office and support function, essentially being self-employed.

The past decade has seen the rise and rise of consultant-led law firms in a self-employed fee share model. Consultant solicitors work under the umbrella of a "back office" regulated law firm, which provides them with the tools that they need to do their job and the insurance and compliance systems required by the regulators, in exchange for a slice of the fees that they generate. Once limited to the realm of partner-level city lawyers, the model is now proving itself in other areas of the profession.

One of the peculiarities of the Legal Services Act is that it effectively creates a competitive environment between the front line regulators. For example, the Council for Licensed Conveyancers (CLC) (which is often seen, rightly or wrongly, as a friendlier regulator with a preferential insurance set up) has actively touted for SRA-regulated firms to switch over to CLC regulation. The SRA has even made that process easier, by removing the requirement for firms to put themselves into run-off when making the switch. This all adds another opportunity for law firms to rethink how to best structure their operations.

Other external factors

Some might argue that, rather than seeing evidence of deregulation, on the front lines there is an ever increasing regulatory burden for lawyers and law firms. Take, for example, the rules around anti-money laundering, which, with every new Directive and set of regulations, have become more burdensome and require more controls at the firm-wide compliance level whilst at the same time putting more emphasis on professional judgement of risk.

Since January 2020, even more legal practice areas have been brought into the realms of anti-money laundering compliance through the broadening of the definition of "tax adviser" and "trust and company service provider". Under the expanded Money Laundering Regulations,[12] litigators, non-transactional commercial and employment lawyers, and those acting as professional trustees have to carefully weigh up whether they are caught by the Money Laundering Regulations. If they are, or they treat themselves as caught for fear of getting it wrong, the compliance burden increases significantly. With more regulation comes the incentive to make areas of compliance – like client due diligence and risk assessment – more efficient. We have seen wide-scale adoption of anti-money laundering e-verification systems using sophisticated technology including biometrics, passport validation, sanctions checks, and international searches. These systems allow firms to onboard and monitor their clients with confidence, even when they do not physically meet them or see original identification documents.[13]

Of course, we couldn't write this chapter without mentioning the COVID-19 pandemic, which itself has brought a driving force of technological innovation in law firms. Some say that 2020 saw many years' worth of innovation in the space of months. Having to work from home, take meetings over the internet, not see clients face-to-face, whilst at the same time having to supervise juniors' work and maintain organizational culture led to an unprecedented switch to legal technology. It could be argued that COVID-19 made technology such as video conferencing and case management systems a necessity rather than nice-to-have, and made vague long-term plans to "go paperless" a pressing matter.

Ten years of ABSs – evolution rather than revolution?

What of the Legal Services Act 2007? This landmark legislation was the culmination of the early 2000s Clementi Review, which was characterized by introducing the specter of "Tesco law", the Doomsday scenario where mighty consumer brands squeeze the smaller incumbents out of the market. (Think high street fishmongers having no option but to work at the in-store fish counter.) As it happens, this has not come to pass, despite significant new players entering the market (The Co-operative, AA, Saga, and BT to name a few). Perhaps this says a lot about the legal profession's ability to adapt, survive, and innovate to avoid being eaten by the bigger fish. Although it is probably fair to recognize that big brands have not shown a huge appetite for legal services… yet. What chance would traditional firms have if Amazon, Google, and Facebook, with their infinite marketing budgets and data-driven insight into consumer behavior, suddenly showed an interest?

The Legal Services Act has fundamentally changed the framework of legal regulation. The main headline for the purposes of innovation was the introduction of licensed bodies, also known as alternative business structures (ABSs). Around 13 percent of all regulated law firms are now ABSs.[14]

The LSB, the oversight regulator, is tasked with implementing the Act and it is notable that its approach appears to prioritize the Section 1 regulatory objective of "promoting competition"[15] above all other regulatory objectives in Section 1 of the Act. More competition in the market, so goes the argument, puts pressure on law firms to innovate in order to avoid being left behind, with the ultimate beneficiary of these market forces being the end user, the client or "consumer".

There is no doubt that ABSs have made previously unthinkable law firm structures entirely possible, which in turn opens the door of opportunity. This is a profession where, not too long ago, the only form of advertising permitted was a brass name plate. Now, law firms are allowed to float stock exchanges, raise huge sums from investors for marketing campaigns, aggressive growth through acquisition, and funding litigation.

It's fair to say that the majority of early ABSs were mostly conservative. Non-lawyer spouses being added as managers and owners, finance directors becoming partners, and obvious tie-ups between claims management companies and solicitors to skirt the referral fee ban.

The regulators expected to see a rush towards multi-disciplinary practices, where lawyers, accountants, insurance brokers, wealth management, and other professionals would team up to create a one-stop shop with cross-selling opportunities. This model has not been as widely adopted as anticipated. Perhaps the most notable example is the "Big Four" firms, who now offer legal services in addition to their core audit, tax, and consultancy services – a model that has been replicated by some mid-tier accountancy firms.

The possibilities of ABS structures are almost entirely limited by the imagination – all sorts of innovative models and joint ventures between lawyers and non-lawyers have been born out of this flexibility.

ABSs allow a regulated law firm to sit within an otherwise unregulated group structure, benefiting from a parent company's access to clients, funding, people, and branding. One of the more popular models is a law firm "bolt-on", where a regulated firm sits underneath or to the side of a non-legal business. The core business then directs clients to the law firm and vice versa, in a symbiotic relationship. It is a proven way to provide added value to clients. Businesses that generate legal work can now capture those clients, rather than waving them off to a separate law firm.

We can expect to see more of these types of niche ABSs popping up. Think estate agents owning their own conveyancing firm, funeral directors offering probate services, and HR consultancies being able to advise on pension schemes. There is also significant scope for law schools to turn their legal advice clinics into ABSs – both as a training ground for future lawyers under the SQE route, and as a low cost legal service to address the unmet legal needs identified by the regulators.

The profession has also seen prominent investors and entrepreneurs, frustrated with delays and inefficiency in a "traditional" practice, asking whether they could do it better themselves. Non-lawyers bring a whole range of transferable skills and experience, and are often much better placed to improve systems, technology, workflows, culture, and client service. Essentially, the elements that are required to modernize the practice of law.

But one of the biggest drivers towards ABSs has to be the ability to attract both investment and human talent. No longer are law firms limited by the capital that the partners can afford to put into the pot. They are vehicles that are increasingly attractive to private equity and capital markets. Nor are they limited by the skills that lawyers can bring to the table; CEOs, HR directors, marketers, and finance professionals can all sit equally with lawyers as owners and managers.

Some critics say that this is an erosion of professionalism, although the counter to that is to point out that ABSs are regulated just like any other law firm and, in any event, lawyers do not have a monopoly on professionalism or ethics. But there is no doubt that the framework allows law firms to act in a way that is or like a modern commercial business rather than a traditional partner-led law firm. Whether that is a good or bad thing is entirely subjective.

Innovation is easier said than done

A word of caution. For all the talk of innovation in this chapter, innovation for the sake of it is probably a fool's errand. Lawyers could burn through countless billable hours and valuable resources chasing the beguiling tag of being an innovative practice. But there must surely be a clear commercial driver when one is seeking to be innovative. Those drivers might include maximizing efficiency, translating to cost reduction and fee maximization. Or maybe better client experiences, giving the firm a competitive edge and better reputation.

Make no mistake, change is hard. Whenever organizations try to implement new or exciting projects, there will always be push back. Change management, therefore, is as much the required skill when innovating a law firm as the innovation itself. New entrants to the market have an unfair advantage in having a blank canvas to work with.

Let's not pretend that innovation purely means having the latest technology and artificial intelligence. In the context of the legal profession, innovation might involve re-engineering a service, setting out proper workflows and process mapping to identify where the inefficiencies and bottlenecks are, where the clients get frustrated, and where team members could benefit from a clearer path. Often, innovation comes from being able to see a service from a different angle, for example from the client's perspective or that of the referrer. It might involve unbundling a service or marketing a firm in a new and exciting way. The law firms that were first to social media were at one time innovators.

There is also lots of opportunity for firms to develop their own intellectual property. Again, we are not just talking about technology, but also ways of working, developing strong brands, harnessing network effects, building referral networks, being early to emerging practice areas and so on. These are another way to add value into a legal business above and beyond selling time and knowledge. In some cases, the added value of innovation in and of itself will attract a premium price.

Many legal services suffer from inefficiency, delay, and in-built incentives to drag things out (here's looking at you, billable hour). The person to solve these problems will improve matters immeasurably for clients and will be rewarded handsomely. Conveyancing, commercial litigation, and wills are obvious candidates – but there are countless examples where a new approach, thinking "we don't have to do it this way", will result in true legal innovation.

References

1 Philip Schieber, "The Wit and Wisdom of Grace Hopper," in OCLC Newsletter, No. 167 (March/April 1987), www.cs.yale.edu/homes/tap/Files/hopper-wit.html.

2 Fred R. Shapiro, *The Yale Book of Quotations*, Yale University Press, New Haven, 2006.

3 SRA corporate strategy 2020 to 2023, www.sra.org.uk/sra/corporate-strategy/.

4 Mari Sako and Richard Parnham, *Technology and Innovation in Legal Services – Final Report for the Solicitors Regulation Authority*, with contributions from John Armour, Ian Rodgers, and Matthias Qian, University of Oxford, www.sra.org.uk/globalassets/documents/sra/research/chapter-1---technology-and-innovation-in-legal-services.pdf?version. The full report is recommended reading for anyone with an interest in this topic, and the executive summary can be found at https://bit.ly/3DmWvfe.

5 SRA News 11 October 2021: "Interested in unbundled services? Get involved in our pilot", www.sra.org.uk/sra/news/sra-update-97-unbundling/.

6 CMA – Legal Services Market Study Interim Report, 8 July 2016, https://assets.publishing.service.gov.uk/media/577f76daed915d622c0000ef/legal-services-market-study-interim-report.pdf.

7 Solicitors Regulation Authority, Transparency Rules, 25 November 2019, www.sra.org.uk/solicitors/standards-regulations/transparency-rules/.

8 SRA – Risk Outlook 2018/19, 25 July 2018, www.sra.org.uk/sra/research-publications/risk-outlook-2018-2019/.

9 *Ibid.*

10 Solicitors Regulation Authority, Standards and Regulations, 25 November 2019, www.sra.org.uk/solicitors/standards-regulations/.

11 Legal Services Act 2007, www.legislation.gov.uk/ukpga/2007/29/part/3/cross-heading/reserved-legal-activities, Section 12.

12 The Money Laundering, Terrorist Financing and Transfer of Funds (Information on the Payer) Regulations 2017, www.legislation.gov.uk/uksi/2017/692/contents/made

13 See chapter six for more information on anti-money laundering.
14 As of March 2022 there were 9,813 regulated law firms, SRA Breakdown of solicitor firms, www.sra.org.uk/sra/research-publications/regulated-community-statistics/data/solicitor_firms/, of which 1,312 were licensed bodies, SRA Search for a licensed body (ABS), www.sra.org.uk/solicitors/firm-based-authorisation/abs/abs-search.
15 Legal Services Act 2007, www.legislation.gov.uk/ukpga/2007/29/section/1, Section 1(1)(e).

About Globe Law and Business

Globe Law and Business was established in 2005. From the very beginning, we set out to create law books that are sufficiently high level to be of real use to the experienced professional, yet still accessible and easy to navigate. Most of our authors are drawn from Magic Circle and other top commercial firms, both in the United Kingdom and internationally.

Our titles are carefully produced, with the utmost attention paid to editorial, design and production processes. We hope this results in high-quality publications that are easy to read and a pleasure to own. Our titles are also available as ebooks, which are compatible with most desktop, laptop and tablet devices. In 2018 we expanded our portfolio to include journals and Special Reports, available both digitally and in hard copy format, and produced to the same high standards as our books.

In 2021, we were very pleased to announce the start of a new chapter for Globe Law and Business following the acquisition of law books under the imprint Ark Publishing. Our law firm management list is now significantly expanded with many well known and loved Ark Publishing titles.

We are also pleased to announce the launch of our online content platform, Globe Law Online. This allows for easy search and networked access across firms. Key collections include the Law Firm Management Collection, Private Client and Energy and the Energy Transition. Email me at sian@globelawandbusiness.com for further details or to arrange a free trial for you or your firm.

Sian O'Neill
Managing director
Globe Law and Business
www.globelawandbusiness.com

www.ingramcontent.com/pod-product-compliance
Ingram Content Group UK Ltd.
Pitfield, Milton Keynes, MK11 3LW, UK
UKHW021849150926
8657IPUK00005B/163

9 781787 429161